Advance Directives and the Pursuit of Death with Dignity

M E D I C A L E T H I C S S E R I E S

David H. Smith and Robert M. Veatch, *Editors*

Advance Directives and the Pursuit of Death with Dignity

Norman L. Cantor

Indiana University Press

Bloomington and Indianapolis

The paper used in this publication meets the minimum requirements of American National Standard for Information Sciences—Permanence of Paper for Printed Library Materials, ANSI Z39.48-1984.

⊗™

Manufactured in the United States of America

Library of Congress Cataloging-in-Publication Data

Cantor, Norman L.
   Advance directives and the pursuit of death with dignity / Norman
L. Cantor.
     p. cm. — (Medical ethics series)
   Includes bibliographical references and index.
   ISBN 0-253-31304-X
   1. Right to die. 2. Euthanasia. 3. Medical ethics. I. Title.
II. Series.
R726.C34 1993
179'.7—dc20   92-46072

1 2 3 4 5 97 96 95 94 93

Contents

On Restraining Life-Preserving Medical Technology

AT ONE TIME, most people wanted to live as long as possible, and the medical profession sought to prevent death at all costs. That approach could prevail so long as medical capabilities to forestall death were limited. In the middle of the twentieth century, however, medical science developed an array of mechanisms able to extend life well beyond previous bounds.

Mechanical ventilators could sustain breathing processes for protracted periods. Techniques for artificial nutrition and hydration could sustain patients whose ingestion-digestion systems had failed. Immunosuppressive drugs made organ transplantation an option. Sophisticated resuscitation techniques could often revive patients whose breathing had ceased. These and many other developments made it possible to sustain life long after the human body had lost its natural ability to perform critical tasks.

For the most part, these developments were salutary. This was particularly so when the new technology assisted in restoring an ailing person to something close to a prior level of functioning. Yet there was and is a downside. Medical technology can sustain—for protracted periods—gravely debilitated, dying individuals who have no hope of recovering their former capacities. This technological capability has cast doubt on the prior strategy of activating all possible life-preserving medical means.

In the modern era, death increasingly results from chronic maladies and gradual body failure. Cancer, cardiovascular ailments, and cerebrovascular diseases often cause progressive degeneration and protracted dying processes.[1] Alzheimer's disease offers an example. Its gradual impairment of mental functions continues inexorably for an average period of 8.1 years. In its final stages, severe dementia necessitates constant care until death ensues from pneumonia, heart disease, or kidney failure.[2] Such possibilities of grave deterioration of mental faculties and total loss of function have implications both for the aging American population and the medical profession.

Many people have come to view a degenerative dying process as a fate worse than death itself. They dread a difficult and protracted dying process, featuring total helplessness and dependence, increasing dementia, and astronomical expenses. The ultimate specter is one of prolonged suspension in a helpless state, sustained by an array of tubes and machines.[3] Medical intervention then preserves the shell of life but is unable to restore the previously vital patient to anything resembling the patient's previous status.

That specter may or may not include physical and emotional suffering. But it almost certainly entails a status deemed degrading by the typical adult considering his or her own demise. People wonder how they can avoid such a fate. They wonder how medical intervention in the dying process might be restrained sufficiently to permit death with dignity or, at least, death without prolonged suspension in a gravely deteriorated state.

The physician's role has inevitably shifted in the face of modern medicine's awesome capabilities. When medical science had very limited means to arrest fatal conditions, it made sense to activate all medical tools to keep the patient alive for the maximum period possible. With the advent of modern capacity to prolong a difficult dying process beyond "natural" bounds and to preserve the patient in a debilitated state, common sense dictated that the lifesaving imperative sometimes be relaxed. Accordingly, the physician's role has changed. The physician has become a *manager* of medical intervention. Not every life-preserving device need be activated, and a device once activated need not be maintained indefinitely. A stage may be reached when further medical intervention is unwarranted and the patient may be allowed to expire.

This altered approach to life-preserving medical intervention has been acknowledged by numerous physicians and medical bodies.[4] The question is how this altered approach will be administered. What are the circumstances in which medical intervention may properly be withheld or withdrawn? What criteria govern conduct which will lead to the death of a patient? How can a person control a post-competence dying process in a fashion which preserves a personal vision of dignity?

One vehicle for controlling medical intervention is an advance directive. By advance directive, I mean a writing issued by a competent person intending to govern post-competence medical care. That directive might contain substantive instructions which stand by themselves, taking the form of what is commonly known as a living will. Such a document is aimed at guiding any and all decision makers responsible at the moment for critical post-competence decisions. (Usually, the decision makers are a close family member in conjunction with an attending physician.) Alternatively, an advance directive might simply designate a health-care agent (sometimes called a proxy or surrogate or attorney-in-fact) who will be charged with making post-competence medical decisions for the patient. Appointment of an agent can be accompanied by substantive instructions to that agent—a course which I vigorously endorse.[5]

This book considers the legal, moral, and practical bounds of advance directives. Because the concept of an advance directive is rooted in respect for self-determination and autonomy, chapter 1 examines the scope which current law accords to medical decisions by competent patients shaping their contemporaneous medical handling. Chapter 2 works from that foundation to consider the scope of any "right" to direct in advance the degree of medical intervention which will be rendered during a post-competence dying process. That chapter considers the inherent difficulties of *prospective* autonomy as confronted in directives governing future medical contingencies.

Chapter 3 looks at the state statutes—whether living-will type laws or durable power of attorney for health-care measures (DPOA-HC)—which are potentially applicable to advance directives. The nature and impact of such measures is analyzed. Chapter 3 then discusses the various formats which might be used for an advance directive in light of the statutory framework.

Chapter 4 turns to the practical task of drafting advance directives. That chapter first surveys the formulations which have commonly been used to instruct health-care agents or other decision makers. It then examines deficiencies in current versions of advance directives and suggests ways in which such instructions might be improved.

Chapters 5 and 6 address problems of administering advance directives. Chapter 5 presents the principles which guide those persons charged with interpreting and implementing an advance directive. It also considers circumstances which might warrant deviation from the apparent terms of a directive. Chapter 6 examines perhaps the hardest issue faced in administration of an advance directive: a conflict between the instructions previously issued and the now incompetent patient's contemporaneous well-being. That chapter treats the moral and legal bounds applicable when such a conflict is encountered. Included are discussions of both professional conscience and institutional conscience as they bear on implementation of advance directives.

Chapter 7 examines the mechanisms which might be available to enforce advance directives. It discusses what might ensue when either a health-care provider or a relative of the patient refuses to comply with the terms of an advance directive.

The final chapter examines New Jersey's recent (effective January 1992) Advance Directives for Health Care Act. That enactment represents perhaps the most comprehensive and forward-looking piece of legislation regulating advance directives. For reasons that are outlined in chapter 8, the New Jersey legislation might well serve as a model for states seeking to update their statutory frameworks for advance directives.

The stakes are high in the modern effort to shape a humane approach to medical technology's capacity to prolong moribund medical patients far beyond previous bounds. Pressures are increasing to employ new responses (such as assisted suicide and active euthanasia) to people's widespread apprehensions of dying in a prolonged, debilitated status. The key question is whether medicine and law can adapt existing techniques for shaping limits to medical intervention in the dying process in order to assure people that they can avoid a distasteful and prolonged demise.

The advance directive is supposed to be an important tool in achieving that goal. Failure of that tool will almost certainly precipitate more widespread resort to assisted suicide and active euthanasia. This book seeks to promote the understanding, use, and effectiveness of advance directives. The hope is that by allowing persons to shape the contours of medical intervention they can secure a modicum of dignity in the dying process.

Advance Directives and the Pursuit of Death with Dignity

1

The Bounds of Autonomy for Competent Medical Patients

FOR PURPOSES of analyzing advance directives, it is useful to understand the bounds imposed on patient autonomy to reject life-preserving medical intervention. Both an advance directive (exercising prospective autonomy) and a contemporaneous decision (exercising immediate autonomy) allow a person to shape his or her own dying process in accord with personal values and preferences. While prospective autonomy is not identical to contemporaneous autonomy,[1] they share a common foundation in self-determination. The judicial determinations concerning contemporaneous patient decisions illuminate both the precise nature of the patient's interests in making such decisions and the conflicting interests which might warrant limitations upon fatal choices. The same kind of interests and the same kind of conflicts sometimes surface in the context of advance directives. Analysis of these tensions in the context of contemporaneous decisions can therefore cast light on similar tensions when an advance directive is applied to an incompetent patient.

The prerogative of a competent individual to determine if and when to receive life-preserving medical intervention is now firmly entrenched in American jurisprudence. Every decision by a highest state court has upheld a competent patient's right to control medical intervention even when the consequence will be the patient's death.[2] And medical sources have largely acquiesced in this precept of patient autonomy.[3]

This legal and medical consensus about patient autonomy was by no means a foregone conclusion. Medical tradition had long favored a view of doctor-patient relations in which the patient's handling was determined primarily by the physician's professional judgment (which usually called for maximum life preservation).[4] And many sources believed—for religious or philosophical reasons—that stricken persons ought not be accorded dominion over their own dying process. Only recently have notions of individual autonomy and bodily integrity come to prevail over medical paternalism. In any event, despite the shaky foundation in medical practice, respect for a competent patient's control over medical intervention has now become both the legal and medical norm. This development reflects a widespread sentiment that individual self-determination is an integral element of human dignity and of humane medical treatment.

Yet there are still uncertainties about the source and bounds of a patient's prerogative to reject life-preserving medical intervention. The roots of patient autonomy are found in common-law sources. The doctrine of battery protected all persons against unconsented invasions of their bodies.[5] The doctrine of informed consent adapted this concept of bodily integrity to the physician-patient context. Informed consent became a key element in the tort law governing the physician-patient relationship. But these common-law protections of medical patient autonomy are not the exclusive legal protections available.

Within the last twenty years, many courts have reinforced the common-law prerogative to reject life-preserving care by incorporating it into the constitutional sphere. Numerous decisions declare that a patient's control of medical intervention is anchored in the federal Constitution's protection of liberty (and often in a comparable state constitutional provision as well).[6] At the same time, these cases note that the constitutional "right" involved is not absolute. The individual's constitutional interest will occasionally yield to some asserted government interest in limiting a patient's decision to reject life-preserving medical care.

It is important to decide the precise degree of constitutional protection accorded to patient autonomy. For if a patient's right to reject life-preserving medical intervention is indeed anchored in a constitutional source, both state legislatures and state judiciaries must respect that constitutional constraint. Constitutional doctrine can thus affect the rules—whether legislatively or judicially created—which govern the substance and effect of advance directives.

Constitutional protections have the potential to overcome governmental policies which purport to confine terminal decisions to patients who are facing unpreventable death within a short time or which limit the types of medical intervention which a patient can reject. (These kinds of constraints will be discussed later in this chapter and in chapter 3.) Further, even in the absence of explicit substantive instructions from a competent patient, constitutional law might impact on terminal medical decisions. It is possible that a person's designation of an agent to make post-competence health-care decisions is entitled to constitutional protection as an exercise of liberty.[7] A state might be constitutionally obligated to respect a person's designation of a surrogate decision maker, and that health-care agent might even be constitutionally entitled to make the same range of decisions that the patient could have made if competent.[8] This last possibility makes it even more important to define the constitutional scope of a competent patient's right to reject life-preserving medical treatment. That right might become the measure of an appointed health-care agent's authority.

IS A DECISION TO REJECT LIFE-PRESERVING MEDICAL INTERVENTION A FUNDAMENTAL ASPECT OF PERSONAL LIBERTY UNDER THE FEDERAL CONSTITUTION?

The starting point for analysis is the June 1990 U.S. Supreme Court decision in *Cruzan v. Director, Missouri Department of Health*.[9] That case addressed the medical fate of a permanently unconscious patient who, according to the trial court's findings, had not issued clear-cut prior instructions. *Cruzan* thus contains no definitive determination about the scope of autonomy of a competent person who issues advance medical instructions. Nonetheless, *Cruzan* was the Supreme Court's first pronouncement concerning the constitutional interests of medical patients. It is, therefore, a source of guidance about constitutional doctrine in the area.

Cruzan dealt with the fate of Nancy Cruzan, a woman mired in a permanently unconscious state in the wake of severe brain injuries sustained in an automobile accident. Ms. Cruzan's parents had sought judicial authorization to act on their daughter's behalf and to end the artificial nutrition maintaining her existence. Ms. Cruzan had previously made informal oral declarations indicating she would not wish to be maintained in a permanently vegetative state. However, the Missouri courts had ruled that there was insufficient evidence to establish the now incompetent patient's preferences in a clear-cut fashion. Without clear and convincing evidence of the patient's wishes, the Missouri Supreme Court refused to permit a guardian's decision to withdraw life-preserving medical treatment from an incompetent patient. The parents appealed to the U.S. Supreme Court contending that Ms. Cruzan's constitutional right to reject unwanted medical treatment had been violated.

The holding, or thrust, of *Cruzan* goes to Missouri's approach to *in*competent medical patients. By a five to four margin, the U.S. Supreme Court rejected the constitutional challenge to Missouri's approach. Chief Justice Rehnquist's majority opinion ruled both that a state may (but need not) confine terminal decisions on behalf of incompetent patients to instances when the patient has previously expressed such a preference and that the state may demand clear-cut evidence of the patient's previous expressions. These precautions were reasonable, the majority declared, in order to safeguard incompetent patients from terminal decisions inconsistent with the patient's preferences and in order to safeguard against abuse of the helpless patients involved.

The U.S. Supreme Court accepted the Missouri Supreme Court's finding that Nancy Cruzan had not made clear-cut expressions about her post-competence medical fate. By definition, then, there was no autonomous patient choice involved in the case. Nonetheless, Nancy's parents had grounded their petition on the premise that their daughter had possessed, as a competent adult, a constitutionally protected right to reject life-preserving medical intervention. Their threshold contention was that the word "liberty" in the due process clause of the Fourteenth Amendment affords a competent adult a right to reject unwanted medical care.[10]

The majority opinion in *Cruzan* assumed, for purposes of discussion alone, that a competent person does enjoy "a constitutionally protected right to refuse life-saving hydration and nutrition."[11] Nonetheless, a number of commentators have suggested that *Cruzan* forebodes a contrary conclusion: that a decision to reject medical treatment is *not* a fundamental aspect of liberty protected by the Fourteenth Amendment.[12] Those commentators base their conclusion on the majority opinion's references to a liberty "interest" in rejecting treatment (as opposed to a liberty "right"). Their premise is that a Supreme Court opinion would not use the term *interest* if it were thought that a fundamental aspect of liberty was involved.

My own analysis is different. To my mind, the *Cruzan* decision lends impetus to the notion that a competent patient's rejection of medical intervention *is* a fundamental aspect of liberty. Use of the term "liberty interest" is explainable by judicial caution in crafting constitutional jurisprudence. The majority was reserving decision about the ultimate scope of a competent patient's constitutional preroga-tive. It had already assumed that a constitutional right existed. There was no need to specify whether that right was part of fundamental liberty or not. The government interests surrounding care of an *in*competent patient were strong enough to prevail in either event.

While the majority opinion in *Cruzan* is inconclusive, there are some indications even in that opinion that a majority of the Supreme Court will ultimately declare that a competent patient's decision to reject life-preserving medical intervention is a fundamental aspect of liberty. The majority opinion surveys (without any hint of disapproval) some of the many state court decisions establishing patients' control of medical intervention in a natural dying process as a right grounded in common law, state constitutional law, or federal constitutional law.[13] The majority acknowl-edges as well that the "logic" of prior Supreme Court cases regarding fundamental liberty interests could easily be extended to the competent medical patient. However, Chief Justice Rehnquist's opinion refuses to go the last step and declare a medical patient's constitutional right. Instead, it "assumes," for purposes of the *Cruzan* case alone, that such a constitutional right does exist.[14]

Justice O'Connor's concurring opinion expresses strong sympathy for the claim that a competent patient has a fundamental liberty interest in rejecting medical care. Justice O'Connor comments: "[T]he due process clause must protect, if it protects anything, an individual's deeply personal decision to reject medical treat-ment."[15] Her opinion, in combination with the four dissenting voices in *Cruzan*, means that there were five Justices in June 1990 who supported that notion. Only Justice Scalia disparaged the idea of a competent person's constitutional right to reject unwanted medical treatment. That leaves current Justices Kennedy, Souter,

Thomas, and Chief Justice Rehnquist (as well as Justice White's successor) free to join Justices O'Connor, Stevens, and Blackmun and acknowledge the fundamental liberty status of the patient's autonomy interest.

Judicial acceptance of a competent patient's autonomy interest as fundamental depends on whether the patient's interest is deemed "so rooted in the traditions and conscience of our people as to be ranked as fundamental."[16] That is the standard used by the modern Supreme Court for defining fundamental aspects of liberty.[17] Employing that standard, there is a considerable basis for deeming the competent medical patient's liberty interest to be fundamental.

As noted, even Chief Justice Rehnquist's majority opinion recounted the string of modern cases upholding a competent medical patient's prerogative to reject life-preserving medical intervention. That line of authority helps demonstrate how self-determination and bodily integrity have become integral aspects of a medical patient's interests. The doctrine of informed consent—a doctrine premised on a patient's prerogative to reject medical intervention—has found universal acceptance in American jurisprudence. Moreover, the doctrine has universally been transposed to life-and-death decisions in the face of medical afflictions. Thus, there is a solid foundation for the conclusion that control of life-sustaining medical intervention has become a fundamental aspect of personal liberty in the context of modern American society.

The *Cruzan* opinions of Justices Stevens (dissenting) and O'Connor (concurring) eloquently explain why autonomy to reject unwanted treatment during a natural dying process can be deemed a fundamental aspect of liberty. Justice Stevens is particularly sensitive to the dilemma posed to modern society by medical technology's capacity to prolong a dying process. He therefore urges application of autonomy principles to the context of human dying. He comments:

> Choices about death touch the core of liberty. Our duty, and the concomitant freedom, to come to terms with the conditions of our own mortality are undoubtedly "so rooted in the traditions and conscience of our people" as to be ranked as fundamental. . . . [18]

Both Justices Stevens and O'Connor elucidate the important human dignity elements which underlie patient self-determination. One element identified is the blow to human dignity which accompanies a patient's inability to secure his or her wish regarding the important and intimate matter of death. Justice Stevens in particular notes patients' interests both in a closure of life consistent with individual values and beliefs and in preservation of a particular self-image during the dying process.[19] Thus, both fulfillment of chosen values and avoidance of subjective degradation or embarrassment (during debilitation in the dying process) are seen as important components of human dignity and personhood. Another element recognized is the indignity or humiliation entailed in the forced subjection of a patient to unwanted medical intervention. Justice O'Connor in particular uses graphic images of physical "restraint" and the patient as "captive" of the care givers.[20]

The Stevens and O'Connor opinions, along with the dissenting opinion of Justice Brennan, highlight how a right to select medical treatment honors the intrinsic worth of human choice in this context. Autonomy is afforded not just to promote a patient's material best interests but to enable a patient to fulfill self-selected values. This focus on self-determination (as opposed to bodily integrity) as the key ingredient within the patient's interests will help define the ultimate scope of the right or interests involved. This focus helps refute the notion that a patient's right is confined to declining particularly invasive or burdensome forms of medical care—a notion that has sometimes been voiced.[21] If autonomy or self-determination is the key interest, even relatively unobtrusive medical interventions (such as blood transfusions or simple medications) may be resisted by the competent patient. A diminished concern with the physical invasiveness of medical intervention is consistent with the trend of state court decisions. Those decisions have attached less and less importance to the invasiveness of the medical intervention being rejected.[22]

Identification of the integral tie between choice and human dignity in the context of death-and-dying decisions follows the path of prior state court decisions in the field. Some of those decisions had stressed the blow to dignity when a patient's autonomous preferences regarding medical interventions are not respected.[23] Other decisions had acknowledged the relation between human dignity and the avoidance of both suffering and a dying process deemed undignified or degrading according to the affected individual.[24] All these voices emphasized the importance of an individual's choice to reject medical interventions deemed distasteful or to decide when a prospective existence is so painful or dismal that life-preserving intervention is unwanted. These judicial expressions form part of the "collective conscience" which will ultimately determine the constitutional status of a patient's autonomy interest.

It isn't just the failure of the majority opinion in *Cruzan* to disparage the jurisprudence linking medical self-determination and fundamental human dignity which encourages me to think that rejection of life-preserving medical intervention will eventually be recognized as a fundamental aspect of liberty. Note that the majority opinion acknowledges the value and importance of self-determination in the death-and-dying context. Indeed, one of the governmental interests which is recognized and upheld in *Cruzan* is an interest in safeguarding a patient's choice.[25] (The majority regarded Missouri's demand for clear and convincing evidence of prior patient expressions as necessary to ensure that any guardian's decision would be consistent with the patient's own wishes.) Chief Justice Rehnquist adds that he doesn't think that due process of law requires government "to repose judgment on these [life-and-death] matters *with anyone but the patient herself* [emphasis added]."[26]

(The irony, of course, is that Missouri's scheme actually frustrated personal choice as applied to Nancy Cruzan and to many medical situations. For example, polls demonstrate that the vast majority of Americans prefer not to be maintained in a permanently vegetative state.[27] Yet Missouri insists on maintaining a permanently vegetative patient in the absence of clear and convincing prior instructions to the contrary. The state's policy accomplishes a result opposite to what the vast majority of patients would want and opposite to the best judgment of what Nancy Cruzan would have wanted.)

It is true that the current Supreme Court is not inclined to expansively define fundamental liberty interests. The marked trend is to confine the notion of fundamental interests to those explicitly mentioned in the Constitution (such as free speech) or to those relating to marriage, procreation, and family living.[28] Even *Roe v. Wade*[29] and its inclusion of a woman's abortion interest within the realm of fundamental liberties was recently assaulted, though not vitiated.[30] Some perspective on this trend is appropriate.

The vulnerability of *Roe v. Wade* lay not in the general concept of fundamental aspects of liberty but in its specific application to an abortion decision. Fundamental liberty is supposed to be rooted in "the traditions and collective conscience of the people." Yet at the moment *Roe v. Wade* was decided in 1973 almost half the states punished the performance of abortions, and a very significant portion of the population regarded abortion as a form of homicide. There was arguably a dissonance between the Supreme Court's 1973 declaration of fundamentality and widespread societal perceptions. A similar dissonance affects the effort to have homosexual relations declared a fundamental aspect of personal liberty. Sexual relations are generally viewed as intimate and part of personal liberty. Yet certain forms of sexual behavior have traditionally been deemed abominable by a very significant segment of American society.

By contrast, there is no widespread aversion to a competent patient's prerogative to reject life-preserving medical intervention. As noted, notions of bodily integrity and control of medical intervention have strong grounding in twentieth century American jurisprudence and in societal attitudes of the last few decades. Self-determination in shaping medical response to a fatal affliction appeals not just to archliberals, like Justice Brennan, but to judicial conservatives as well. A prime example is former Chief Justice Warren Burger. While still a lower court judge in 1964, Warren Burger authored a ringing judicial endorsement of the notion of individual autonomy to reject life-preserving medical intervention.[31]

To be sure, respect for self-determination of a medical patient is not universal. There are right-to-life groups which are opposed to allowing preservable patients to expire. Some religious groups view life-and-death decisions as exclusively within the domain of a divine being (rather than in the dominion of the patient). But in a pluralistic society, there are almost no universal moral precepts. These ripples of dissent do not undermine the basic point that a competent patient's prerogative to reject life-preserving medical intervention has wide-ranging support in modern American society. That support—as well as the roots in well-established concepts of bodily integrity and informed consent—bode well for eventual Supreme Court recognition of a patient's prerogative as a fundamental aspect of liberty. Another positive sign is that post-*Cruzan* state court decisions continue to view a competent patient's rejection of life-preserving medical treatment as a fundamental aspect of liberty under both the federal and state constitutions.[32]

Calling something a fundamental aspect of liberty does not determine the ultimate contours of the right involved. Even fundamental liberties can be impinged in response to "compelling" governmental interests. There is still need, then, to define the scope of a competent patient's right to reject life-preserving medical intervention.

IS A PATIENT'S INTEREST IN REJECTING LIFE-SUSTAINING TREATMENT OUTWEIGHED BY A STATE INTEREST IN PRESERVING LIFE OR IN PRESERVING RESPECT FOR THE SANCTITY OF LIFE?

Many state supreme court decisions have considered a competent patient's decision to reject life-sustaining medical intervention where the patient was preservable for a considerable period of time. Those decisions commonly confront a putative governmental interest in the "sanctity of life." That sanctity-of-life interest can be divided into two components. One element is the protection of individuals against the harm normally entailed in the deprivation of life. A second element is promotion of societal respect for the concept that human life is sacrosanct. This element arguably includes maintaining social respect for all human existence by preventing human intermeddling which prematurely shortens a preservable life. Government could argue that any patient's judgment that a life is no longer worth living is morally offensive and that the state refuses to condone such a judgment. Or government might argue, as some people have done, that allowing debilitated persons to choose death broadcasts a message that life is not worth living for some handicapped persons. The concern is that this message will devalue the lives of handicapped persons and will weaken the social fabric.[33]

The legitimacy of a governmental interest in the preservation of life is indisputable. Such an interest suffuses much of American criminal law and significant parts of tort law. The question, though, is how this interest plays out when arrayed against what has been identified as an individual's fundamental liberty interest in shaping life-sustaining medical intervention. While a government interest in preserving life is potentially a compelling one, is it predominant in the context of competent medical patients rejecting life-preserving care?

Several state supreme court decisions declare that a competent patient's autonomy interests simply outweigh government interests encompassed within the sanctity-of-life rubric. The New Jersey Supreme Court's pronouncement is fairly typical: "[T]he state's indirect and abstract interest in preserving the life of the competent patient generally gives way to the patient's much stronger personal interest in directing the course of his own life."[34] The U.S. Supreme Court's *Cruzan* decision does nothing to undermine this determination. Indeed, eight of the Justices there seemed ready to rule that if Nancy Cruzan's wish to resist life-preserving medical intervention had been clearly expressed, it would have prevailed against any asserted state interests.

Some commentators have wondered why autonomy interests so easily prevail against sanctity-of-life concerns in the medical context.[35] To my mind, the judicial balance in favor of patient control of medical intervention is correct. But the balance deserves further explanation, beyond merely stressing the importance of a patient's autonomy and bodily integrity interests.

As noted, one legitimate governmental concern is protection of each individual against the harm entailed in deprivation of life. Yet that individual interest is really a protection against *unconsented* conduct which threatens a premature demise. Government can and should protect individuals against life-threatening abuse and mistreatment. But where a patient makes a deliberate determination that medical intervention will precipitate a status worse than death (from the perspective of that patient), government frustration of that choice does not promote the individual patient's self-defined interest. From the patient's perspective, the death which ensues is not a harm but, rather, a chosen and timely relief. (Government does have an interest in ensuring an informed and deliberate choice—but not in frustrating a considered choice.)[36]

Alternatively, government might assert—under the sanctity-of-life rubric—a collective interest in frustrating what government terms a morally offensive determination that some life is no longer worth living. The major defect in this argument is the premise that a person's choice not to struggle against a potentially fatal affliction is morally offensive. Modern medicine's capacity to preserve life long beyond previous bounds has undermined that premise. There is now societal understanding that prolonged suffering or prolonged indignity in the face of a fatal affliction can be a fate worse than death. People understand that a cancer patient may prefer death to the subjectively intolerable consequences of chemotherapy. People understand that an ALS patient (a victim of amyotrophic lateral sclerosis, a degenerative disease of the muscles known also as Lou Gehrig's disease) may reach a stage of helplessness and debilitation where continued respirator maintenance is intolerable.

In short, no moral condemnation currently accompanies the proposition that not every life-extending medical means must be maintained in the face of a naturally occurring dying process. There is widespread acknowledgment that, for some persons facing fatal afflictions, nonexistence may be preferable to medical maintenance. Once the morality of that posture is accepted, it makes eminently good sense to respect an individual's judgment that the dying process has become sufficiently torturous or degrading to warrant the cessation of medical intervention.

No one can assess the individual's suffering or sense of indignity better than the individual. Thus, it is not surprising that a competent patient's self-determination interests have been deemed dominant over the state interest in promoting respect for the sanctity of life.

The final government interest in this context is in avoiding endorsement of judgments that certain lives are not worth preserving. It is understandable that government wishes to avoid conveying a public message that *it* sees certain lives as so lacking in quality that further protection is unwarranted. But that is not the necessary consequence of government acquiescence in a competent patient's determination that medically maintained existence is so painful or dismal as to warrant foregoing life-sustaining treatment.

Judicial upholding of a patient's control over medical intervention does not constitute government endorsement of a determination that a particular life is not "worth living" or preserving. Indeed, judges upholding a patient's decision to reject life-preserving medical treatment frequently disclaim any judgment that the patient's decision is wise, desirable, or commendable.[37] Judicial respect for the patient's decision can therefore be viewed as an affirmation of human dignity as embodied in the patient's exercise of self-determination.[38] As one judge explained, with respect to a decision to terminate life support made by a woman suffering from a fatal degenerative muscle disease (ALS):

> This poor woman is not anti-life and her decision is not anti-life. . . . She has suffered much. It simply is not wrong in any sense for this good woman to want relief from her suffering. Hospitals and health care providers do not deal with life in the abstract. They deal with living people. Eventually, all those living people become dying people, and those people must be dealt with in a way which fully respects their dignity, including as part of that dignity the right to choose one's treatment.[39]

The New Jersey Supreme Court has added that "the value of life [is] desecrated not by the decision to refuse medical treatment but by the failure to allow a competent human being the right of choice."[40] In sum, when a competent, dying patient makes a determination that prospective physical or mental pain warrant rejection of continued medical intervention, this is not seen as an antilife posture undermining the state interest in promoting sanctity of human life. A person's coming to terms with a natural dying process is not seen as an affront to respect for the value of life.

IS THE RIGHT TO REJECT LIFE-PRESERVING MEDICAL INTERVENTION CONFINED TO TERMINAL PATIENTS NEARING THE END OF LIFE?

The answer to this question has implications for advance directives. Many people's directives seek to avoid prolonged medical maintenance in a stable, but severely debilitated, status. At the same time, termination of medical treatment to a stabilized patient, preservable for an extended period, has been attacked as a form of medical homicide which ought not be tolerated. Insight into this tension can be gleaned from consideration of competent patients who have rejected medical intervention capable of preserving their existence for long periods.

Is the patient's prerogative to reject life-sustaining medical intervention confined to the last stages of an inevitably terminal illness or condition? Early cases dealing with a patient's rejection of life-preserving medical treatment cautiously suggested that the governmental interest in preserving life could be overridden only because the patient's existence was nearing its end anyway.[41] According to that early perspective, the state's interest in preservation of life diminished as the duration of preservable existence diminished. Under such an approach, the patient's constitutional right to resist life-sustaining treatment might be limited to situations where an unpreventable death is near. Otherwise, the governmental interest in sanctity of life would prevail and a state could (if it wished) dictate continued life-preserving medical intervention.[42]

There are at least two reasons why the long potential duration of a patient's existence cannot determine the scope of a patient's right to resist life-preserving medical intervention. First, the government interest in sanctity of life does not increase just because the potential life span is longer. The government concern is both with promoting general respect for life and with the implicit judgment that a patient's quality of life is no longer worth preserving. That state interest is present and constant whether the patient's death is imminent or whether the dying process could be extended for years. (Even if the treatment rejected could only extend life for an hour, there is an implicit judgment that the hour of life was not worth preserving.) Second, the patient's autonomy interest in controlling medical intervention in a naturally occurring dying process[43] actually increases as the preservable existence lengthens. The patient's principal interest is in determining when a prospective existence (following contemplated treatment) would be so painful, distasteful, or degrading that further medical intervention is unwanted. The long prospective duration of a dying process only enhances the importance of the patient's choice. That is, the longer a prospective dying process, the more important choice is to a patient who views the prospective existence as torturous or degrading.

A number of state court decisions confirm this judgment: that a competent patient's autonomy interest prevails regardless of the duration of the preservable existence in issue.[44] That judicial posture is easiest to understand where the motive for the patient's rejection of treatment is avoidance of suffering. (The relevant cases generally involve patients afflicted with degenerative diseases or severe chronic debilitations.) Judges express understanding of a patient's powerful self-determination interest where medical intervention, while extending the patient's existence, will leave the patient in a gravely debilitated status. They understand that such a patient may wish to avoid the suffering and/or indignity which the patient associates with prolonged incapacitation. They also recognize that a patient's suffering is subjective—largely beyond judicial capacity to measure and weigh—and that such suffering can continue for a protracted period.[45] Accordingly, the cases uniformly refuse to supplant a competent patient's judgment that, for that patient, the prospective existence following continued medical intervention will be intolerable.[46] In that fashion, the courts avoid endorsing any particular judgment that a quality of life is so deteriorated as not to be worth preserving, and they avoid having to determine what length of preservable existence would override a patient's normal autonomy interest.

All the discussion so far goes to the right of a competent patient who is faced with an unpreventably fatal condition. A harder question is whether the competent patient's constitutional prerogative extends beyond terminal patients. (By terminal patients, I mean those afflicted with a pathological condition triggering an inexorable dying process—whatever its duration. I am including within terminal conditions both diseases such as ALS, which themselves cause a patient's death, and diseases such as AIDS, which affect the body's systems and lead to death from intervening causes.)[47] The hardest application of the issue comes when a medical patient is salvageable to a "healthful" existence and nonetheless seeks to reject lifesaving medical intervention.

Some state court decisions do mention the incurable status of the patient when discussing why a state interest in the preservation of life may be overridden.[48] Such a position is at least understandable. The offense to the state interest in sanctity of life seems intuitively greater if the patient is curable. A patient who resists treatment which could restore him or her to a healthful existence is behaving in a manner reminiscent of a suicide. (The interest in preventing suicide will be addressed separately in the next subsection.) The patient is not simply acquiescing in an unpreventable dying process. Many people see a salvageable patient's decision to resist medical intervention as morally less defensible than an inexorably dying person's decision.[49] It would, then, be theoretically possible to distinguish between the prerogative of an inexorably dying patient and a patient restorable to a "healthful" status.[50]

The likelihood is that a competent patient's medical autonomy will be upheld regardless of whether the patient is facing unavoidable death. One context in which competent, salvageable patients have been accorded a right to resist lifesaving medical intervention involves religiously motivated patients. (The typical case involves a Jehovah's Witness opposing a lifesaving blood transfusion.) Numerous decisions uphold the religiously motivated patient's decision, usually invoking constitutional grounds.[51]

The religious patient's autonomy interest is reinforced by the federal Constitution's explicit protection of religious freedom. However, it is unlikely that a competent patient's prerogative will be confined to religiously motivated patients.

The general patient interests reflected in medical decisions—self-determination, bodily integrity, and maintenance of dignity—are likely to reach the same constitutional plane as freedom of religion. Not surprisingly, then, the most recent state supreme court decision upholding a religiously motivated patient's rejection of treatment is grounded on constitutional interests in liberty and privacy (without reliance on the free exercise clause).[52]

This suggested constitutional approach to the religiously motivated patient is consistent with recent decisions upholding, as a matter of common law, a salvageable patient's right to resist life-preserving medical intervention.[53] The premise of such cases is that a competent patient's self-determination and bodily integrity interests simply outweigh the state's interest in preservation of life—even when the patient is preservable to a healthful existence. Such determinations regarding the common-law scope of the patient's right will in turn help shape the ultimate bounds of the constitutional right in issue.[54] (This is so because the constitutional right is shaped in part from the "traditions and collective conscience" of the people. State common law is one important index of the collective conscience.)

Just as a patient is entitled to resist life-preserving medical intervention even if that patient is salvageable to a healthful existence, a patient is entitled to resist intervention which would leave him in a chronically debilitated condition (though preservable for an extended period). A variety of patients fit this category. There is the gangrene patient facing an amputation operation. There is the patient with acute kidney disease who is sustainable for many years but will be perpetually dependent on burdensome medical intervention (kidney dialysis). There is the quadriplegic patient who is dependent on a mechanical respirator or on artificial nutrition because of chronic pathological conditions. In all these instances, courts have upheld competent patients' decisions to refuse further life-sustaining medical intervention.[55]

This result is sound. It would not be sensible to confine a patient's autonomy right to those patients who are beyond recovery (i.e., unpreventably dying). An inevitable issue under such a standard would be the definition of patient "recovery." Can the patient with gangrene "recover" (and therefore be deemed nonterminal and not entitled to resist life-preserving intervention) if the contemplated operation will leave him or her an amputee? Is the cancer patient with a fifteen percent chance of recovery a dying patient? And what about the patient with acute kidney disease who is salvageable for many years but can't stand the burden of the dialysis process? If the competent patient's constitutional prerogative depended on the length and quality of the preservable existence, courts would be implicated in the assessment of when the nature of the salvageable life is so dismal or uncertain as to preclude state interference with the patient's decision. This is a troubling specter for the judiciary.[56]

All this makes sense. Yet, when a patient's condition has stabilized and the patient is preservable for an extended period, a decision to forego further treatment (knowing that the result will be death) has overtones of suicide. The similarity to suicide warrants examination.

IS RELINQUISHMENT OF AN EXISTENCE PRESERVABLE FOR AN EXTENDED PERIOD INCOMPATIBLE WITH SOCIETY'S TRADITIONAL ANTIPATHY TOWARD SUICIDE?

When the issue of rejection of life-sustaining medical treatment arose in the 1950s and 1960s, hospitals argued that society's long-standing antipathy toward suicide warrants medical refusal to cooperate with a patient's rejection of treatment. The argument had appeal, particularly where the patient was salvageable to a healthful existence or where the patient's condition had stabilized and the patient was preservable for an indefinite period. In such instances, a decision to reject or discontinue medical support precipitates a prompt and foreseeable death. Isn't that suicide? This contention found some early judicial support.[57] And the contention was recently echoed by Justice Scalia in his opinion concurring in the result in *Cruzan*.[58]

Despite Justice Scalia's plaintive cry, the basic assertion has been thoroughly repudiated. Every decision of the last fifteen years has refused to equate suicide with a competent patient's rejection of life-sustaining medical intervention.[59] The only issue is the precise rationale for this result.

One common explanation is that suicide entails a specific intent to die and that a person declining medical intervention lacks such an intent. That rationale is convincing with regard to some patients. For example, a patient motivated by religious tenets (such as a Jehovah's Witness refusing a blood transfusion) has no specific intent to die. That patient hopes and expects a healing process to ensue and is merely adhering to a religious injunction in rejecting the particular treatment at hand. Likewise, a patient rejecting a highly expensive lifesaving procedure might well lack any specific intent to die.

However, the specific intent rationale is more problematic as applied to a terminally ill patient seeking to avoid a distasteful dying process. If the patient's main objective is avoidance of suffering or indignity, and that objective can be achieved only by death, then the intent behind the rejection of life-preserving treatment is close to the specific intent of any suicide who finds existence painful or meaningless.[60] Thus, the element of specific intent does not provide a comprehensive basis for distinguishing suicide.

Another basis to distinguish suicide from rejection of medical treatment is to see the former as involving a self-initiated destructive action.[61] This conforms with the commonsense understanding of suicide. When we think of suicide, we commonly think of taking pills, slitting wrists, or firing a shot. By contrast, rejection of medical treatment entails acquiescence in a natural disease process or trauma not initiated by the patient. Letting nature take its course is seen as different from inflicting an injury upon oneself.[62]

There is a simpler explanation for the distinction between rejection of life-preserving treatment and suicide. Over the past twenty-five years, both popular and judicial perceptions have come to regard a patient's decision about medical intervention in the face of a critical condition as part of a competent person's fundamental self-determination prerogatives.[63] A decision to resist life-preserving medical intervention involves important elements of both bodily integrity (resisting bodily invasions) and self-determination (shaping one's dying process). Recognition of these elements as engendering "rights" in the context of a critically stricken medical patient has simply removed the matter from the realm of suicide.[64]

It was inherent in the recognition of informed consent in the context of critical medical care that the patient would sometimes choose to die. Often, the patient's motive in rejecting medical intervention was distaste for the prospect of a gravely debilitated existence. (Among others, we're talking about the cancer patient, the gangrene patient, or the quadriplegic dependent on artificial aids.) Such refusal of medical intervention might well entail a suicide-like thought or state of mind. But no court could accept the notion that a patient might be foreclosed from exercising a right to refuse treatment because the patient might be deliberately preferring death over the anticipated, subjective hell of continued existence. A recent Massachusetts opinion commented: "There is a clear distinction between respecting the right of individuals to decide for themselves whether to refuse treatment and endorsing the idea that it is acceptable for individuals to take their own lives."[65]

Once the patient is deemed to be exercising a right to self determination, the motives behind the action are irrelevant. This is not such a surprising notion. For example, if a death-row prisoner waives a promising appeal or refuses to assert a possible defense, this is seen as a legitimate exercise of self-determination and part of the person's human dignity.[66] So long as the prisoner is competent, it shouldn't matter if he has an underlying wish to die because of a belief that the prospective punishment is warranted. While the prisoner's decision might be loosely analogized to a suicidal step, common sense tells us that it is not suicide.

The competent patient's decision to resist life-preserving medical treatment falls in the same realm. There is no occasion to differentiate among decisions motivated by religious convictions, by economic concerns, by distaste for a particular form of treatment, or by distaste for the dismal, debilitated condition facing the patient if treatment is accepted. The decision, whatever the precise motive, lies within the patient's self-determination prerogative.

The above perspective on a patient's acquiescence in death from natural causes applies even when the patient's condition has stabilized and life could be extended indefinitely. Some poignant examples have involved quadriplegics dependent on medical machinery (either respirators or artificial nutrition) who have been permitted to terminate life support.[67] Despite both the patient's specific intent to die and the fact that the withdrawal of medical intervention would be a "but for" cause of death, the withdrawal has been regarded as a permissible rejection of medical care and treated as distinct from suicide.[68] The underlying disease or trauma which is permitted to run its course by removal of the artificial intervention is considered the determinative legal cause of death.

A further wrinkle on the suicide theme occurs where the patient's condition has not only stabilized, but the medical support has been in place for an extended period. This situation triggers an assertion that life support has become such an integral part of the patient's being that any removal of life support constitutes a self-destructive, suicide-like act.

That contention recently surfaced in a dissenting opinion in *McKay v. Bergstedt*,[69] a Nevada case. In that instance, a thirty-nine-year-old quadriplegic sought to cease life-sustaining mechanical ventilation after twenty-three years of such treatment. The majority upheld the patient's decision. Judge Springer's dissent argued that the ventilator should be viewed as an integral part of the dependent patient so that its withdrawal would constitute a self-destructive act.[70] He saw the act as equivalent to removal of a pacemaker, prosthetic device, or artificial organ from a stabilized patient.

My perspective is that medical intervention doesn't cease to be medical intervention even if maintained for a long period and even if installed within the body. With degenerative ailments and with experimental treatments, it is understood that a patient's condition might deteriorate and reach a point when maintenance of the technology becomes intolerable. This is the case, for instance, with kidney dialysis. Many patients accept that treatment for years before ultimately deciding to terminate the burdensome intervention. A respirator, a pacemaker, or an artificial organ ought to fall into the same category. If, after months or even years, the patient's condition deteriorates or the patient's emotional tolerance is exhausted, a halt to medical intervention ought to be possible. Judge Springer's effort to anthropomorphize the medical machinery in order to make the process seem more like suicide is neither helpful nor persuasive.

There are situations where a person's self-harmful behavior exceeds mere rejection of medical intervention and is closely akin to suicide. A healthy person's attempt to donate a liver or other vital organ to a needy recipient might be an example. No health-care provider would cooperate with such an enterprise, even if it were motivated by admirable altruistic motives. At the same time, a person stricken with a potentially fatal pathology could reject medical intervention with the intention of dying and donating an organ to a needy recipient. This is only to say what was already asserted: that the prerogative to reject medical intervention may be exercised by a competent patient no matter what the patient's motive.

Another patient behavior which exceeds mere rejection of medical intervention is a refusal to accept oral feeding. The usual context is an elderly, grievously debilitated person who refuses to eat even though swallowing and digestive capabilities are still intact. I'll address this matter below, in the context of rejection of nutrition.

DOES A COMPETENT PATIENT'S RIGHT TO CONTROL MEDICAL INTERVENTION INCLUDE REJECTION OF ARTIFICIAL NUTRITION AND/OR MANUAL FEEDING?

Trauma or degenerative disease sometimes causes loss of a patient's swallowing reflex or disruption to the normal ingestion-digestion system. A range of interventions (including insertion of a nasogastric tube or surgical installation of a gastrostomy tube) may be available to sustain the patient's life. Does the competent patient's self-determination prerogative encompass refusal or withdrawal of such artificial nutrition? (I use artificial nutrition here as a shorthand applicable to artificial hydration as well.) The issue has provoked strong emotions and controversy over the last ten years.[71]

If there were strong grounds to distinguish artificial nutrition from regular medical intervention, it might be possible to exclude artificial nutrition from the scope of the patient's constitutional prerogative to control medical intervention. Even a fundamental liberty interest can be circumscribed when certain applications exceed the accepted or traditional bounds of the liberty principle involved.[72] In the case of artificial nutrition versus conventional medical treatment, the kind of distinction which would warrant separate constitutional handling probably does not exist. This conclusion flows from consideration of the claims raised by those commentators who seek to differentiate artificial nutrition from conventional medical intervention.[73]

One common assertion is that because cessation of nutrition inevitably leads to the patient's death, such cessation is tantamount to killing the patient. The patient is allegedly being dehydrated (or starved) to death instead of merely being permitted to die from a natural disease process.[74]

There is another perspective on causation. From this latter perspective, the trauma or disease process which incapacitated the patient's alimentary system ought to be viewed as the legal cause of death. This pathology, which permanently ended the patient's ingestion-digestion capacity, created the need for artificial intervention to maintain the patient's existence. Absent artificial nutrition, the patient would have died naturally from the underlying illness or trauma. Removal of that artificial nutrition merely allows the natural dying process to follow its terminal course. Death through dehydration stems from the original incapacitating trauma and not from introduction of a new external element into the scenario. While dehydration may be a "but for" cause of death (along with the underlying pathology), the death may still be viewed as "acquiescence in the natural shutting down of a critical bodily function."[75] The underlying pathology can be deemed the legally determinative cause of death so long as the withdrawal of artificial nutrition accords with the applicable standards of physician responsibility to a competent patient.[76]

From the perspective of causation, the situation is not significantly different from a patient who rejects life-preserving mechanical ventilation or kidney dialysis. Legal responsibility for withdrawal of life-preserving intervention is assessed according to the scope of medical duty to the particular patient. This approach prevails whether the intervention is a respirator for lung or heart malfunction, a dialysis machine for kidney malfunction, or artificial nutrition for alimentary malfunction. In all these instances, the normal medical duty to preserve life is modified by the competent patient's instructions.

A separate claim is that the provision of nutrition has a special symbolic significance which differentiates it from medical treatment. Some commentators contend that feeding is inherently a symbol of human interdependence and caring, a symbol which should always be preserved.[77]

Yet any symbolic distinction between artificial nutrition and conventional medical care seems forced. The caring embodied in artificial feeding seems little different from the caring involved in furnishing antibiotics, blood transfusions, medicines, or chest massage. While feeding normally carries a salutary symbolic message, that is not always the case. In the context of a competent, fatally afflicted patient, feeding may carry no benefit for the patient; the act may lose its usual symbolic cast.[78] This is especially so when the patient is undergoing a torturous dying process being prolonged by artificial nutrition. When that stage is reached, it is palliative care (nursing care aimed at easing the pain, anxiety, or discomfort of the patient) which may connote the caring and humane consideration that people expect and deserve.

Some health-care providers may have special qualms about withdrawing artificial nutrition. One survey indicated that as late as 1983, seventy-three percent of physicians surveyed would continue artificial nutrition even for a hopelessly comatose, terminally ill patient.[79] Intravenous fluids were apparently considered by some to be an entrenched therapy at that time. Yet the survey is deceptive. As of that time, there was still uncertainty about the legal consequences of withdrawing artificial nutrition. Recall that some of the first legal expressions concerning refusal of medical intervention spoke in terms of a prerogative to reject "extraordinary" means. Most of the early cases dealt with respirators or other forms of regular medical intervention. Only between 1983 and 1985 did the courts begin to indicate that artificial nutrition could be regarded like conventional medical intervention.[80] Moreover, physicians in 1983 may have had concerns about the pain and aesthetics involved in a death by dehydration, concerns which have since been largely resolved.

When the issue of withdrawing artificial nutrition first arose, an effort was made to portray the consequences for the "starving" patient as painful and repulsive. A Massachusetts lower court in 1986 devoted twenty pages to the gruesome consequences allegedly attached to death by dehydration.[81] However, contemporary medical opinion repudiates that portrayal.[82] By use of basic palliative techniques (including sedatives, analgesics, and moistening of passages) health-care providers can mitigate the harsh effects of death from dehydration. One expert analogizes the end stage (following cessation of artificial nutrition) to the process by which patients often died thirty years ago, before artificial nutrition techniques were available.[83]

Having repudiated the specter of agonized, grotesque creatures being starved to death, the medical community has tended to regard artificial nutrition like other forms of medical intervention. A wide range of physicians' groups and ethicists have adopted the position that no logical distinction exists between removal of artificial nutrition and removal of other life-preserving technology. For example, the American Medical Association Council on Ethical and Judicial Affairs includes artificial nutrition among those life-prolonging medical interventions which may ethically be foregone at some phase in the decline of a terminally ill patient.[84] Similar stands were taken both by the President's Commission for the study of Ethical Problems in Medicine and by the Hastings Center Task force on Death and Dying.[85]

Not surprisingly, the judiciary has adopted the same perspective. State cases virtually unanimously view artificial nutrition as a form of medical intervention that is governed by standards applicable to conventional medical procedures.[86] Respirators, dialysis machines, and artificial nutrition are all seen as medical technology performing bodily functions when the body's normal processes have shut down. All are therefore subject to the patient's prerogative to control medical intervention. The Supreme Court's tacit acceptance of this proposition in *Cruzan* speaks thunderously for this conclusion. Although the justices were well aware of the arguments seeking to distinguish nutrition from medical treatment, no opinion embraces that idea.

The only dissonance in this emerging attitude toward artificial nutrition comes from state legislative voices. In some states, living-will type laws or durable power-of-attorney measures differentiate between nutrition and other forms of medical intervention. That dissonance and its limited practical effect will be discussed in chapter 3, which deals with the legal status of advance medical directives.

If a competent patient has a prerogative to reject artificial nutrition, does that prerogative include a right to reject manual feeding? The issue seems to arise when a patient is afflicted with debilitating chronic conditions, none of which yet necessitates life-sustaining medical intervention. The patient may seek to accelerate death by declining oral feeding while simultaneously refusing permission for artificial nutrition. (The assumption here is that the patient is capable of ingesting food without distress but simply chooses not to.) Some persons would avoid this juncture by a pill overdose or other means of suicide. Other persons, though, will be so physically incapacitated, weakened, or isolated that suicide is not a viable alternative. Because a food-rejecting course of conduct is sometimes prompted by extreme depression, the competency of the patient deserves careful scrutiny.[87] However, such scrutiny may well disclose that the patient is competent and the legal issue must then be faced.

All discussion to this point recognizes a legal prerogative to reject *medical intervention*. A threshold question, then, is whether hand-feeding is medical in nature. The answer is probably negative. While such feeding is commonly provided in institutional settings by health-care providers, the same assistance could presumably be provided by lay persons. There may be borderline cases, as when oral nutrition is being provided through a syringe or where professional guidance is crucial to shaping the patient's diet. Nonetheless, simple hand-feeding in most instances may be deemed to fall outside the bounds of medical intervention. The Illinois Supreme Court recently commented that spoon-feeding and bottle-feeding are "analytically distinguishable" from the artificial nutrition considered part of medical intervention.[88]

There is also a causative relation problem when hand-feeding is equated with the medical intervention previously discussed. In one sense, the patient may be tired of coping with chronic afflictions and may be seen as acquiescing in a natural dying process. Yet if a chronically ill patient is capable of ingesting and digesting, a death by starvation (or dehydration) is arguably not a proximate result of natural processes. (This is unlike the situation where ALS or some other degenerative disease disables the patient's swallowing capacity.) The decision to stop eating is a self-initiated deviation from customary human conduct in a fashion which jeopardizes survival. It is also undertaken with the intention of dying. The conduct closely resembles suicide—even though it involves passive behavior and is, therefore, technically distinguishable from typical means of suicide.

All these factors suggest that rejection of manual feeding is not part of a person's fundamental constitutional prerogative to reject life-sustaining medical intervention. The patient's accepted prerogative is to decline medical intervention in the face of a naturally occurring pathological condition. This does not encompass a patient's decision to prompt a life-threatening condition by refusing to ingest food.[89] Consistent with this view, the majority opinion in *Cruzan* remarked: "We do not think that a State is required to remain neutral in the face of an informed and voluntary decision by a physically able adult to starve to death."[90]

This conclusion—that a competent patient does not have a constitutional right to reject manual feeding—is also supported by the bulk of cases which have dealt with hunger strikers. Especially where the hunger striker was a prisoner seeking to extract concessions in return for resumption of eating, the judiciary has rejected the striker's reliance on a right to decline medical intervention.[91] It might be tempting to distinguish these cases on the ground that they involve unfair coercion being utilized by prisoners to blackmail administrative officials; that is, a prison administrator ought to be free to make policy judgments without the emotional blackmail of a prisoner's life hanging in the balance. Yet judicial hostility has also surfaced where the prisoner refusing nutrition has sought no concessions.[92]

The likely explanation is that courts see a moral distinction between self-initiated distress situations, such as hunger strikes, and situations where natural afflictions have prompted the necessity of artificial nutrition. Where a healthy person simply refuses to eat, this is seen as an act of passive suicide differentiable from a decision whether to accept medical intervention in the face of natural disease.

At the same time, there are a few cases where lower courts have indicated unwillingness to interfere with a debilitated elderly person's determination to refuse all nutrition (even though the person was physically capable of receiving such nutrition).[93] These courts have refused petitions by health-care providers to authorize forced feeding of the persons in question.

I suggest that the explanation for such results is revulsion at the prospect of physically restraining (for extended periods) persons who are both competent and determined to resist nutrition. This demeaning restraint constitutes such a significant harm to human dignity and self-respect that courts may be unwilling to interfere, at least where the person is already involved in an inexorable dying process.[94] Many sources have noted the distasteful specter projected by forcible restraint of a patient.[95]

This concern for the indignity of restraints has not always prevailed. The forced treatment of hunger strikers provides one example. In addition, courts have sometimes authorized forcible medical intervention toward resisting medical patients.[96] But this intervention usually occurs where an *in*competent patient is engaged in self-destructive behavior. That is, restraints are frequently used for patients who uncomprehendingly tend to harm themselves or others.[97]

The judicial attitude may well be different where competent patients facing serious afflictions determine to resist all forms of nutrition. In that context, the likelihood is that solicitude for the competent patient's dignity will impel courts to refrain from interference when nutrition is knowingly declined by wearied chronic patients. This approach might well prevail in the future even where hunger-striking prisoners are involved (so long as they are not seeking to exert coercion on administrators or others). That is, the revulsion toward forced administration of nutrition against the considered will of competent individuals may well overcome the moral qualms about acquiescing in a form of passive suicide.

IS A PERSON FACING A FATAL AFFLICTION ENTITLED TO ACCOMPLISH DEATH BY MEANS OTHER THAN REJECTION OF MEDICAL INTERVENTION?

Some commentators have sought to expand the notion of a right to refuse life-preserving medical treatment to include a "right to die."[98] These commentators see the self-determination implicated in rejecting treatment as encompassing a prerogative to dictate the circumstances in which life may be ended. This would include not only self-administered suicide but assistance from others in committing suicide.

Some persons would even include active euthanasia (the introduction by others of external agents, such as poisons, to end a patient's life).

As a matter of constitutional law, the argument that recognition of a patient's right to decline medical intervention compels recognition of a right to die is not very persuasive. The tradition which impelled acknowledgment of a right to refuse life-preserving medical intervention was grounded in bodily integrity and self-determination as reflected in the doctrine of informed consent. Bodily integrity has included a prerogative to resist many bodily invasions. But bodily integrity has never meant a prerogative to introduce whatever elements into the body that a person wishes. Laws against narcotics, prostitution, and consensual sodomy tend to refute such a notion. And laws against assisting suicide tend to undermine the notion that there is a traditional prerogative to control the timing of one's demise or to use active means to terminate one's existence.

Consider the healthy person who decides to contribute a vital organ to a critically ill person. However commendable the motivations involved may be, any physician who performs such an organ-harvesting operation is probably committing homicide. The same analysis is applicable to the technician who freezes a patient to death pursuant to the patient's wish to utilize cryonics. The motives of all parties involved may be life-preserving or life-exalting in nature, but the deed is still a homicide unlikely to find constitutional protection.[99] The motive for accomplishing another person's death has not generally provided a legal defense. (Self-defense and defense of others constitute exceptions.) There is certainly room for legislative change if and when resurrection of frozen corpses becomes a realistic possibility. In the meantime, freezing persons to death will likely remain a crime.

All this is not to say that persons suffering natural afflictions will never be accorded a "right" to secure a quick and painless death. Assisted suicide and even active euthanasia deserve careful analysis as society devises responses to the modern life-extending capability of medical technology. The conflicting policy considerations surrounding those issues are beyond the scope of this book. My only point here is that if such steps are to take place, they will follow from legislative authorization or from common-law development and not from constitutional law.

2

Advance Directives and Problems of Prospective Autonomy

MODERN MEDICINE'S ability to preserve persons indefinitely in gravely debilitated states has prompted a search for ways to cope with technology. One such way is patient control over medical intervention. Chapter 1 described the evolution of legal doctrine aimed at permitting competent individuals to govern their contemporaneous medical fates. This chapter addresses the adaptation of this autonomy principle to future-oriented decisions.

Advance directives have emerged as a vehicle for people to control post-competence medical intervention in a dying process. The object is to permit individuals to prescribe personal preferences in advance and so to maintain a measure of autonomy even after incompetency. I refer to this technique as *prospective autonomy*.

By formulating advance instructions, a declarant (directive maker) can seek to shape future medical handling according to his or her personal values. An advance directive may also designate an agent who will ultimately be responsible for implementing the declarant's instructions or, in the absence of discernible instructions, for making medical decisions on behalf of the incompetent patient. Such a person is variously known as a health-care agent, representative, surrogate, attorney-in-fact, or proxy; but I'll use the term health-care agent. (Note also that in this book the term *advance directive* includes an instruction directive, a directive appointing an agent, or a document combining both elements.)

The potential benefits of an advance directive are plain. Not only can persons prospectively promote personal values and concepts of dignity, but the ultimate decision makers on behalf of the incompetent patient can receive crucial guidance. An advance directive can guide health-care providers as to the agent to be responsible for decision making, as to substantive wishes of the declarant regarding care, or both. A health-care agent or, in the absence of a designated agent, any person acting as formal or informal guardian of the incompetent patient also can receive guidance as to the wishes of the patient. This guidance might mitigate the anxiety, uncertainty, or conflicts sometimes surrounding terminal decisions on behalf of incompetent patients.

As noted, an advance directive exercises prospective autonomy. Prospective autonomy is clearly different in some respects from the contemporaneous personal choice described in chapter 1. Those differences raise certain practical problems. One problem flows from the complexity of decision making in the death and dying area. Future-oriented decisions may involve hypothetical facts and a multitude of prospective circumstances which complicate decision making.[1] To formulate a comprehensive advance directive, a person might have to consider a spectrum of potential mental states (within the range of incompetency), infinite combinations of mental and physical dysfunction, and a variety of possible factors bearing on a decision whether to receive life-sustaining medical intervention.

Additional problems in formulating advance directives flow from the limited perspective of a person looking toward future, post-competence events. A directive may not always be drafted proximate to the moment of its implementation, so it may involve prediction about remote and abstract developments. A person's feelings about death and incapacity might even change with maturity or greater proximity to critical events. Moreover, a person shaping future medical handling is speculating about feelings and sentiments (in a future state of incompetency) which are inherently unknowable in advance.

These difficulties concerning the complexity, remoteness, and perspective of future-oriented death-and-dying decisions prompted initial uncertainty about the legal status of advance directives.[2] In the early 1970s, it was thought that an advance directive constituted a hortatory instrument—an instruction that the declarant *hoped* would be followed but which had no legally binding effect. It was assumed that extending life was an integral part of a guardian's and health-care provider's responsibilities toward an incompetent, dying person. There was no confidence that removal of life support would be consistent with traditional responsibility to act in the "best interests" of a helpless ward. In that era, even if a now incompetent patient would apparently have preferred to relinquish life-preserving medical intervention, the doctrine of parens patriae (a state's authority to protect incompetent persons) loomed as a possible basis to override the patient's prior choice. That implication might have been drawn from cases of the period ordering lifesaving treatment for Jehovah's Witnesses despite their previously stated religious objections.[3] A possible reading of those decisions was that an incompetent patient's guardian should be guided by the patient's current health interests rather than by the patient's prior values and expressed preferences.

Subsequent legal doctrine has repudiated those initial hesitations. Courts have come to recognize that prospective autonomy in shaping medical intervention is not only a legitimate concept but an integral part of the self-determination which society respects. This judicial posture was reached only by overcoming both the practical concerns mentioned above and skepticism about the role of autonomy in the context of incompetent beings. The arguments which countered the initial concerns are worth attention. Their persuasiveness will determine the ultimate scope accorded to advance directives.

DO THE PRACTICAL DIFFICULTIES AFFECTING
PROSPECTIVE AUTONOMY OBVIATE THE UTILITY OF
THE ADVANCE DIRECTIVE INSTRUMENT?

As noted, practical difficulties confront a person formulating instructions concerning future medical handling in a state of incompetency. First, incompetency can encompass a wide spectrum of mental states—from total unconsciousness to acute awareness (but lacking the mental ability to process the impressions being absorbed).[4] A person's attitudes toward future handling may vary widely across this spectrum of possible states. Further, a person might ultimately face a wide range of physical afflictions and disabilities. This range of afflictions in turn engenders a host of medical contingencies. Each affliction carries its own prognosis uncertainty as well as a multitude of possible combinations of physical and mental dysfunction.

A patient contemplating this range of mental and physical states must also consider a multiplicity of factors in planning future medical intervention. Personal attitudes toward physical pain, physical appearance, physical incapacity, diminished mental function, helplessness, dependence, religious precepts, economic burdens, and well-being of surrounding family and friends represent some of the elements which might influence a person's future-oriented medical decisions. The sheer complexity of the issue therefore raises concern about a person's ability to make an informed and considered choice about dying in a future state of incompetency.[5]

Despite the difficulties involved, the multiplicity of prospective medical situations should not prevent effective advance directives. While a comprehensive directive anticipating all possible situations might not be possible (given the limits of human imagination), every competent person is capable of addressing a few precepts or guidelines regarding future medical care.[6] A person can articulate certain principles—whether grounded on religious scruples, personal philosophy, or personal notions of dignity—which will be relevant across a wide spectrum of medical conditions.

Religiously based principles are likely to be simple (such as an aversion to blood transfusions or a belief that life should be preserved to the maximum extent possible). Dignity-based principles may be more complex, but they may also be reducible to understandable terms. First, a person may have well-developed dignity concepts about a particular status, such as permanent unconsciousness. Such a preference can be expressed in a simple and clear-cut fashion. Second, even if a person is seeking to avoid a conscious, but severely debilitated, existence, it may be possible to describe a few key factors (such as level of dementia) which would make life-sustaining intervention unwanted regardless of the particular medical condition at hand. In short, an outcome-oriented directive—one that describes a debilitated status which is personally intolerable—cuts across a wide range of potential medical interventions.

Additional problems regarding future-oriented decisions flow from the distance of the competent person looking toward future events.[7] A person might well formulate medical instructions far in advance of the anticipated events. (Indeed, this is sound policy because one can't know when an unexpected accident might precipitate a permanent state of incompetency.) This distance sometimes necessitates predictions about remote and abstract circumstances.

This problem of immediacy generates several concerns. One is that the abstract nature of the initial decision making reduces the scrutiny and consideration which would otherwise be given to deviant or morally problematic decisions.[8] A patient making a contemporaneous decision to reject life-preserving medical intervention (e.g., because of religious scruples or views about post-treatment indignity) will likely be subjected to counterarguments and supplications by surrounding staff and concerned observers. The person drafting a directive to shape prospective treatment may not receive similar input or confrontation. This can make the advance decision less informed or considered than might be ideal.

Another concern relates to the fact that the directive may be based on projections about feelings which might not in fact materialize. Professors Rebecca S. Dresser and John A. Robertson argue that the difficulty of foreseeing personal interests in a remote and abstract state make an advance directive an unreliable device.[9] They observe that a person's condition, feelings, and sensations (as they materialize in a future state of incompetency) might be radically different from those contemplated at the time of making an advance directive. For example, a debilitated status which in advance seems demeaning may turn out to have some redeeming value to the incompetent patient. If that is the case, a lack of proximity to actual events may have distorted the substance of the directive. A healthy declarant may have undervalued the potential satisfactions of a debilitated status.[10]

A further concern is the hypothetical nature of projected feelings in a future state of incompetency. A person shaping future medical handling is speculating about feelings and sentiments which are inherently unknowable in such a state. A person cannot precisely anticipate the feelings and experiences of an incapacitated existence—whether positive feelings of satisfaction or negative feelings of frustration and humiliation.[11] If a person can only *guess* about the nature of personal reactions to a future debilitated state, should society respect life-and-death judgments made from such a divorced perspective? In some other contexts, significance is attached to the abstract perspective of the decision maker toward actual consequences. For example, there is great reluctance to bind a woman to prebirth decisions regarding the adoption or future custody of a prospective child.[12] An inability to accurately envision the feelings of childbirth and bonding supposedly undermines the reliability of the advance decision.

The difficulties of remoteness and perspective in making future-oriented death-

and-dying decisions ought not preclude giving binding effect to advance medical directives. While a person cannot be certain what conditions will develop post-competency, it may well be that a declarant correctly anticipates the suffering and/or debilitation associated with his or her dying process. And there is no reason to assume (absent contrary evidence) that a declarant's views or priorities have in fact changed since the advance directive was signed. An adult may have well-developed and firm attitudes about some important issues (e.g., a vision of personal dignity or concern for the surrounding family's emotional and/or fiscal interests) which apply across a spectrum of medical conditions and which are likely to remain firm.

Those sources who oppose prospective autonomy on grounds of remoteness and lack of proximity have yet to explain what chronological lines could be drawn. That is, it is evident that some prospective autonomy must be honored. If a competent person gives instructions about the scope of prospective surgery, that instruction will be honored while the patient is under general anesthesia the next day. This is an exercise of prospective autonomy. The same is true if the surgery is to take place in a week or a month. Unless there were some material reason to think that the patient had altered his or her decision, the initial, competently made instruction would govern. If the initial instruction speaks to the situation later encountered, at what point is the instruction too remote to be upheld?

Of course, a person's philosophy and attitude toward death *might* change over time. It is, therefore, appropriate for the eventual administrator of an advance directive to examine whether the patient's values did vary or change after the directive was issued. Yet the *potential* changeability of people's feelings should not be a basis to bar future-oriented directives.

Certainly, law does not withhold enforcement of future-oriented disposition of property by will, irrevocable trust, or contract, even though the disposer's inclinations might change over time. In those contexts, documents are enforced as written even if it is later shown that the disposer's inclinations changed in fact (but no alteration was made in the relevant document while the actor was still competent). In the context of advance medical directives, it should at least be assumed that a directive maker's wishes persist over time unless there is some showing to the contrary.

The unknowability of a person's prospective feelings in a state of incompetency should also not constitute a bar to advance directives. This unknowability factor ought to impel some serious deliberation (by the declarant) about the content of an advance directive. A person ought to ponder the possible range of feelings in various debilitated states before dictating the rejection of life-preserving intervention in those states. But a person is generally capable of contemplating states of incompetency and fixing his or her basic parameters of personal dignity in those states. Sometimes, prospective feelings or sensations will not be particularly important, as when the condition being contemplated is an unconscious or semiconscious state. Even if future feelings are relevant, a person is capable of making an informed prediction about those feelings and of considering the importance of such feelings in relation to other elements relevant to post-competence medical intervention.

Consider some illustrations. For some persons, an altruistic concern for the interests and well-being of surrounding loved ones will be an overriding factor even if prospective existence does not entail great suffering. For some persons, a personal vision of dignity—grounded on the image which the person wants to leave for posterity—will be a determinative factor even if a feared sense of embarrassment or humiliation does not in fact materialize. In short, the problems of remoteness and perspective associated with advance directives dictate care in formulating such instruments but do not vitiate their utility.

Nor does remoteness (and the possible abstract nature) of a determination mean that inadequate deliberation has gone into the advance instructions. We are considering a written document drafted with the expectation that it will govern life-and-death decisions. A person would indeed be well advised to consult with someone knowledgeable and caring concerning the practical and moral implications of the person's advance instructions. But the reduction to writing and the signing themselves have a cautionary impact on the declarant, thus impelling reflection.

A prerequisite that an advance directive be signed only after certain consultations would entail costs likely to make such instruments accessible only to upper income people. Again, the nature of the deliberation surrounding an advance directive might be a proper inquiry for any health-care agent (or other person) eventually implementing the instructions. That agent might inquire whether the declarant was aware of the considerations making a particular instruction problematic. (Chapter 5 explores this and other aspects of administration of an advance directive.) But the signing of an advance directive ought to be presumed—subject to rebuttal—to carry with it sufficient deliberation to make it binding. Every person knows that he or she might be disabled tomorrow, and so the specter of incapacity has to prompt a certain amount of contemplation even if the maker of an advance directive is currently hale and hearty.

There is no better way to respect future-oriented self-determination than an advance directive. A person's own projections about preferred choices are more likely to accurately reflect that person's will than the approximations and reconstructions of that will performed by other parties at a later date when the subject is incompetent. Thus, if society wants to uphold self-determination in the context of medical decisions for incompetent patients, advance directives must be respected.[13]

A public policy which upholds advance directives is likely to benefit the peace of mind of competent persons in general and persons afflicted with degenerative disease in particular. Many persons experience anxiety in contemplating the prospect of prolonged existence in a status regarded by them as degrading. That anxiety can be acute for persons who see a protracted, severely debilitated dying process as a significant detriment to a lifetime image. Some persons may even be so wary of the aggressiveness of health care providers as to forego treatment for life-threatening disorders. For all such persons, the knowledge that advance instructions will be honored may be a source of relief and reassurance.[14] Limited studies tend to confirm both that loss of control over events prompts patients to suffer negative physical and emotional effects[15] and that discussion of advance directives causes patients to worry less.[16] Future-oriented control of medical intervention may also promote competent persons' self-respect.

Such factors as reduced anxiety and increased self respect add a general, morale-promoting value to a public policy upholding advance directives. Another utilitarian benefit is the saving of public resources. That is, widespread use and implementation of advance directives might well result in reduced resort to expensive life-preserving medical machinery. This would be an incidental public benefit flowing from the upholding of future-oriented autonomy. I am not contending that these general public benefits provide a morally sufficient basis for enforcing advance directives. They do, however, reinforce the self-determination arguments for upholding a competent person's advance directive.

IS A RIGHT TO SELF-DETERMINATION MEANINGFUL IN THE CONTEXT OF AN INCOMPETENT PATIENT?

Self-determination normally entails a conscious weighing of the options at hand. For a medical patient, this means considering and weighing the consequences of nontreatment or various forms of treatment. By definition, an incompetent patient is incapable of performing these functions. Many sources therefore argue that notions of autonomy and personal decision making have no place in regard to an irreversibly incompetent patient.[17] For those sources, a right to refuse medical treatment is dependent upon capacity for choice.[18]

The obvious response is that an advance directive reflects a competently made declaration of a person's wishes and, therefore, is an exercise of self-determination. Not everyone is satisfied with this response. Some commentators insist that the problems of uncertainty, proximity, and perspective mentioned in the previous section subvert the notion of autonomy with regard to advance medical directives. For them, a person contemplating a prospective dying process can never be sufficiently informed in advance to make an effective and binding determination.[19]

The counterarguments were presented above. I argued that prospective autonomy is entitled to respect despite the practical difficulties of anticipating future medical scenarios. The advance directive mechanism for self-determination may not be perfect. There will always be some residual doubt about whether the declarant fully grasped the implications of his or her determination or whether the declarant might have changed his or her mind in the interim. But these flaws don't destroy the importance of advance directives in a society which highly values self-determination.[20]

A declarant ought to be presumed to have deliberately formulated and constantly adhered to the sentiments of an advance directive unless the record rebuts that presumption. A dying process—particularly a protracted dying process—is too integral a part of a person's life to be removed from the realm of self-determination. People care mightily about the image and memories to be left during a period of decline and death. People strive to cultivate an image during a lifetime, and they don't want to see that image despoiled by a protracted demise in a gravely debilitated condition.[21] These personal aspirations seem worthy of respect. Disregard of prior choices relegates the now incompetent patient to the status of an object whose fate is determined for it rather than of a human who has etched his or her own fate.

The question now is which view will prevail. Do obstacles of proximity and perspective bar recognition of prospective autonomy in the context of death and dying? Or are people entitled to shape in advance the degree of medical intervention provided in their post-competence existences?

In law, the concept of prospective autonomy has been almost universally accepted—as a matter of state common law, state constitutional law, or federal constitutional interpretation. A number of state court decisions ascribe to an incompetent person the "same right to autonomy in medical decisions as a competent patient."[22] This broad declaration ignores the cognitive incapacity of an incompetent patient and cannot be taken literally. But at the least, the statement means that a person who has competently expressed his or her wishes (as in an advance directive) is entitled to have post-competence medical care shaped according to those wishes.

Judicial willingness to preserve self-determination in the context of an incompetent patient spawned what is known as the "substituted judgment" approach. The idea was to decide the incompetent patient's fate in the same manner the patient would decide if the patient were miraculously competent for a few moments.[23] Replicating a patient's choice might be a difficult goal to attain, at least in the absence of the patient's considered judgment about life-sustaining medical intervention. But an advance directive can constitute an explicit judgment about that issue. Most authorities therefore recognize that a person's advance directive is the best evidence of the now incompetent patient's wishes.[24] And all authorities endorsing the substituted judgment approach regard the patient's competently expressed wishes as binding.

Recognition of the binding effect of prior expressions could have come through common-law development (judicial structuring of the physician-patient and guardian-patient relationships). As courts began to recognize a constitutionally based right to reject life-sustaining medical intervention, however, they quickly acknowledged prior expressions as a source of constitutional rights for an incompetent patient. That is, the courts readily viewed implementation of the prior wishes of an incompetent patient as fulfilling a constitutional "right" of self-determination.[25]

The ready acceptance of prospective autonomy reflects judicial appreciation of the importance of self-determination and personal visions of dignity in shaping a dying process. Many of the relevant cases arose in the context of permanently unconscious patients who, while competent, had indicated that they would not want life-preserving medical treatment if reduced to a permanently vegetative status. Those cases regard a prior declaration as a statement about what the declarant would regard as a degrading existence. They regard such a declaration as a way for a person to preserve humanity and dignity in the face of an incapacitating condition. And they regard this determination as an integral part of the self-determination which properly belongs to an individual either under the common law or the Constitution.

The U.S. Supreme Court's disposition of *Cruzan* does not alter this judicial pattern. I've already argued that *Cruzan* does not repudiate the notion that a competent person's rejection of medical intervention is a fundamental aspect of liberty. *Cruzan* holds only that it is constitutional for a state to prevent withdrawal of life-sustaining care *in the absence of clear-cut instructions* from the previously competent patient.

The *Cruzan* decision may even reinforce the respect which has been accorded to advance directives as a vehicle of prospective autonomy. Eight of the nine justices seemed to indicate that if there had been clear proof of the incompetent patient's previously expressed wishes, the state would have been required to respect that determination. This would be consistent with prior Supreme Court acknowledgement that rights involving choices for incompetent persons can only be given meaningful expression via agents acting on behalf of the incompetent individuals.[26] *Cruzan* may well mean that the clear exercise of future-oriented autonomy will be deemed to prevail (as a matter of constitutional law) against a state's asserted interest in promoting sanctity of life principles. An advance directive is, potentially, a clear expression of the patient's autonomy.

This possible constitutional status for advance directives has significant implications for efforts of some states to circumscribe the scope of living wills or other advance directives. The next chapter examines those implications while setting out the legal framework governing interpretation and administration of advance directives.

Before turning to that topic, some last words about *Cruzan*. The Supreme Court ruled there that in the absence of clear-cut prior expressions, a comatose patient's constitutional liberty interest was not violated by a state requirement of continued medical intervention. That ruling was probably sound in terms of a liberty interest in self-determination. That is, in the absence of a patient's prior expressions on the topic of life-sustaining medical intervention, no genuine choice can be attributed to the now incompetent patient.[27]

Self-determination, though, is not the only constitutional interest which could have surfaced in *Cruzan*. The practical effect of Missouri's legal framework was to relegate to an indefinite limbo every incompetent patient who had not left prior instructions. Absent prior expressions, Missouri mandated continued life support no matter how painful or degraded the status of the incompetent patient. This course denied the guardians of Nancy Cruzan any option to act in her best interests or in order to preserve her dignity. This preclusion of medical approaches consistent with the best interests of the incompetent patient deprived Nancy Cruzan of a highly humane course and relegated her to a permanently insensate status. The Missouri statute was thus arguably unconstitutional in denying liberty—liberty not in the sense of choice but in the sense of a range of humane treatment options.[28] Denial of that range of options relegates some patients to an indefinite, undignified status arguably inconsistent with constitutional respect for human dignity.

In sum, it would have been possible to rule in *Cruzan* that liberty and due process under the Fourteenth Amendment demand that states respect the basic dignity of incompetent patients. That would mean, at least, that the standard fixed for guardianship must permit a medical decision consistent with the incompetent patient's best interests, including personal dignity.

This idea—that the due process clause compels states to use guardianship decision-making standards which permit choices consistent with the well-being and dignity of an incompetent being—has implications beyond the death-and-dying area. Liberty as dignity would mean, for example, that a state must furnish protection and at least a minimum level of dignified care to any incompetent whom the state decides to shelter.[29] Similarly, a state could not preclude a sterilization (or other medical procedure) for a gravely mentally disabled person if such a procedure were necessary to that person's happiness and well-being.

The topic of rights of incompetents (in the absence of competently expressed, advance instructions) is beyond the scope of this book. My only point here is that *Cruzan* could have been resolved on a basis broader than Nancy's self-determination interest or her parents' familial decision-making authority. As it is, *Cruzan* does not constitute an impediment to advance directives. But that case could have been better argued (and decided).

3

Choosing the Best Format in Light of the Statutory Framework for Advance Directives

IN ORDER to decide on the proper format and content for an advance medical directive, it is important to understand the governing legal structure. There are variations from state to state, so before counseling anyone, an adviser must check the statutes in effect in the particular locale.[1] However, there are common features, and this chapter examines the most prominent patterns.

Parallel to the post-1976 development of judicial doctrine establishing the importance of prior expressions (as described in the previous chapter), state legislatures have widely endorsed the concept of advance directives designed to govern medical handling of incompetent patients. This legislative recognition of prospective autonomy has taken two forms. The most prevalent vehicle is living-will legislation—laws recognizing the binding effect of prior instructions reduced to writing in accord with certain formalities. Another vehicle is legislation authorizing a competent person (a principal) to appoint a health-care agent charged with making the principal's post-competence health-care decisions. The principal may also accompany appointment of a health-care agent with written guidelines or instructions to the agent.

In the next sections, I'll look at the strengths and weaknesses of these respective techniques for shaping post-competence care. Thereafter, I'll suggest a preferred format for an advance directive.

LIVING-WILL TYPE LEGISLATION

Starting with California's fledgling effort in 1976, forty-seven states have endorsed the use of written substantive instructions aimed at governing future medical intervention.[2] These living-will type measures typically provide that a now incompetent patient's prior instructions should be given binding force. The typical statutory preamble declares legislative recognition of the autonomy and dignity of incompetent patients and dictates respect for living wills ₊ ₐ means to promote those values. The typical statute then prescribes certain formalities for creation of a living will, usually the witnessing of a declarant's signature by two persons. In a few states, the statute provides a form document which must be followed; more often, the statute provides a sample form which can be adopted or varied at the option of a declarant.[3] Usually, the statute mandates that health-care providers either honor the terms of a living will or act to transfer the patient to a provider who will cooperate with the patient's will. (The sanction for noncompliance is usually stated as "professional discipline".)

The potential utility of living-will type legislation was considerable.[4] In the many states where the judiciary had not addressed the issue, living-will statutes removed any legal cloud over the concept of future-oriented autonomy. The legislation clarified that a now incompetent patient's prior instructions could and should be given binding force. It also clarified that medical compliance with a living will would not be deemed assistance to suicide or any other impropriety. Indeed, health-care providers were assured by the legislation that good-faith compliance with a living will would immunize providers from legal liability.

Living-will type legislation also offered considerable practical promise. By encouraging written documentation of a person's wishes regarding life support, such legislation seemed to promise important help to future decision makers acting on behalf of incompetent patients. A written format provides the opportunity for elaboration of a person's preferences and for deliberation on the complex issues involved. As an evidentiary tool, a writing is clearly preferable to testimony about prior oral declarations. As a practical aid, an instruction directive might reduce the uncertainty and anguish of those decision makers responsible for the medical fate of an incompetent patient. Accordingly, a directive might reduce disagreement and conflict among decision makers.

Despite the considerable potential of living-will type laws, major disappointments must be noted regarding the bulk of such legislation to date. (New Jersey provides an exception, for reasons to be explained in chapter 8.) First, the legislation in most jurisdictions is seriously flawed. The state political processes have clearly been impacted by a variety of interest groups: health-care providers, religious groups, and right-to-life organizations, as well as patients' rights advocates.[5] The result has been serious limitations on the circumstances in which state legislatures have given their endorsement to the implementation of living wills. (The nature and effects of these limitations are considered below.) Second, the living will has not yet emerged as a popular tool for the exercise of control over a future dying process. The best estimates are that only fifteen to twenty-five percent of adults have signed a living will, though the percentage is higher for persons over age sixty-four.[6]

There are significant obstacles to the widespread use of living-will type instruments. One obstacle is people's common unwillingness to confront their own mortality. That unwillingness has always been reflected in the low percentage of people who draft regular wills, and it is probably a factor contributing to the low percentage who draft instructions regarding terminal medical treatment.[7]

Another obstacle may be a public perception that living-will instruments will not effectively control critical medical decisions.[8] There is some empirical evidence which would explain such a perception. One recent study and some anecdotal reports show that physicians in charge of medical intervention in a dying process may be influenced more by the wishes of surrounding family members than by the incompetent patient's living will.[9] This order of influence flows in part from physicians' sensitivity to the possibility of lawsuits.[10] In the typical terminal care scenario, it is the surrounding family which looms as a litigation threat if their wishes are contravened and not the helpless, moribund patient. A similar phenomenon has occurred in the context of prior instructions regarding organ donation, where the surrounding family's wishes tend to prevail in practice.[11]

Two developments in 1990 might provide impetus to the use of living-will type documents. The July 1990 *Cruzan* decision received extensive publicity and highlighted the importance of clear-cut prior instructions in the context of incompetent patients. In the months following *Cruzan*, right-to-die oriented organizations received over a million requests for living-will forms. And in October 1990, Congress passed the federal Patient Self-Determination Act[12] requiring health-care institutions receiving federal funds to provide to their patients information about advance medical directives.[13]

These two 1990 developments have certainly promoted public consciousness about advance directives, including living-will type instruments. The ultimate success of a living will depends, however, on its utility in achieving the basic goal—extensive control over medical intervention in a subsequent dying process.

As noted, the living-will legislation in most jurisdictions is flawed. And the principal flaw stems from provisions in many living-will laws significantly qualifying the circumstances in which legislative endorsement is accorded to implementation of advance instructions.[14] Because such legislation appears to limit the scope of a declarant's autonomy (in contrast to the broad common-law acceptance of prospective autonomy), it threatens to have a negative effect on the responsiveness of health-care providers to living-will type instruments. Statutory restrictions may well cause health-care providers to have hesitations about the legal effect of certain living-will instructions. The providers' risk-aversive tendencies would then prompt irresolution and thus hamper the implementation of advance instructions. The statutory limitations therefore warrant examination.

STATUTORY CONSTRAINTS CONTAINED IN LIVING-WILL TYPE LAWS

Living-will type statutes almost universally confine authorized removal of life support to a patient in a "terminal condition."[15] The precise definition of a terminal condition varies from state to state, but the thrust of many such provisions is to limit legislative endorsement of cessation of life support to unpreventably dying patients in the last stages of decline (as opposed to gravely debilitated individuals whose lives are indefinitely preserveable despite serious medical pathology). A legislative limitation of this sort is unresponsive to the needs of people who dread protracted maintenance in a chronic, debilitated status or of people stricken with degenerative disease and on the brink of what will be inexorable decline toward total helplessness. "Persons suffering from Alzheimer's disease and strokes, from chronic kidney failure, or from certain malignancies may not be terminal but nevertheless consider aggressive, life-sustaining medical interventions to produce a disproportionate burden."[16]

A number of living-will statutes define a terminal condition as an "incurable and irreversible" condition which, "regardless of" medical intervention, makes death imminent.[17] The irreversibility notion raises the possibility that the technical maintenance of lost bodily functions can preclude finding a terminal condition and thus undermine an advance directive aimed at preventing indefinite lingering in a gravely debilitated condition. For example, dialysis machines can substitute for the waste-disposal function of damaged kidneys. And artificial nutrition can substitute for normal ingestion of food after brain trauma incapacitates the swallowing reflex. Yet, end-stage kidney disease may so ravage the patient that dialysis merely prolongs the dying process without relieving suffering or restoring a meaningful level of function.[18] And artificial nutrition may sustain a patient in a permanent vegetative state, forestalling death but leaving the patient utterly insentient. In short, if a condition is deemed "reversible" when medical intervention can preserve bodily function (but the patient is left with insidious consequences from the pathological condition), then the purpose of many advance directives would be frustrated.[19]

As noted, a number of living-will statutes define a terminal condition as one which, *regardless of* medical intervention, will cause death imminently. If the words "regardless of medical intervention" are read literally to mean death will result imminently even with medical intervention, then such a provision is pointless. Where death is imminent anyway with or without medical intervention, the prerogative to relinquish further medical intervention has no practical consequence.[20]

A few state courts have recognized the pointlessness of such language and have ruled that proximity of death must be assessed without regard to the particular medical intervention in dispute. The Illinois Supreme Court recently commented: "If the very delay caused by the [life-preserving] procedures [in dispute] were allowed to govern the assessment of imminence, the Act's definition of a terminal disease would be rendered circular and meaningless."[21] That court ruled that imminence must be judged "as if the death-delaying procedures were absent."[22] This means, for example, that if a respirator is sought to be detached from a patient with chronic respiratory incapacity, the condition would be deemed terminal if death would be imminent without the disputed respirator. However, there is no assurance that all state courts facing similar statutory language will similarly interpret their living-will legislation.

Even where the "terminal condition" limitation is understood to mean terminal

in the absence of the disputed medical intervention, a problem occurs with living-will statutes which include a proximity of death limitation. For example, some
statutes in defining a terminal condition require that death be "imminent" (in the
absence of medical intervention). A narrow interpretation of such a provision
would exclude conditions involving artificial nutrition and would necessitate extended treatment for many cancers. Moreover, where a gradual illness, like pneumonia, afflicts a severely demented and incapacitated person whose underlying
physical condition is stable, such a provision apparently means that antibiotics
must be provided. In all these instances, death might not be considered imminent
even in the absence of medical intervention. (Also, there is a hazard that the intervening pneumonia might be deemed a curable or reversible condition, so that
the stabilized, deteriorated patient might still not be in a terminal condition.)

In some jurisdictions, the imminence requirement has been altered to say that
death must occur "within a relatively short time" in the absence of medical intervention.[23] Even this relaxation of the requisite time proximity between cessation
of treatment and death does not fully meet the exigencies of advance directives.
For one thing, the phrase "a relatively short time" is imprecise and subject to
grudging interpretation by health-care providers so inclined. In addition, people
ought to be able to provide in advance for medical response to protracted dying
processes such as cancer or other degenerative diseases. "The two leading killers
in the U.S.—heart disease and cancer—as well as degenerative diseases—M. S.
and Alzheimer's—and any of the immune disorders—such as AIDS—are all
chronic illnesses that frequently lead to a [protracted] terminal period of incompetence."[24] In the absence of living-will legislation, the judicial proclivity would
probably be to respect clear prior directives without respect to death proximity or
life-expectancy limitations.[25]

The impetus for the original legislative tendency to endorse advance directives
only for the last stages of unpreventable dying processes is understandable. Legislators were influenced in part by the early judicial formulations of a competent
patient's prerogative to resist life-preserving treatment. These early formulations
had hinted that the patient's prerogative might be limited to situations where unpreventable death is near.[26] It was thought that, otherwise, government interests in
promoting sanctity of life might override even a competent patient's self-determination prerogative.[27] In addition, legislators were concerned about helpless beings
and their possible exploitation in a medical setting. When most living-will laws
were adopted, there had been little experience with standards and practices of removal of life support. The specter of government-endorsed quality-of-life judgments
about indefinitely preservable beings alarmed some people.[28] Finally, legislative
hesitancy to endorse full-blown autonomy in the context of future-oriented terminal
medical decisions also stemmed from political pressure. State legislative processes
have commonly been impacted by a variety of interest groups (including religious
groups and right-to-life organizations).[29] Right-to-life organizations, in particular,

have sought to circumscribe the circumstances in which living wills might lead to a patient's demise via removal of life support.

The problem is that confining advance directives to the last stages of an un-avoidable dying process intolerably restricts the scope of future-oriented autonomy. Many persons drafting advance directives are concerned with the effects of pro-gressive deterioration of organ systems and the combined effects of chronic dis-orders. Previously vital persons often wish to oppose medical intervention capable of prolonging existence for extended periods if the status preserved entails extreme suffering or a gravely incapacitated and (subjectively) degrading status. When medical intervention cannot restore an individual to even a semblance of a former status, that individual may seek the prerogative to reject further medical intervention via an advance directive. The "terminal illness" limitation—as contained in some living-will type legislation—inhibits the exercise of that prerogative. (Later in this chapter I'll suggest means to circumvent this limitation for persons preparing an advance directive in jurisdictions with restrictive legislation.)

Other common restraints within living-will statutes relate to the scope of "life-sustaining procedures" deemed rejectable pursuant to a living will. One common subject of special attention is artificial nutrition and hydration. (For simplicity's sake, I'll use the term nutrition as a shorthand for both nutrition and hydration.)

As noted in chapter 1, some commentators sought to draw a distinction between artificial nutrition and other forms of life-sustaining medical treatment. There were two contentions. One was that provision of nutrition carries a symbolic import—commitment to the well-being of fellow humans—absent in other types of medical intervention. A second contention related to causation; withdrawal of nutrition was claimed to cause a patient to starve to death, while withdrawal of mechanical life support would merely allow a natural disease process to run its course.

Almost all courts addressing the issue have rejected the notion that artificial nutrition is differentiable from other medical intervention. A wide range of phy-sicians' groups and ethicists have also rejected the asserted distinctiveness of arti-ficial nutrition. I already explained the reasons for this triumph of logic and common sense. Nonetheless, the living-will statutes in a number of states still single out artificial nutrition. This statutory distinction poses a serious concern for a declarant (maker of an advance directive) who is fearful of being mired either in a permanent vegetative condition or in a barely conscious state caused by severe strokes or other brain trauma. In those situations, a person may well wish to forego artificial nutrition as well as other forms of medical intervention.

The statutory constraints on rejection of artificial nutrition take a variety of forms. As of 1986, seventeen states had excluded artificial nutrition from the scope of treatment rejectable pursuant to a living-will. Since that time, a number of those seventeen state legislatures have mitigated that exclusionary policy. Several of those states now include nutrition within rejectable life support.[30] Several others among them now allow for the withdrawal of artificial nutrition if the declarant has explicitly authorized that course.[31]

There are still approximately six states which seek to bar withdrawal of artificial nutrition pursuant to a living will.[32] And a few other states closely confine the circumstances in which nutrition can be withdrawn. For example, Illinois bars withdrawal of nutrition if it "would result in death solely from dehydration or starvation rather than from the existing terminal condition."[33] North Dakota allows nutrition cessation only if continued nutrition would be "harmful or painful" to the patient.[34]

The overall picture with regard to artificial nutrition is more permissive. In the majority of states, artificial nutrition is either not mentioned (thus leaving room for judicial determinations equating nutrition with other forms of life support) or can be foregone if the declarant has explicitly authorized such a course. Nonetheless, as noted, a number of states' living-will laws still seriously circumscribe a declarant's options regarding artificial nutrition.

A more minor legislative constraint is found in living-will statutes excluding "comfort care" from life-sustaining measures which can be withheld pursuant to a living will.[35] The legislative intent is to require provision of palliative care—meaning drug relief of pain or anxiety, skin care, hygiene, and grooming. In large measure, such a requirement coincides with people's preferences. The vast majority of people presumably prefer to receive intervention promoting their own comfort. However, there may be some patients who have religious or philosophical reasons for opposing drugs which will diminish suffering and/or alertness. And there may be instances when "palliative" relief would incidentally either shorten or prolong a dying process and therefore be unwanted by a declarant. In some instances, then, a legislative mandate of comfort care would impinge on the preferences of persons formulating an advance directive.

There is another objectionable feature of some living-will laws as to the scope of rejectable "life-sustaining procedures." A number of state statutes include a sample form which must either be substantially followed or is at least suggested (and even if not "suggested" would often be adopted as a matter of convenience by unsophisticated declarants). Many declarants will find the prescribed form inadequate for the declarant's needs.

Often, the prescribed or suggested form describes the treatment to be withheld as that which "only prolongs the process of dying."[36] This formulation for unwanted treatment is extremely opaque and uninformative.[37] A prime object of a living will is to indicate a level of deterioration and incapacity and/or suffering at which the formerly vital individual no longer desires life-sustaining intervention. Yet the form declaration does not describe factors which would determine when a patient's condition is so dismal or painful that treatment "only" prolongs the dying process. Is it the intendment of the formulation that any possible benefit from further existence, any iota of interactional capacity, means that treatment should be extended because it does not only prolong dying? Even if the incompetent patient's condition is burdened by unrelievable suffering? Even if the patient is physically helpless and severely demented—a status which would be deemed intolerably demeaning by many people directing their own future medical fates? And how does the notion of treatment only prolonging a dying process relate to chances for a temporary and partial remission? Does a one percent chance of a brief remission mean that treatment is not "only" prolonging the dying process? In short, the typical "forms" suggested by living-will laws are deficient in their vague formulation of the circumstances in which life-preserving medical intervention is to be withheld. (Chapter 4, on drafting advance directives, suggests solutions.)

There exist other minor defects in typical living will legislation. One example is a provision in approximately thirty living-will laws which suspends the effect of such a document while a female declarant is pregnant.[38] The defect is minor only in the sense that it will impact on few people. But at least in the approximately twenty jurisdictions which nullify a declarant's directive during an entire pregnancy, the defect is major in that the provision is unconstitutional. A sweeping nullification during an entire pregnancy disregards the viability line drawn by *Roe v. Wade* and would be struck down.[39]

Another common defect is a revocation clause providing that the maker of a living will revokes the document by any statement or expression to that effect, regardless of the maker's mental state at the time of the expression.[40] Such a provision has been roundly criticized as inconsistent with the living will's underlying object of promoting autonomy. To quote one source:

> The revocation of a declaration by an incompetent patient or one unable to understand what he or she is doing should not be effective, since it negates the very essence of what the act seeks to promote: self-determination.[41]

A broad revocation policy has been defended as erring on the side of life and as reflecting commitment to respect for human life.[42] Yet a revocation provision ignoring the mental status of the declarant creates considerable potential for the manipulation of an incompetent patient who possesses a living will. Under it, a severely demented patient could repeatedly be asked whether he or she wants to rescind the prior directive, and eventually a positive response would be forthcoming. Or an observer might simply misrepresent that verbal repudiation of the directive had occurred.[43] It makes more sense to say, as some state laws do,[44] that the competently expressed desires of a declarant at all times supersede any inconsistent expression contained in a prior directive.

Alternatively, any expression by an incompetent patient apparently inconsistent with a prior directive ought to provoke reassessment of the patient's mental capacities and desires. It is conceivable that an incompetent patient might have enough cognitive understanding so that a desire to continue to receive life-sustaining treatment ought to be respected. This requires some comprehension of death (and of the significance of the decision) on the part of the incompetent patient. However, a patient's expression ought not be followed without regard to the level of dementia involved.[45]

The preceding discussion about the meaning of terms like "terminal condition" and "life-sustaining procedures" showed how some living-will statutes appear to constrict the autonomy of makers of living wills. The prime objectives of living-will statutes were salutary: to offer an approved vehicle for prospective autonomy and to reassure health-care providers about legal liability. The results, as shown, were sometimes confusing and problematical. A leading commentator, Professor Alexander Capron, has suggested that living-will statutes "have sown much confusion and have probably detracted as much from patients' real rights as they have added."[46]

The key question—at least in jurisdictions whose statutes bear some of the defects previously addressed—is whether to utilize the living-will vehicle provided by the state legislature. Before resolving that issue, it is useful to examine another possible vehicle for exercising prospective autonomy: appointment of a health-care agent.

ADVANCE DESIGNATION OF A HEALTH-CARE AGENT

It is usually important to make advance selection of a person—whom I call a health-care agent, although alternate names include proxy, surrogate, attorney-in-fact, or health-care representative—who will be responsible for post-competency medical decisions. The assumption is that a reliable person will be chosen as future agent and that such agent will be conversant with, and sympathetic to, the declarant's wishes regarding medical intervention in the dying process.

If such a trustworthy person is available, selection of a personal agent offers an extremely useful means to promote self-determination in the dying process. In the first place, selection of a personal agent should provide an occasion for the principal (the person designating an agent) to contemplate and discuss the substance of future-oriented instructions regarding medical intervention. The principal naturally needs to discuss the contents of instructions with the contemplated agent in order to be sure that the agent both understands and sympathizes with the principal's goals. Indeed, no self-respecting person would agree to serve as agent without understanding at least the essence of the principal's wishes. Second, an agent serves as an authoritative source to whom health-care providers can turn regarding critical decisions. The presence of a designated agent can thus mitigate confusion about decision-making authority and reduce conflict among relatives or others surrounding a moribund patient.[47] Finally, an agent can serve both as an advocate and potential enforcer of a patient's wishes in the event that health-care providers seem to be ignoring or deviating from those wishes.[48]

A health-care agent's advocacy role is important during the current era in which advance directives are still an unfamiliar device. As noted, there are indications that physicians in charge of terminal care may be influenced more by the wishes of surrounding family members than by the incompetent patient's prior instructions.[49] Yet, if advance directives are to become a widespread and effective vehicle, people will have to be reassured that their wishes will in fact be implemented. Presence of a trusted agent (with authority to act as an advocate) ought to increase the probability that an advance directive will be faithfully observed. No one can be certain that a trusted agent won't turn renegade and deviate from prior instructions. But the chances of faithful adherence to prior wishes would seem to be better through a specially selected and instructed representative than through reliance on the happenstance of which family members are on hand at critical moments.

Assuming that a suitable person can be found to act as agent, a question may arise about what legal mechanism to utilize for appointment of that agent? The object, of course, is to secure binding effect for the agent's determinations and to afford the agent full authority to implement the principal's wishes.

In a growing number of states (now approximately twenty), the living-will legislation permits a declarant to designate a person to be in charge of implementing the declarant's living will. The problem with this mechanism is that the designated agent is presumably confined by the limitations contained within the relevant living-will statute. This means that in some states constraints described in the preceding section—concerning a "terminal condition" and "life-sustaining treatments"—would apply.[50]

A more promising mechanism is use of a durable power of attorney (DPOA). This is a simple document giving the named agent (sometimes known as a proxy, surrogate, or attorney-in-fact) authority to make post-competence decisions on behalf of the principal. The DPOA document is effective without any judicial proceedings, and the principal can generally define the scope of the agent's authority. Statutes providing for durable powers of attorney exist in every state.

A first task, though, is to make sure that the jurisdiction in question will recognize the authority of the DPOA holder (the agent) to make decisions as to life-sustaining medical intervention. The general DPOA statutes were primarily intended to cover property-related decisions for incompetents, and the statutes usually did not mention health-care decisions (let alone terminal medical decisions). There was doubt in many jurisdictions whether authority over intimate and personal life-and-death decisions could be delegated in a regular DPOA. However, the uncertainty has been resolved in many states in a manner allowing a DPOA to be used for medical decisions.

Legislatures in approximately thirty states have adopted special statutes authorizing a durable power of attorney for health care (DPOA-HC).[51] (The mechanism might be called appointment of a health-care proxy, as in New York, or of a health-care representative, as in New Jersey; but the concept is the same.) A competent person (principal) appoints an agent who will have binding authority over post-competency medical decisions, including authority to reject life-preserving medical intervention.

Even in the absence of a DPOA-HC law, a person may well have authority to designate an agent who will have power to make critical medical decisions. In several states, the general DPOA statute mentions health-care decisions and will likely be interpreted to include critical medical decisions. Moreover, several courts have indicated that written designation of a prospective health-care agent should be respected either under a general DPOA law (even without statutory mention of health care decisions) or as a matter of common law.[52]

Even if a mechanism exists for appointment of a health-care agent, a question remains whether that agent will possess full authority to implement the principal's wishes. (Again, the answer may vary from jurisdiction to jurisdiction, but certain generalities can be described here.) Most DPOA-HC laws do afford the agent full authority. Many such measures instruct a health-care agent to carry out the principal's wishes as gleaned from the appointing document or elsewhere. And the agent is given authority to make the same range of decisions regarding life-preserving medical intervention that the principal could make if competent.[53] For example, New York's enactment empowers an agent to make "any and all health care decisions on the principal's behalf that the principal could make."[54]

By potentially enabling a health-care agent to make the same range of decisions that the principal could have made if competent, these broad DPOA-HC type laws permit the maximum scope possible for prospective autonomy aimed at shaping post-competence medical handling. The only clear limitations are those (like bans on assisted suicide or active euthanasia) which would be imposed even on the decisions of competent patients. (A further possible limitation—conflict between a principal's instructions and the contemporaneous best interests of the now incompetent patient—will be discussed in chapter 6.)

Not all DPOA-HC type statutes confer plenary authority on a health-care agent to carry out the wishes of the principal with regard to life-preserving medical intervention. In a few instances, a DPOA-HC measure replicates the same kind of restrictions contained in the state's living-will law.[55] As noted, this usually means a "terminal condition" restriction on the circumstances in which life support may be withdrawn and some restraint on removal of artificial nutrition. Other constraints may also exist. For example, Kentucky does not require an agent to carry out the wishes of a principal; rather, the agent must consider physicians' recommendations as well as the patient's best interests in shaping medical handling.[56] Nonetheless, the majority of DPOA-HC type laws offer a broad, effective device for exercising prospective autonomy.

CHOOSING A FORMAT FOR AN ADVANCE DIRECTIVE

The principal modes for advance directives have now been described: a living-will type document (instruction directive) and appointment of a health-care agent. Which format, or combination of formats, is best suited to effectuating a declarant's object of controlling post-competence medical intervention?

Circumstances may dictate the appropriate response. If there is no trustworthy, sympathetic, and willing person to serve as a health-care agent, then a declarant's only option is an instruction directive aimed at directing anyone who is eventually in charge of the incompetent patient's medical care. Also, the particular statutes within a state—their degree of deference to a declarant's autonomy—will help determine what format to employ.

If we assume both that a suitable person is available and that the particular state's DPOA-HC law (or comparable statute) affords an agent broad authority to carry out a principal's wishes, it makes good sense to utilize that statutory mechanism to designate an agent. In the absence of a designated agent, attending medical personnel would customarily turn to an incompetent patient's spouse, or next of kin, or other close acquaintance willing to assume responsibility for medical decision making. This might seem like a satisfactory arrangement, depending on the declarant's circumstances. That is, a person might be confident that his or her spouse (or other trusted person) will be on hand at the critical moments and that the spouse will faithfully implement the incompetent patient's wishes.

Yet, there are almost always good reasons to formally appoint an agent. First, if there are children or siblings in the picture (among those likely to be on hand during a dying process), there is always potential for disagreement and confusion. One child or sibling (or other relative, for that matter) may become so grief-stricken or guilt-ridden as to oppose implementation of the patient's wishes. Or that child or sibling may have a different interpretation of what the patient's wishes actually are. Designation of a single authoritative agent (as well as alternate agents in the event the main agent is unavailable) will diminish the disruption and confusion which might otherwise prevail.

A second reason to formally designate an agent is to enhance that agent's authority in the event of opposition from health-care providers. This is particularly a concern if the now incompetent patient's wishes are idiosyncratic or otherwise not to the tastes of the surrounding medical personnel. In many states, in the absence of designation as a health-care agent, the spouse or next of kin (or whoever is on hand) has no formal legal authority to make decisions on behalf of the incompetent patient. Health-care providers commonly rely on the decisions of surrounding family only as a matter of convenience. At the moment that an attending physician is troubled by the course which the family is seeking in reliance on the patient's wishes, the physician can contend that the family has no formal legal status. To regain control, the family might have to institute costly and time-consuming guardianship proceedings. By contrast, an agent appointed pursuant to a DPOA-HC law (or comparable statute) is armed with explicit authority to implement the wishes of the now incompetent patient.

The problem of who's in control of decision making is mitigated somewhat in the approximately nineteen states which have adopted statutory provisions regarding surrogate decision making for incompetent persons. These provisions list, in order of priority, the persons authorized to make medical decisions on behalf of an incompetent patient who has not designated his or her own agent. The list of authorized surrogates usually begins with a spouse and then reaches blood relatives in a descending order of proximity.[57]

These family-surrogate decision-making provisions will often be unsuited to declarants seeking to shape their post-competence medical fates. First, the close relative delegated decision-making power by statute may not be the person whom the declarant believes would be most suited to the task. Second, there may be disagreements or frictions among relatives of equal status (disputes among children or siblings or relatives of another degree). Third, many of these provisions appear within the state's living-will type statute and are therefore subject to the constraints (such as a terminal condition limitation) found in the relevant living-will type statute.[58] In other words, these legislative efforts may not satisfactorily fill the void when a declarant has failed to designate a health-care agent.

My only hesitance to use a statutory mechanism for appointment of a health-care agent would arise where the relevant DPOA-HC contains limitations on an agent's authority which are distasteful to the principal. (This might be the case, for example, where the DPOA-HC law itself imposes a narrowly defined "terminal condition" limitation.) In that instance, I would recommend a "nonstatutory" designation of a health-care agent. That is, the principal's appointment document would be signed with the same formality (number of witnesses, etc.) dictated by the DPOA-HC law, but the principal would make clear that he or she was relying on common-law and constitutional prerogatives rather than the DPOA-HC statute. In that fashion, the appointed agent could assert that he or she is not bound by the distasteful (to the principal) restraints contained in the DPOA-HC law. This effort to escape the unwanted limitations of a particular DPOA-HC law might not succeed, but it's probably worth a try.

If an agent is designated—whether through a DPOA-HC type law or otherwise —a question arises as to whether the document should contain substantive instructions (beside just naming an agent and alternates). My response is affirmative.

There are important reasons to accompany designation of a health-care agent with substantive instructions representing the principal's basic perspectives on post-competence medical handling. In the first place, any decision maker, including a designated agent, ought to be instructed on several critical considerations. These include the principal's personal attitudes toward pain, incapacitation, and indignity, as well as financial costs and the emotional interests of surrounding family and friends.

Reliance on familiarity with the principal's general values, as culled from the agent's casual interactions with the principal, is probably inadequate. A recent study shows a significant divergence between competent chronic patients' actual wishes (regarding CPR) and the perceptions of family members and physicians close to the patient.[59] This divergence tends to emphasize the need for precise articulation of the principal's wishes regarding terminal care. Moreover, even pointed discussions about a principal's medical preferences may be inadequate. Oral conversations may considerably predate the critical events, and an agent ought not rely on memory alone.

Written instructions to the health-care agent can be useful for reasons beyond assuring the agent's full understanding of the principal's wishes. Written instructions will help repel any challenges or objections posed by family or medical staff opposed to the incompetent patient's wishes.[60] A written substantive directive can thus serve as an important evidentiary tool for the agent, especially where the directive's content reflects idiosyncratic wishes of the patient which otherwise might be opposed by family or staff.

Even in a jurisdiction which ostensibly accords an appointed agent potential power to make the same range of decisions the patient could make if competent, the presence of written instructions may well assist the agent in securing adherence to the principal's wishes. The agent is supposed to be acting according to the wishes of the principal. The agent may contend that the principal's wishes were communicated orally; but if those purported wishes are unusual or controversial (e.g., a rejection of all life-sustaining care should the principal be placed in a nursing home), health-care providers may be reluctant to accept that contention. Then, in the absence of written confirmation of the incompetent patient's wishes, the agent may be hard put to implement the principal's wishes. For if the agent can't show that the patient's wishes were in fact consistent with the controversial course which the agent is seeking, then the health-care providers might well refuse to follow the course sought. Moreover, even recourse to the courts may be unavailing in such a case. When the wishes of the principal are unknown (or, as in the present hypothetical, unprovable), an agent is supposed to act in accord with the patient's best interests. And those contemporaneous best interests might diverge from what the principal really wanted, but didn't express in writing, and now can't be proven.

Of course, an agent may be able to convince the surrounding health-care providers even in the absence of written instructions. That is, an agent in some instances might credibly and persuasively argue that he or she is following the principal's wishes as orally conveyed. But there is a risk that the agent's representations will be disbelieved. And even the presence of a broad statutory authorization to make any decision the patient could have made, if competent, may not be enough to overcome physicians' or other observers' doubts (in the absence of written instructions).

Written instructions also serve as a check against an agent's abuse of authority. Because the principal has provided a written standard or guideline, medical staff or other observers can be reassured that the agent's decisions conform with the incompetent patient's previously expressed wishes.[61] Again, a health-care agent is a fiduciary entrusted with carrying out a patient's wishes. If an agent unjustifiably deviates[62] from the principal's instructions, health-care providers are supposed to resist (and secure judicial appointment of a guardian to supplant the designated agent).

Nothing prevents use of written substantive instructions in a jurisdiction which provides for appointment of a health-care agent. Indeed, such laws generally require the agent to implement the principal's wishes and thus contemplate existence of instructions. Nothing prevents the reduction of such instructions to writing, whether the instructions are incorporated into the document appointing an agent or contained in a separate writing. (The substantive instructions might be lengthy; and while appointment of a health-care agent can usually be accomplished by a short form, the instructions might be contained in an attachment or appendix incorporated by reference into the appointment document.)

In some jurisdictions, it may be important to label the instructions as adjuncts to appointment of a health-care agent rather than as a separate living-will document. This would be true, for example, where the state living-will law contains unwanted (by the principal) limitations on implementing a declarant's wishes regarding terminal care. It would also be true in the odd jurisdiction, such as Illinois, whose DPOA-HC law states that appointment of an agent makes a living will inoperative.[63]

So far, I've suggested that the ideal format for an advance directive is a document appointing a health-care agent together with written substantive instructions. While these instructions are intended primarily to direct a health-care agent, they should also bind any future decision maker on behalf of the incompetent patient. This is so because almost all states give effect to clear-cut prior expressions by the now incompetent patient in shaping the bounds of medical intervention.[64] As a precaution, even if written instructions accompany appointment of an agent and are labeled accordingly they ought to include a sentence clarifying that the same instructions are intended to bind any eventual decision maker (if the agent is unavailable for any reason).

What about the person who cannot recruit a suitable health-care agent? What advance directive format should that person follow? In a state like New Jersey whose living-will type legislation accords broad autonomy to a declarant, that statutory mechanism should be utilized. (By "statutory mechanism" I mean personalized instructions complying with the formalities of a living-will statute, not necessarily any sample form recommended within the statute itself.) A living will fully conforming to the applicable statute should likewise be the format if the particular state's limitations on declarant autonomy don't conflict with the declarant's preferences.

A statutory living will binds all decision makers ultimately in charge of an incompetent patient's medical handling (including health-care providers and surrounding family).[65] Using the living-will statute also reassures physicians that they will be immune from liability for good-faith compliance with the document. At the same time, any statutory penalty for noncompliance with a declarant's instructions will be applicable.

In a state whose living-will type statute contains unwanted constraints, a non-statutory advance directive—which I will call a *nonstatutory instruction directive*[66]—appears to be the best course. This is a writing, signed and witnessed in accord with the formalities demanded by the jurisdiction's living-will law, expressing the declarant's personal wishes with regard to post-competence medical intervention. (Compliance with the statutory formalities is designed to demonstrate the requisite seriousness and deliberation which the relevant legislature deemed appropriate to an instruction directive.) The distinctive feature of this nonstatutory document is that it invokes the declarant's common-law and constitutional prerogatives rather than the statutory authority provided in the relevant living-will law.[67]

The object of a nonstatutory instruction directive is to prescribe post-competence medical handling while avoiding the substantive statutory constraints of most living-will laws. Can these statutory "restrictions" be so easily circumvented?

The answer is probably yes. Most living-will statutes explicitly preserve the legal prerogatives of persons who have not invoked the statutory living-will mechanism. A typical "preservation-of-rights" provision specifies that the living-will law "shall have no effect or be in any manner construed to apply to persons not executing a directive pursuant to this [living-will law] nor shall it in any manner affect the rights of any such persons. . . . "[68] This language preserves common-law rights, including any rights applicable under the doctrines of substituted judgment or best interests of the patient. Under those judicially developed doctrines, persons charged with responsibility for incompetent patients are expected to follow the patients' expressed wishes.[69] Accordingly, courts have used an instruction directive as convincing proof of the patient's wishes even in a jurisdiction which did not have a living-will law.[70] And several courts have dictated compliance with oral instructions which exceeded the "terminal condition" or artificial nutrition limitations of living-will statutes.[71]

How can this be, you ask? What was the point of living-will legislation if its "restrictions" can so easily be circumvented?

The answer requires historical perspective. State legislatures adopting living-will laws wanted to endorse the concept of prospective autonomy, but in a restrained fashion. The legislators were generally wary about shaping the fate of helpless patients (only since 1976 have the courts and legislatures seriously dealt with this issue), and they were sensitive to political pressure from right-to-life oriented groups. At the same time, the legislators did not seek to disrupt the judicial doctrines which had developed or to foreclose continued judicial developments. The typical legislature adopting a living-will law was saying in effect: "We approve advance directives, and we'll even provide explicit immunity for health-care providers who comply with advance directives. But our official stamp of approval applies only so long as the patients affected are in a terminal condition (or aren't deprived of nutrition, or are 'only' having their dying process prolonged by medical intervention). We are wary about encouraging living wills beyond these bounds. But we are willing to leave it to the courts, if they are intrepid enough, to shape people's autonomy rights regarding medical intervention in the dying process."

If this interpretation of legislative intent is correct, then nonstatutory instruction directives exceeding the ostensible legislative bounds ought to be enforceable. The legislative object was to withhold *its* endorsement from instruction directives going beyond "terminal illness" or "life-sustaining procedures" (as defined by the living-will statute) but not to make such provisions unlawful or unenforceable by the courts.[72] Such an interpretation would be reinforced in a jurisdiction which has adopted a DPOA-HC type law conferring authority on health-care agents to implement their principals' instructions in circumstances beyond those mentioned in that jurisdiction's living-will law. Such a DPOA-HC underscores the legislature's willingness to permit terminal decisions beyond the bounds endorsed in the living-will statute.

There are two major problems with reliance on a nonstatutory instruction directive—at least until there has been authoritative judicial confirmation of the approach. First, health-care providers may be influenced in practice by the apparent facial limitations of a living-will statute's language. Physicians and health-care administrators are notoriously sensitive to possible traversing of legal bounds. Even when the health-care provider is confident of winning a legal test, there may be reluctance to incur the time, expense, and publicity accompanying litigation. The provider may therefore choose to follow the superficial meaning of the statutory language (constraints like terminal condition) rather than the underlying statutory intent described above. (Indeed, there is a danger that health-care providers will ignore the preservation-of-rights clause and regard the living-will mechanism as the exclusive one for withholding life-preserving care. In other words, there is a hazard that health-care providers would infer that the statutory immunity conferred under a living-will law implies that liability is possible for any provider who removes life-preserving care in circumstances beyond those enumerated in the living-will law.)

The primary solution to this misapprehension of the legal framework is vigorous education of health-care providers as to the legal status of a nonstatutory directive. It will be incumbent upon agencies concerned about advance directives—including state health departments and voluntary professional or consumer organizations—to inform health-care providers about the common-law and constitutional rights embodied in nonstatutory instruction directives.

That informational task will be supplemented, over time, by health-care agents acting pursuant to DPOA-HC and comparable laws. Those agents will act as advocates of incompetent patients' interests, and they will no doubt press for adherence to principals' instructions despite the ostensible constraints of some living-will type statutes. However, the topic at this point is use of nonstatutory instruction directives where a person could not find a suitable agent and where the relevant living-will law is narrow and confining. In the absence of an agent, compliance with the incompetent patient's nonstatutory instruction directive may be dependent on the degree of awareness of legal rights and responsibilities among the surrounding medical staff. Again, a conglomeration of health-care consumer groups, medical professional organizations, and state and federal agencies will have to endeavor to apprise health-care providers about the legal effect of a nonstatutory instruction directive. (It would be nice if they circulated large quantities of this book as part of that endeavor.)

Some commentators suggest that a nonstatutory instruction directive be used as a *supplement* to a conventional living will conforming to all statutory limitations.[73] That is, they recommend signing a statutorily correct document *and* a nonstatutory instruction directive. The latter is supposed to "amplify" the declarant's wishes and, by invoking common-law and constitutional rights, avoid the limitations of the relevant legislation. This nonstatutory instruction directive would state that the declarant's signing of the prescribed living-will form should not be construed as limiting the nonstatutory document's instructions—the latter representing the declarant's genuine wishes.

I can understand the rationale for this approach. By signing a conforming living will, the declarant hopes to secure whatever benefits (such as sanctions for noncompliance with instructions and assurance of nonliability for good-faith compliance) that the relevant statute provides. Medical personnel are presumably bound by this document meeting all statutory conditions. At the same time, the medical personnel are presented with an expanded document (a nonstatutory directive) expressing the patient's real wishes without reference to statutory restrictions like a "terminal condition" constraint. The commentators' hope is that the medical personnel can be persuaded to follow the more expansive wishes expressed in this nonstatutory instruction directive.

While I understand and sympathize with this strategy, I can't endorse it. The effect is to present two documents which on their face seem inconsistent or contradictory. That situation seems rife with potential uncertainty and confusion, and it may even be an invitation to obstructionism. It is true that the reasons for two documents are readily understandable, as explained above. The declarant is hoping to effectuate the minimum provided by statute and to expand upon that minimum by invoking other legal sources. Yet, purposeful preparation of inconsistent instructions seems quite problematic. The problem would be even greater if it happened that the conforming living will were prepared *after* the nonstatutory directive—the obvious hazard being that the latter document would be viewed as controlling despite the declarant's contrary intention.

My own preference, as stated, is to prepare a single, nonstatutory instruction directive. This unequivocal expression of the declarant's wishes, explicitly relying upon common-law and constitutional prerogatives, ought to be effective. As noted, the nonstatutory directive would be prepared with all the formality (witnesses, etc.) prescribed in the living-will statute, so its seriousness of purpose could not be questioned. And the document should fall within the preservation-of-rights provision contained in most living-will laws.

The down side of my strategy seems modest. True, the enforcement machinery provided by a living-will statute would not technically be applicable to a nonstatutory document. But the enforcement machinery provided under a living-will statute is minimal anyway (a point to be discussed in chapter 7, which deals with enforcement of advance directives). Similar enforcement devices can be utilized for a nonstatutory directive.

It is also true that voluntary medical cooperation might be more easily obtained pursuant to a conforming living will than pursuant to a nonstatutory instruction directive. This is because the immunity from liability provision of a living-will statute is, technically, not applicable to a nonstatutory directive. Nonetheless, use of a conforming living will (along with a nonstatutory advance directive) would risk either thwarting the desired scope of the declarant's substantive instructions or creating confusion because of inconsistent instructions. On balance, my advice is to spell out a declarant's actual preferences in the format of a single, nonstatutory instruction directive.

A second problem with a nonstatutory instruction directive may be that not all courts will adopt the generous view of legislative intent which I have outlined. An alternative view of legislative intent is that statutory limitations on living wills—such as those relating to terminal conditions or artificial nutrition—express a public policy antagonistic to any activity exceeding those limitations. Under this view, the public policy expressed in a living-will measure might be extended to decision makers deciding the fate of all incompetent patients, even without a statutory living will in the picture. The restrictive legislative policy might then be applied to a nonstatutory instruction directive, to prior oral expressions, and to incompetent patients who left no prior instructions at all.

This was the approach suggested by the Missouri Supreme Court in the *Cruzan* case.[74] The Missouri living-will law excluded nutrition from rejectable life-sustaining medical procedures. Ms. Cruzan, a permanently unconscious patient, had made certain verbal statements indicating that she would not want life-preserving intervention in such a status, but she had not issued a living will. The court chose to respect the policy reflected in that living-will law (supposedly opposing any withdrawal of artificial nutrition) even though no living will was actually involved in the case.[75]

A similar approach was followed by an Ohio appellate court in a case called *Couture v. Couture*.[76] Ohio's DPOA-HC law[77] had restricted a health-care agent's authority with regard to nutrition and with regard to a patient in a nonterminal condition. Even though no power of attorney was involved in the case, the *Couture* court relied on the public policy expressed in the DPOA-HC law to circumscribe the authority of a guardian seeking to implement an incompetent patient's prior oral instructions.[78]

In a jurisdiction where the inclination of lower court judges is to give broad public policy effect to the limitations contained in living-will or DPOA-HC laws, the ultimate resort for patients' advocates is constitutional attack on those limitations. Chapter 2 described prospective autonomy (as exercised via an advance medical directive) as an extension of a competent individual's fundamental liberty interest in shaping medical intervention in a dying process.[79] That perspective has prevailed in decisions both under the federal constitution and under some state constitutions.

This possible judicial responsiveness to constitutional claims has important implications for state statutes restricting the circumstances under which life-preserving medical intervention can be withdrawn. For example, a statutory bar to withdrawal of artificial nutrition would appear to be unconstitutional in the face of a patient's prior authorization of nutrition cessation.[80] Several state courts have already reached that conclusion, relying primarily on state constitutional provisions.[81] And that conclusion is probably reinforced by the U.S. Supreme Court's 1990 decision in *Cruzan*. None of the justices there endorsed a distinction between nutrition and other forms of medical intervention. Indeed, the majority opinion even recounted, with no hint of disapproval, prior state judicial determinations upholding the withdrawal of artificial nutrition.

There is also significant doubt about the constitutionality of statutory provisions confining implementation of advance directives to patients in a "terminal condition." A number of courts have suggested that the "rights" of incompetent patients with regard to prior autonomous expressions rejecting treatment are identical to those of competent patients.[82] At the same time, numerous decisions have indicated that competent patients are entitled to reject life-preserving medical intervention even in circumstances when the patient is not in a terminal condition (meaning that death might still be forestallable for years). At least where a patient has left clear-cut contrary instructions, then, a statutory terminal-condition limitation would appear to be unconstitutional. A few courts have already subscribed to this conclusion.[83]

Ultimate resort to a constitutional attack is likely to provide small consolation to the lingering, gravely debilitated patient in a jurisdiction with broad public-policy constraints on the permissible scope of advance instructions. If the particular state judiciary is inclined to expansively interpret the import of statutory limitations on a declarant's autonomy, those same judges may prove unsympathetic to constitutional attacks on the statutory restrictions. Even if the constitutional attack is ultimately successful—for example, at the state supreme court level—the litigation will entail substantial delay and expenditures.

Hopefully, the constitutional attack strategy will only be necessary in a few states. Many jurisdictions have legislation giving expansive scope to declarants' autonomy by means of appointment of a health-care agent. And most jurisdictions should be willing to respect nonstatutory instruction directives invoking common-law and constitutional prerogatives. That result should be reachable without extensive litigation.

I've now indicated the preferred format for an advance medical directive. In a jurisdiction providing for a DPOA-HC or other means to appoint a health-care agent with broad authority to implement a declarant's wishes, that mechanism should be utilized. That appointment document should be accompanied by substantive instructions to the agent. For the person who cannot find an appropriate agent, a living will should be utilized, unless the state's statutory limitations on declarant autonomy are distasteful to the particular declarant. In the latter event, a nonstatutory instruction directive provides an appropriate vehicle. In all these instances, the declarant issues substantive instructions to guide those ultimately in charge of decision making on his or her behalf. I turn now to the problem of formulating those instructions.

4

Drafting Advance Instructions

THE OBJECTIVE of an advance medical directive is to design a good death, a death with dignity as personally defined by the declarant. That definitional task might be easy for some people. For example, there are some persons who want all available means to be used to forestall death. This approach might appeal to someone who believes that all life, whatever its quality, is preferable to death. Or to someone who believes that dominion over death is solely a divine prerogative. Or to someone who doubts the ability of others to make appropriate "terminal" decisions, even with the benefit of advance instructions. For all such persons, it should be easy to dictate maximum medical intervention. One formula reads: "I want my life to be prolonged to the greatest extent possible without regard to my condition, the chances I have for recovery, or the cost of the procedures."[1]

Variations on this maximum-intervention theme are easily imaginable. A person could prescribe that all life-preserving measures are to be undertaken and continued *until* irreversible coma ensues. Or one could dictate medical intervention until death is, according to medical judgment, unpreventably imminent (specifying the brief time span intended by the word imminent). The thrust of this approach is that life support is to be vigorously maintained until the patient is really in extremis.

The task of defining a death with dignity is much harder for most people. Most people believe that circumstances do exist in which life-preserving medical intervention would be unwanted—circumstances in which existence for the individual would constitute a fate worse than death. Defining these circumstances entails fixing a stage in a future dying process at which life has become intolerably painful or undignified. For most people, this means defining a level of mental and physical dysfunction which is personally unacceptable. That, in turn, can be a daunting task. As noted in the discussion of prospective autonomy in chapter 2, a multitude of problems hamper this definitional task.

There are an infinite number of potential medical situations which may occur in a dying process. There are infinite gradations of mental deterioration and physical disability. There are infinite combinations of mental and physical dysfunction. There are always uncertainties attached to medical diagnosis and prognosis, including chances of error and statistical possibilities of remission or recovery. Moreover, a plethora of factors might shape a person's conception of dignity in the dying process.[2] Physical pain, emotional suffering (feelings of embarrassment, frustration, and dependency), immobility and physical helplessness, mental incapacity, use of physical restraints, and physical appearance are common elements in defining an undignified or degrading state. Beyond personal well-being and dignity, a person might wish to consider the interests of surrounding persons—for example, loved ones and health-care providers. The interests of surrounding persons might include the emotional strain of protracted care, the economic costs of care, and the allocation of medical resources.

The multitude of variables involved makes it impossible to anticipate and specifically provide for all post-competence health-care decisions. One consequence is that considerable disagreement exists about the best strategy for designing advance instructions. Advice ranges from leaving nothing in writing to articulating detailed instructions about forms of unwanted medical treatment, or about a level of debilitation deemed personally intolerable, or about both. In the following pages, I'll comment on some of the major approaches before describing my own preferred solution.

THE "NO WRITTEN DIRECTIVE" OPTION

A couple of years ago, a noted physician in the bioethics field published an article explaining why she would not prepare an advance directive.[3] She was confident that her next of kin would be present during any critical moments in her future dying process and that those persons could be counted on to understand and implement her preferences regarding medical intervention. Likewise, she was confident that the health-care providers likely to be on hand would be compassionate, understanding, and cooperative. Finally, she was dubious whether a typical instruction directive would be very informative to the ultimate decision makers.[4] She regarded the typical instructions as too vague to be useful.

My first quarrel is with the good doctor's failure to designate in writing a health-care agent. In the previous chapter, I described the inevitable potential for confusion or dispute if more than one close family member or loved one is on hand for critical decisions. Naming an authoritative agent (and alternates) seems to me a vital step in avoiding that hazard.

My second quarrel goes to the absence of written instructions. Is it enough to appoint an agent and orally instruct that agent?

This ·is a tempting option for the multitudes of people who are repulsed or intimidated by the prospect of spelling out their vision of an intolerable, incapacitated existence. An attorney active in the field of death and dying described to me her clients' common impulse to rely on appointment of a health-care agent. She explained:

Most people are not caught up in the details of medical conditions in which they would or would not want to be maintained. Rather, they feel that if there is no chance they would be restored to a quality of life they define as worthwhile, they would not want treatment continued. They believe that the people who know them and love them understand their values enough to draw the cutoff lines, and they are willing to abide by the decision those people would make. They usually feel more strongly about the decisionmaker than the decision itself—they trust the decision their loved ones would make and do not trust a decision that would be made by others involved, including hospital personnel and (in the worst possible situation) courts. Thus, the most crucial aspect of the advance directive is the appointment of the health care representative. (It seems to create a feeling of security comparable to appointment of a guardian in a testamentary will to take care of one's children.) Indeed, for many people who do not want to contemplate all of the possible medical conditions which could arise, completing a proxy directive, without more, fulfills their concerns.[5]

There is another argument (besides aversion to the seemingly complex and morbid drafting job) against issuing written instructions. When the time arrives for implementing instructions, a hazard exists that some observer (relative or friend of the patient, or health-care provider) will use the imprecision of the advance directive to contest and obstruct implementation of the now incompetent patient's wishes. Many such documents use language leaving considerable room for interpretation, including room for a grudging interpretation by anyone so inclined. A person disagreeing with a health-care agent's interpretation of an advance directive can seek intervention from hospital administrators, from an institutional ethics committee, òr even from the courts. Such intervention might disrupt or delay the smooth effectuation of the principal's wishes.[6]

I am totally unconvinced of the wisdom of refraining from written instructions. In the first place, I feel that helpful and informative instructions *can* be prepared, even for people who are reluctant to confront their mortality and contemplate the circumstances of their eventual demise. (This chapter is largely devoted to that drafting enterprise.) Second, reliance on prior oral instructions (or, worse, impressions from prior general interactions between the agent and principal) seems quite unsound. Memories fade, and the time span between instructions and implementation can be considerable. Third, the eventual health-care providers may not be as cooperative as anticipated so that some reinforcement of the agent's chosen course of treatment might be necessary. Written instructions can serve that function. This tool is especially useful if the instructions are unusual or idiosyncratic.[7] Fourth, written instructions may serve as a check on the designated agent or other decision maker. That is, an observer may in good faith note that an agent is being swayed by personal predilections rather than the declarant's instructions. Returning the agent to the declarant's prescribed track may then be entirely consistent with the declarant's wishes.

Having articulated my strong preference for written advance instructions, I'll now examine several approaches to that drafting problem.

THE SHORT-FORM OPTION

The multiplicity of potential medical situations during a dying process and/or common aversion to spelling out an intolerable debilitated status have often prompted resort to short, sweeping formulations of the criteria for withdrawing life-preserving medical intervention.[8] Many short-form living wills (or instruction directives) condense the operative language to one sentence. One of the first living-will forms was drafted in 1969 and distributed to over 500,000 persons over the years by the Euthanasia Education Council, an organization later known as Concern for Dying.[9] The operative portion of that directive read:

> If a situation should arise in which there is no reasonable expectation of my recovery from physical or mental disability, I request that I be allowed to die and not be kept alive by artificial means or heroic measures. I do not fear death itself as much as the indignities of deterioration, dependence, and helpless pain.[10]

The deficiencies of that form are patent. Ambiguous language such as "heroic measures" is one weakness. Terms such as "heroic" or "extraordinary" are too often used in instruction directives to describe types of unwanted medical intervention. The terms have no commonly understood content and serve only to confuse.[11]

The even more serious fault is the opaque phrase used to define the point at which life-sustaining intervention is to be omitted. The form refers to "physical or mental disability" from which no recovery is reasonably likely. No definition is provided for the level of disability expected to trigger withholding of life-sustaining intervention. Does the form really intend to reject intervention from the point at which mental incapacity (according to its legal definition) is reached? Aren't there some degrees of mental incapacity which would be tolerable, at least if the declarant is restorable to physical health? And aren't there some physical incapacitations which would be tolerable (to the typical declarant) so long as the incompetent patient were still mentally capable of pleasure and interaction with the environment?

More recent short-form efforts fare only slightly better. One living-will version, distributed as of late 1990 by the Society for the Right to Die,[12] reads:

> If I should be in an incurable or irreversible mental or physical condition with no reasonable expectation of recovery, I direct my attending physician to withhold or withdraw treatment that merely prolongs my dying. I further direct that treatment be limited to measures to keep me comfortable and to relieve pain.[13]

Another 1990 model reads, in operative portion:

> If I am permanently unconscious or there is no reasonable expectation of my recovery from a seriously incapacitating or lethal illness or condition, I do not wish to be kept alive by artificial means.

These forms provide precious little guidance as to the nature and degree of deterioration which the declarant considers a fate worse than death.[14] One possible interpretation of the latter form is that once the declarant becomes incompetent (i.e., loses decision-making capacity for serious medical decisions), life-sustaining care should be omitted starting from the onset of any incurable, "seriously incapacitating" chronic condition. Does the typical declarant really want to reject all life-preserving care at that point, even if the incompetent patient is capable of enjoying continued existence? How "serious" must the incapacitating condition be?

As mentioned in the preceding chapter, the sample living wills sometimes provided within living-will statutes are even more problematic. In the first place, they commonly state that the patient must be in a "terminal condition" as defined in the particular statute.[15] As noted, such a limitation may well be inconsistent with a typical declarant's wish to avoid a prolonged, highly debilitated existence or a protracted period of decline associated with degenerative diseases. Second, statutory short forms frequently employ the opaque language dictating removal of care which serves "only to prolong the dying process."[16] It is dubious that such statutory forms satisfactorily reflect the wishes of the majority of persons seeking to shape a dignified dying process.

Numerous other efforts have been made to condense a declarant's substantive instructions into a single sentence or paragraph. Professor Robert Veatch prescribed cessation of life-sustaining care "which is either . . . gravely burdensome to me or will sustain life in a way that is gravely burdensome to me or others."[17] Another example is contained in a "power of attorney for health care" prepared by Charles P. Sabatino for the A. B. A. Commission on Legal Problems of the Elderly. Beside providing for appointment of a health-care agent, that document offers an interesting option regarding substantive instructions to the agent. It mentions "best interests" of the patient as a general standard, but it contains the following language as well:

> I do not want my life to be prolonged nor do I want life-sustaining treatment to be provided or continued if my Agent believes the burdens of the treatment outweigh the expected benefits. I want my Agent to consider the relief of suffering, the expenses involved and the quality as well as the possible extension of my life in making decisions concerning life-sustaining treatment.[18]

Short-form documents of this nature are not entirely useless. They provide a statement that the declarant does not want life-sustaining medical intervention in all circumstances. This is important information dispelling any notion that the patient seeks maximum medical maintenance. These documents also express the declarant's concern about indignity in the dying process and about the burdens upon surrounding parties. Given an agent who has consulted with the declarant and understands the precise intendment of the language, and given sympathetic and cooperative health-care providers, such a document *might* work very well.

A short-form effort like the Sabatino document thus seems appealing. It appears to maximize a health-care agent's flexibility in interpreting the declarant's wishes regarding a dignified dying process. It obviates the daunting task of spelling out the kinds of deteriorated conditions which would be intolerable for the declarant.

To my mind, however, the Sabatino formulation is still too spare. There is not much practical guidance for the ultimate implementers of the instructions, particularly as to the deteriorated quality of life which the declarant deems intolerable. The deficiency is especially acute if there is no health-care agent in the picture, and the de facto decision makers are not familiar with the details of the declarant's wishes. Even if a health-care agent has been designated, the criteria or guidelines are so spare that they create a risk of nonimplementation in the event that any surrounding party (family, friend, or health-care provider) challenges the agent's interpretation of intolerable indignity.

An illustration is provided in a 1987 New York case.[19] A stricken AIDS patient had named a health-care agent and specified that treatment should be withdrawn when "extreme mental deterioration" made a "meaningful quality of life" no longer possible. The patient deteriorated, became incompetent, and reached a stage at which the trusted agent sought the removal of life support. A court refused to order the hospital to cooperate, finding the term "meaningful quality of life" to be too amorphous to be enforceable.

My own feeling is that it is usually important to provide detailed guidance to the ultimate decision makers. If the indignity of a debilitated condition is a declarant's central concern, I would at least seek to define the main attributes of indignity which would make existence intolerable for that declarant. The issue is how to accomplish this objective without making the task so complex and distasteful as to deter masses of people from going beyond the short forms described above.

THE OPTION OF SKETCHING OUT INTOLERABLE DEBILITATION

A number of sources agree with me that it is desirable to provide detailed substantive instructions in an advance directive.[20] We agree that detailed instructions can amplify otherwise vague directives, can reinforce a health-care agent's determinations, and can help establish the thoughtfulness and seriousness of the declarant.[21] Questions exist, though, about how to inject the desired detail without intimidating or frustrating the declarant and without investment of long professional hours in counseling the declarant.

One undesirable technique is to address a whole spectrum of medical interventions, from routine and simple diagnostic tests to complicated procedures (i.e., from blood tests, to various machines, to receipt of organ transplants). There are authorities who recommend specifying the kinds of medical intervention which the declarant would or would not want.[22] I am not one of them. From my perspective, the crucial guidance in an instruction directive goes to the criteria for an intolerable quality of life—particularly the level of debilitation which renders existence degrading to the declarant. In other words, the substantive instructions should be result oriented, focusing on the consequences of medical intervention for the patient's status rather than the nature of the medical procedures.[23]

Of course, there are exceptions to this principle. A declarant's attitude about artificial nutrition ought to be registered, because nutrition constitutes a controversial subject warranting explicit guidance. Or a person might have a particular aversion to some form of treatment (such as a permanent respirator) which would warrant special mention. Beyond such instances, detailed consideration of a spectrum of medical treatments seems superfluous to me. I would concentrate on defining the kind of existence which the declarant deems intolerable.

In defining an intolerable status, most people view some level of dementia as a critical element. For example, the vast majority of people regard maintenance in a permanently unconscious state as a pointless burden on the emotional and financial resources of those surrounding the patient's dying process. They see no benefit to be derived from lingering in a permanently insentient state.

Many people also consider lesser forms of dementia intolerable, though viewpoints obviously differ. A number of commentators focus on the point at which an incompetent patient can no longer recognize the persons around them. From their perspective, interaction with loved ones is a sine qua non for a meaningful existence. Other persons stress the mental capacity to understand and communicate with surrounding persons. Some people insist on full mental capacity, expressing unwillingness to receive life-sustaining medical intervention once mental competence is irretrievably lost.[24]

For many people, physical debilitation accompanying mental incapacity may be an important factor in determining an intolerable quality of life. Immobility, helplessness, dependence, or being an emotional and/or financial burden on others may be extremely distasteful prospects.[25] For some people, an intolerable level of physical incapacity might be readily definable. It is not unusual, for example, to see a living will which renounces life-sustaining medical intervention if the patient becomes permanently dependent on nursing care. That degree of helplessness and dependence, together with mental incompetence, represents an intolerably degrading specter for these declarants.

For most people, though, it seems extremely hard to identify the levels and combinations of mental and physical dysfunction which would make continued existence intolerable, warranting the cessation of life-sustaining medical intervention. A sample form circulated by the New Jersey Bioethics Commission illustrates one approach to the problem. That form first provides an operative paragraph in which the declarant accepts the principle that a debilitated existence may be so personally degrading and distasteful as to be intolerable. That paragraph states:

> I realize that there may come a time when I am diagnosed as having an incurable and irreversible illness, disease, or condition which may not be terminal. My condition may cause me to experience severe and progressive physical or mental deterioration and/or a permanent loss of capacities and faculties I value highly. If, in the course of my medical care, the burdens of continued life with treatment become greater than the benefits I experience, I direct that life-sustaining measures be withheld or discontinued. I also direct that I be given all medically appropriate care necessary to make me comfortable and to relieve pain.[26]

The document's drafters apparently recognized that "severe . . . deterioration [to the point that] burdens of continued life . . . become greater than the benefits I experience" is an imprecise formula. They therefore added a paragraph suggesting that the declarant spell out the kinds of debilitation which would make existence personally intolerable. That explanatory paragraph reads:

> [The above paragraph] covers a wide range of possible situations in which you may have experienced partial or complete loss of certain mental and physical capacities you value highly. If you wish, in the space provided below you may specify in more detail the conditions in which you would choose to forego life-sustaining measures. You might include a description of the faculties or capacities, which, if irretrievably lost, would lead you to accept death rather than continue living. You may want to express any special concerns you have about particular medical conditions or treatments, or any other considerations which would provide further guidance to those who may become responsible for your care.

The idea is sound. Ideally, declarants should specify the levels of debilitation which would make continued life support unwanted. Yet the reality is that most people are either unwilling (because of refusal to face their mortality) or unable (because of unfamiliarity with the relevant terms and concepts) to articulate the desired guidelines.

There are a couple of possible solutions, besides reversion to the short forms previously described. One is to adopt or adapt my own existing effort to express in detail a vision of an unacceptably degrading medical status. Another solution is to utilize a "values profile" in which the declarant is asked to fill out—by checking the relevant boxes—a form covering attitudes about critical elements of degradation in a dying process. I'll address those "solutions" in succession.

THE CANTOR OPTION

In 1990, I first drafted my advance directive.[27] (It was then labeled a living will, though it was really a comprehensive advance directive including both appointment of a health-care agent and substantive instructions.) An updated and shortened version of that directive appears herein as Appendix A. At this juncture, I will articulate the major features of my directive, describing the objectives and concerns which governed my preparation of the document. In particular, I want to show how I handled the dignity-related criteria designed to govern post-competence medical intervention.

The first part of my directive names a health-care agent to be responsible for administering the directive. I strove to select someone reliable, sympathetic with my concerns (as expressed in the document), and who would not be overly affected by the emotional difficulty of "letting go." An alternate agent is designated in the event of unavailability of the primary agent.[28] (As previously noted, in the absence of a designated agent, attending medical personnel would customarily turn to an incompetent patient's spouse or next of kin or other close acquaintance willing to assume responsibility for medical decision making. But for reasons already articulated, I preferred to designate an authoritative agent familiar with my wishes and presumptively able to implement my instructions in a clear-headed fashion.)

It might be advisable explicitly to detail certain authority intended for the health-care agent, such as power to access medical records, to hire and fire health-care personnel, to move the incompetent patient to a different setting, and to initiate litigation.[29] The health-care agent might ultimately have to act as an advocate, and even enforcer, of the directive—if health-care providers refuse to cooperate with its instructions. An enumeration of powers is intended to facilitate the agent's performance of these administrative and enforcement functions. Enumeration would be unnecessary, however, in a jurisdiction whose DPOA statute already confers the desired authority.

Having appointed a health-care agent, I devote most of the advance directive to providing substantive guidance for the agent or any other ultimate decision makers. An introductory paragraph relates to types of medical intervention. There is no effort to enumerate attitudes about a full range of treatments. Rather, a few summary principles are set out.

My concern was threefold in mentioning these "principles" relating to types of care. First, I wanted to clarify that all forms of medical care are, for me, potentially rejectable—not just "extraordinary" or "heroic" or complex means. Second, I wished to clarify that artificial nutrition holds no magic significance for me and should be considered part of potentially rejectable medical intervention. Third, I specified my general preference for palliative care—meaning maintenance in a clean and comfortable environment and relief of extreme pain. This provision regarding palliative care was probably unnecessary, ranking as intuitively self-evident. I included it in an excess of caution only because the use of advance directives is still at a primitive stage of development.

In the section relating to substantive instructions, I present a short statement of criteria or guiding principles for my agent or any other decision maker on my behalf. There, I invoke "best interests" in the sense of burdens of prospective existence exceeding benefits. My intendment is that burdens in this context include any discernible suffering (physical or emotional) and that benefits include any possible gratification from interaction with the environment. This is consistent with the customary meanings given the terms *burden* and *benefit*.

My advance directive also makes it clear, however, that considerations of dignity, as defined in the body of the advance directive, are to be deemed an integral part of my best interests. This latter point is important because often, when a patient has reached a severely deteriorated and debilitated status, commonly understood burdens such as physical and emotional suffering are difficult to assess.[30] It is useful to specify that notions of indignity and degradation are to come into play as part of the best-interests formula. This is consistent with an emerging realization that existence can be burdensome not just because of pain but because of indignity or other subjectively intolerable considerations (like emotional drain on others).[31]

A substantial part of my advance directive then seeks to define my concept of a status sufficiently undignified to warrant withholding or withdrawing life-preserving medical intervention. The instructions are not confined to a "terminal condition" in the sense of an unpreventably fatal illness. Rather, I have sought to control intervention in the face of any potentially life-threatening pathology once a certain level of deterioration and dysfunction has been reached or when the result of medical intervention would be to relegate me to such a deteriorated status.

Such a level of deterioration might be reached suddenly, as through trauma to the brain, or gradually, as the result of a degenerative process. In the latter case, there will not be any single magic moment when a degrading status is reached; the deterioration will be gradual, both in physical and mental terms. Nonetheless, a stage may ultimately be reached when my status has become degrading according to my agent's good-faith application of my criteria.[32] At that stage, I would want no further life-preserving intervention to combat potentially life-threatening pathology. This is consistent with one of my basic objects: the avoidance of prolonged lingering in a self-defined, degrading status.

The first substantive instruction regarding dignity relates to permanent unconsciousness or a permanent vegetative state (PVS). An existence devoid of all awareness is to my mind a demeaning state for a human being, and I don't wish to be maintained in such a condition. I make it clear that all life-preserving medical intervention, including artificial nutrition, should be withheld if such a condition occurs. Medical criteria have been developed for definitive diagnosis of permanent unconsciousness,[33] and I ask only that sound medical practice be followed in verifying the diagnosis.

PVS represents an easy case. The harder task is defining the degree of mental and physical debilitation which—while an individual is still conscious or semiconscious—constitutes an intolerably undignified state for a previously acute and active individual. For me, as I imagine for most people, not all mental incapacity can be deemed degrading. Obviously, a person lacking competence (unable to understand and process data at a level sufficient to make his or her own decisions) can still derive enjoyment and benefits from existence. A person can be "pleasantly senile" despite significant loss of mental faculties. Even though I don't relish being remembered in such a deteriorated state, I don't instruct that life support be withheld solely because of this level of mental dysfunction.

At the same time, my mental dysfunction could become so extreme that my condition would be demeaning or degrading for me. One clear index of such a status would be permanent inability to recognize and/or interact with my relatives or loved ones. I have therefore made this a per se determinative criterion of an undignified status warranting withholding of life support.

This does not mean that such profound dementia is to be the exclusive determinant of an intolerably demeaning status. I further explain that lesser but still extreme mental deterioration (such as the inability to read and understand simple material) would constitute a significant element of indignity to be considered in conjunction with other indices of indignity and suffering in assessing my overall best interests.

Extreme physical disability is articulated as another factor to be considered under the rubric of indignity in assessing my best interests in an incompetent state. As with the case of mental dysfunction, I make it clear that not all levels of physical incapacity are to be deemed intolerable (even in combination with the mental incompetence which is a prerequisite to any application of an advance directive). My assumption is that I am life-affirming enough in character to adjust to a significant degree of physical incapacity. Of course, if my mental deterioration deprives me of the ability to cope with whatever physical disabilities are involved, that fact will have to be included in calculating my best interests. That is, a level of physical incapacity together with extreme mental deterioration may result in discernible suffering or dignity loss to the point that my best interests dictate the cessation of medical intervention in the face of a life-threatening condition. This thought concerning the interrelation of mental and physical incapacity is expressed in my advance directive.

My advance directive also specifies some aspects of physical dysfunction which are particularly relevant to an assessment of indignity. In my mind, certain types of incapacity are associated with extreme helplessness and dependence and may well evoke feelings of frustration and embarrassment. My advance directive mentions three such factors: inability to feed myself, inability to dress (or bathe) myself, and incontinence necessitating either diapering or being otherwise attended. Each of these elements is labeled a significant blow to dignity to be considered in the best-interests calculus. While none of these elements is deemed sufficient, by itself, to prompt a finding of intolerable indignity, each is a relevant consideration.

It may well be that in a debilitated mental state I will not actually sense the frustration, humiliation, or degradation which I associate with an undignified status.

Nonetheless, it is important to me (and, I imagine, to most people) to be remembered in a certain fashion. I have therefore directed that my prospective medical intervention be shaped with my conception of indignity in mind regardless of the extent of perceptible suffering. I also assume that my lingering in a severely degraded status would extract a significant toll from surrounding relatives and friends. This furnishes an additional impetus for bringing indignity into play whether or not I will sense that indignity in a state of incompetency.

All this is not to say that contemporaneous, perceptible feelings will not be factors in the best-interests calculus. My directive specifies that irremediable physical pain (or pain that is remediable only through drug intervention producing a prolonged stuporous state) should be considered a significant factor adverse to best interests. The same instruction applies to perceptible emotional pain (embarrassment, frustration, anxiety, or whatever). The problem, again, is that these various elements of suffering are not susceptible to accurate measurement when a person has reached an extremely debilitated mental state. For that reason I have taken pains to define indignity as a potentially determinative factor.

Any person seeking to formulate a comprehensive advance directive ought to ponder some interests extrinsic to the incompetent patient's own personal status. Principal candidates for attention would be the emotional and financial interests of surrounding loved ones. Most persons, myself included, care about the emotional toll extracted from loved ones by a prolonged deathwatch or chronic care of an extremely deteriorated person. Beyond the anguishing mental and physical burdens imposed upon surrounding persons, the economic costs of terminal care may be relevant. Economic concerns can range from a diminished estate for descendants to actual dependence on the resources of others.

My personal strategy was to try and regulate medical intervention in my dying process in a fashion which would minimize the burdens imposed on others. My advance directive aims to avoid a prolonged dying process at a level of suffering or indignity likely to extract a severe toll from others. In that fashion, I express my solicitude for the anguish or burden suffered by those around me during my dying process. At the same time, I have not explicitly instructed my agent to weigh these extrinsic interests.

An alternative strategy would be to articulate economic costs and/or emotional burden on others as relevant factors in assessing best interests. For example, one could say that if a decision regarding best interests is otherwise borderline, the extreme expense of prospective care and the anguish of loved ones should be considered as factors weighing against initiation or continuation of life-preserving medical intervention.

My advance directive defines one level of mental incapacity (inability to recognize and/or interact with loved ones) as per se so undignified as to warrant cessation of life-preserving medical intervention. In addition, I specify that lesser degrees of dementia, together with other incapacities, would make my existence intolerably demeaning. In order to assist my agent in applying the concept of a demeaning existence, I identify several factors as "significant blows" to dignity. But the ultimate judgment about a demeaning condition is left to my health-care agent.

A difficult issue is presented when a person reaches an extremely debilitated mental status but is still physically healthy. (By "healthy," I mean that there are no current life-threatening conditions, even if there are chronic disabilities.) How should preventive or curative medical care be handled at this juncture? I am referring to future pathological conditions which by themselves are not life-threatening but which, if not treated, will develop into fatal conditions. These include both minor infections which are treatable with antibiotics and minor organ dysfunctions which are curable but which will lead to fatal dysfunctions if not treated. Once what has been defined as a demeaning state has been reached, should preventive and curative measures be withheld in order to facilitate the onset of a liberating dying process?

My personal disposition was to dictate the qualified omission of such medical measures once I have reached a demeaning status. Thus, if I become either permanently unable to recognize relatives and friends or otherwise trapped in a self-defined degrading existence, I anticipate that even medical intervention for curable infections and organ dysfunctions will be withheld. My one major caveat is that the sequelae of nontreatment be considered in applying the governing best interests standard. That is, any pain, discomfort, or indignity which would accompany the ensuing dying process (following nontreatment) must be considered. The decision makers must weigh whether the prospective negative consequences of nontreatment (any additional suffering or additional indignity during the ensuing dying process) outweigh the relief which death would, by definition, provide from a currently demeaning status.[34]

My determination to renounce even preventive and curative intervention—once my condition has reached a self-defined demeaning status—may be controversial. The consequence is to relinquish life for a being (my future, incompetent persona) who is still aware of the environment and perhaps capable of extracting some net pleasure from interactions with that environment. (I'm thinking here about a state of extreme, but "pleasant" senility, for example.)

Some moral issues arise in this context. First, some persons might question my moral right to dictate the demise of a helpless future persona not actually suffering from the deteriorated (though undignified) status. My response to this objection is presented at length in chapter 6. There, I argue that individual self-determination includes a moral prerogative of shaping a post-competence dying process according to a personal concept of dignity—even if that vision of dignity does not coincide with the contemporaneous well being of the incompetent persona. A person who has developed a character during a lifetime deserves an opportunity to shape post-competence recollections of that character. Just as I think I have a right to dispose of my property—even in a way which might disadvantage my future, incompetent persona—I think I have a right to dictate my post-competence medical fate.

Second, there may be tension between my preferences regarding preventive and curative care and the conscientious positions of some medical personnel. I have no desire to force medical personnel to violate their scruples. In the event that attending medical personnel cannot in good conscience implement my preferences, my health-care agent will be expected to seek alternative personnel who can willingly cooperate. In the event that an institutional host (such as a private hospital or nursing home) has conscientious objections to my prescribed course of treatment (or nontreatment), my agent might seek my transfer to another facility in which cooperation is available. Only if these recourses are not viable would I want my agent to seek to legally coerce the objecting personnel or institution. (Chapter 5, which deals with administration of advance directives, devotes further attention to the issue of conscientious scruples of health care providers.)

THE VALUES-PROFILE OPTION

When my advance directive was published in 1990, one criticism voiced was that the document was so elaborate that only persons who could afford a fancy lawyer (and/or medical consultant) would be able to utilize such an instrument. Frankly, I was surprised by this criticism. My conceit had been that my prescription about intolerable debilitation and indignity represented an "every (wo)man" position that would capture the fancy of masses of people. Judging from the dearth of reprint requests, my conceit was sadly misplaced. Apparently, people's preferences about life-sustaining medical treatment are too diverse to be captured in any single document, or standard form. (I hasten to point out, however, that at least a few friends and relatives have replicated my advance directive reprinted herein as Appendix A).

If people's advance directives must be individually constructed, with careful consultation about each element, the prospects for widespread usage of advance directives will diminish. (Recall that best estimates indicate that only between five and twenty-five percent of people currently have an advance directive, even in the prevalent short-form formats). People are notoriously reluctant to deal with the "grisly" task of designing their own dying process. They will be even more reluctant if they have to pay significant sums to accomplish the already distasteful task. Yet if an advance directive is to be a detailed, hand-tailored document, then some expense may well be entailed for medical and/or legal consultations.

Nor are physicians and other health-care providers anxious to perform the consultative function. Physicians have heavy demands on their time and are reluctant to deal with the "hypothetical" death-and-dying process of a healthy person. "[T]he [consultative] process is unfamiliar, time consuming and inherently distasteful to many physicians who have been trained to preserve life whenever possible."[35] There is generally little economic incentive to perform the consultative function, as third-party reimbursements (government and private insurance) usually don't cover the fees involved.

A possible solution is to allocate the consultative task to nonphysicians. Authorities assert that consultation and guidance must initially be available to declarants and that an interactive process is essential (either contemporaneous with or after preparation of a directive) in order that declarants can explain their choices.[36] It is not at all clear that physicians or lawyers are essential ingredients in the initial consultative process.[37] A social worker, patient's advocate, physician's assistant, or other medical-staff person might be trained to fulfill the function of introducing people to advance directives and even assisting in preparation of the documents.

For anyone responsible for initially assisting a declarant in preparation of an advance directive, as well as for the ultimate administrators or decision makers, a "values profile" might serve as an important adjunct or supplement to an advance directive. A values profile is basically a questionnaire aimed at eliciting a declarant's attitudes toward issues commonly arising in the context of medical intervention in a dying process.[38] This device offers the potential both for succinctly laying out the critical issues for a declarant and for providing a handy format for a range of responses. At the very least, an appropriate questionnaire can furnish a useful guide to issues to be raised by a person seeking to assist a declarant in preparation of an advance directive. Even better, the profile could get attached to the directive itself and become an interpretive guide in the ultimate implementation of that directive.

To my mind, efforts to formulate an effective values profile have not been very successful. One effort in the direction of a values profile is called a "values history" and was prepared at the Institute of Public Law of the University of New Mexico Law School.[39] That document provides a series of open-ended questions concerning general attitude toward typical forms of life-preserving medical intervention (e.g., respirators and dialysis machines), permanent unconsciousness, diminished mental and physical function, and chronic illness. This values history seems deficient for a couple of reasons. First, it does not pointedly focus either on particular elements of indignity or on identifying a person's minimally tolerable level of function. Second, its open-ended solicitation of subjective responses may not sufficiently focus respondents' attention upon those critical issues. Moreover, it is difficult for the average declarant to formulate responses to open-ended inquiries.[40]

Another relevant document, called a "medical directive," was prepared by E. Emanuel and L. Emanuel.[41] Its distinctive feature is a questionnaire asking the respondent to signal choices about various forms of medical intervention in four paradigmatic illness circumstances. As with the values history, the object is to explore the declarant's wishes about "the process of dying."[42] However, the four scenarios covered relate only to two extreme stages of mental incapacity: severe dementia, to the point where the patient is unable to recognize people or to speak understandably, and PVS. No inquiry is made about lesser forms of mental incapacity, or about physical deterioration, or about an overall definition of intolerable indignity. This medical directive anticipates that a designated health-care agent will deal with circumstances not covered in the document itself.

The medical directive was published in 1989. In 1990, the Emanuels published an expanded version.[43] Their questionnaire scenarios continue to focus on a rather narrow range of dementia. However, they have added inquiries touching on physical immobility, dependence on others, ability to communicate, and place of habitation. These additions represent an improvement. Yet the added inquiries are still not phrased to identify what the declarant would consider an intolerable status—a fate worse than death.

These previously published documents point in the right direction. The object is to provide a questionnaire format focusing on issues critical to most persons thinking about post-competence medical intervention. Moreover, the questionnaire should supply a list of possible responses allowing the declarant to identify an intolerable existence without having to formulate new language.

My own effort to draft a values profiles is set out herein as Appendix D. It focuses on dementia, physical immobility, helplessness, expense, pain, and burden on others. The hope is that this sample document will advance the pursuit of a values profile which can serve as a handy tool for masses of people to amplify what they really mean by the language of a short-form advance directive.

MISCELLANEOUS OPTIONAL PROVISIONS

To my mind, the central issue in an advance directive is preparation of substantive instructions which convey a declarant's wishes concerning post-competence medical intervention. That instructional task is particularly important if the declarant does not have a health-care agent to administer the advance directive. For that reason, the prior two subsections in this chapter focused on methodology for conveying detailed substantive instructions about post-competence care.

Robert Veatch offers an additional way to provide interpretive guidance as to the meaning of general instructions.[44] His living will is innovative in listing individuals who can be consulted in the course of administering the document. It mentions both persons whose views on post-competence care coincide with the declarant's and medical professionals whose judgment the declarant respects.

There are a variety of other provisions which, at a declarant's option, might be included in an advance directive. A person who cares particularly about the locus of post-competence care (e.g., someone with an aversion to a nursing home) can use an advance directive to articulate that preference. An advance directive could also contain provisions relating to donation of organs or bodily tissue, performance of an autopsy, or even burial instructions.

It might be useful to include an immunity clause expressing the declarant's wish that the ultimate administrators of a directive (including any health-care agent and attending medical personnel) be immune from liability. One option would be to absolve these actors for "good-faith" adherence to the directive.[45] An alternative approach would be to relieve health-care providers from liability only for conduct that meets "reasonable medical standards." This is the standard imposed on decision makers under most living-will type statutes.[46]

The effect of a good-faith standard of immunity might well be to relieve an agent or health professional from liability for negligent conduct. For example, a careless (but good-faith) judgment about the hopelessness of an incompetent patient's condition would be immune from liability. Only reckless conduct would incur liability under a good-faith standard.

The advantage of a good-faith standard is its reassurance to the eventual administrators; they receive a message that the declarant intended to encourage implementation of the directive by conferring immunity for good-faith adherence to instructions. The good-faith standard does not seem like an excessive risk. Many commentators argue that overly aggressive medical intervention poses a greater hazard than undertreatment, at least in hospital settings.

A propos of overly aggressive intervention, one source has suggested a clause threatening dire consequences for physicians' failure to implement an advance directive's request for termination of life-sustaining treatment. The clause provides:

> I will consider such treatment [i.e., medical continuation of life-preserving care] an act of criminal assault, and want my proxy to file a criminal assault and battery complaint against those involved in this violation of my basic right to refuse treatment. Additionally, I want my family members to file a multi-million dollar civil damage suit against those involved in treating me against my will.[47]

My own thoughts on enforcement methods are set out in chapter 7. At this point, I'll just comment on the above paragraph. In essence, the paragraph is bluster aimed at intimidating recalcitrant health-care professionals. The chances of launching a criminal-assault proceeding in the context of a moribund, incompetent patient are somewhere between zero and nil. The chances of launching a successful "multi-million-dollar" damage suit are slim—for reasons to be articulated in chapter 7.

The above effort at bluster and intimidation is a matter of strategy. Personally, I don't see the above paragraph's threats as doing much to promote good will and sympathy from the attending medical personnel. I prefer an approach which reassures the personnel that good-faith implementation of instructions will incur no liability. Of course, a health-care agent or surrounding family member might some day have to threaten suit against recalcitrant personnel or a recalcitrant institution. But I would hold such threats in abeyance in the hope and expectation that they would never become necessary. On the other hand, I can understand an argument that the above paragraph graphically conveys the declarant's seriousness and determination about renouncing life support in accord with the advance directive.

5

Interpretation and Administration of Advance Directives

THE CHALLENGE of interpreting an advance directive is almost inevitable. Millions of short-form directives have been distributed containing only the most rudimentary instructions.[1] This effectively means that hundreds of thousands of people have now dictated a halt to medical intervention which "only prolongs the dying process" once the declarant has become incapacitated with "no reasonable hope of recovery."

The language "*only* prolongs the dying process" cannot be taken literally. Even for a person diagnosed as permanently vegetative, there is some infinitesimal hope either of a misdiagnosis or of a miraculous recovery which would restore some measure of function. Arguably, continued life support then wouldn't *only* prolong the dying process. Yet the declarant's intention was presumably to avoid continued medical intervention in circumstances of grave incapacity and indignity. The challenge is to interpret the imprecise language in a manner fulfilling the declarant's actual wishes.

Even if an advance directive seeks to provide detailed instructions—as in my own document, Appendix A—considerable interpretive discretion may well be lodged in the health-care agent or other person charged with administration. Because "the number of plausible combinations and permutations of [medical] interventions and clinical contexts is virtually limitless . . . ,"[2] even a lengthy document cannot provide for all situations. A common response will be for an advance directive to articulate a general standard or guideline, such as "best interests" of the declarant, in addition to particularized instructions.

A general standard usually confers broad discretion on decision makers acting on behalf of the incompetent patient. For example, a best-interests standard incorporates notions like pain, suffering, indignity, and countervailing benefits—leaving a delicate balancing task in the hands of the agent or other administrator. Application of such a best-interests standard entails a weighing of largely unquantifiable benefits and detriments. The eventual decision makers must make a judgment not only about the extent of suffering being incurred by an incompetent (and perhaps noncommunicative) patient[3] but also about the patient's potential for satisfaction despite a debilitated condition. Elements of indignity must be brought into the balancing process if consistent with the declarant's wishes.

The use of a generalized standard, as well as the frequent imprecision of advance directive terminology, underlines the importance of consultation between a declarant and those persons (including health-care agents and medical professionals) likely to be involved in administration of an advance directive. Virtually every commentator on advance directives stresses the utility of such communication. These conversations have a dual purpose. They illuminate the real wishes of the declarant via amplification of unclear language. And they give the agent or health-care provider a chance to express any discomfort or hesitancy about implementation of the declarant's wishes. In the event of tension between the declarant's wishes and the decision makers' willingness to cooperate, a declarant can either modify those wishes or seek alternative agents or health-care providers.

It would theoretically be possible to demand, as a prerequisite to a binding advance directive, a showing that the document is the product of consultation. Certainly, awareness of all the document's implications and reflective deliberation are a desirable foundation for such a fateful document. Nonetheless, such a heightened standard for validity of an advance directive would impede the utility of such directives and would be unwise.

Any requirement of consultation with a medical or legal source would impose economic costs and diminish people's accessibility to the advance directive mechanism. It might also be difficult to establish in retrospect (sometimes years after the event) that the advance directive was prepared with sufficient consultation (or deliberation). A consultation prerequisite would be subject to manipulation by any physician (or other eventual decision maker) uncomfortable with the substance of an advance directive.

The normal standard for documentary capacity—the ability to understand and appreciate the nature and consequences of the decision—should govern the validity of advance directives.[4] Some commentators suggest that "informed consent" be a prerequisite for a directive (drawing an analogy to the consent expected for a contemporaneous decision to forego medical intervention). This would require receipt of information about the nature of the pathology, the benefits and risks of contemplated medical intervention (or nonintervention), and the available alternatives.

Such an informed-consent or consultation prerequisite for an advance directive would impose an impossible burden where a declarant is healthy and simply anticipating the eventual prospect of incapacity and a dying process. (And that is the usual situation surrounding the making of an advance directive.) The myriad of variables makes customary informed consent impractical. Even if a declarant is aware of particular pathology at the time of making an advance directive, the normal standard for documentary capacity should prevail.

If emotional trauma apparently surrounded making of the directive, that would be a basis for investigation of competency by the health-care agent or other decision maker. That is, a health-care agent aware of traumatic circumstances surrounding preparation of a directive should seek assurance that the declarant at least understood the nature and consequences of the document being signed. It is conceivable that temporary depression or other severe upset unduly influenced the content of an advance directive. However, the starting presumption should be that a declarant who signed an advance directive in the presence of two witnesses was competent to understand the nature and consequences of the decision.

THE BASIC GUIDELINE: THE DECLARANT'S WISHES

The central guideline for any health-care agent or other administrator of an advance directive must be implementation of the desires and preferences of the now incompetent declarant. This conclusion applies whether the advance directive takes the form of a statutorily approved living will, a nonstatutory living-will type document, or a durable power of attorney for health care (or similar mechanism for appointment of a health-care agent).

As the preambles to most living-will type statutes attest, the thrust of such legislation is to recognize a person's autonomy in shaping medical intervention in a future dying process. Not surprisingly, then, the statutes—subject to limitations earlier discussed—anticipate fulfillment of a declarant's wishes.[5] Physicians are commonly accorded legal immunity for compliance with a living will. Under some statutes, a legal proceeding is explicity authorized against a party (whether health-care agent or medical professional) acting inconsistently with the declarant's instructions.[6]

The legal injunction to interpret and apply a declarant's wishes applies to a nonstatutory advance directive as well. That result would follow in most jurisdictions under the judicially developed doctrine of "substituted judgment."[7] A precept of that doctrine is respect for a person's autonomy to shape medical intervention. If a now incompetent patient's previous wishes can be determined, those wishes govern provision of post-competence medical care. The U.S. Supreme Court's decision in *Cruzan* only lends impetus to this judicial trend by suggesting constitutional status for the clearly expressed wishes of a previously competent patient. A written instruction directive will constitute an important index of those wishes.[8]

A similar framework—giving preeminent force to a declarant's wishes—applies to a durable power of attorney or other mechanism for designation of a health-care agent. The typical DPOA-HC statute requires the agent to act in accord with the principal's wishes or, if those wishes are unknown, in accord with the patient's best interests.[9] This approach is consistent with law's traditional approach to fiduciaries acting on behalf of legal incompetents. A guardian, trustee, or other fiduciary is supposed to implement the discernible or inferrable wishes of a ward (expressed while the ward was competent).[10] A health-care agent is a form of fiduciary and is expected to adhere to the patient's wishes.[11]

This does not mean that a declarant's wishes must be comprehensively or precisely expressed in order for a designated agent to seek withdrawal of life-sustaining medical intervention. An important object of a designated-agent mechanism is to secure a person to implement the principal's vision of a dignified dying process without forcing the principal to spell out detailed instructions. When a DPOA-HC statute prescribes that an agent shall act according to "best interests" when the patient's wishes are "unknown," the agent is being enjoined to act consistently with the principal's articulated values and preferences even if an explicit instruction covering the situation at hand is not available. The designated agent is being authorized to interpret and apply the principal's will; the agent's interpretation should prevail so long as that interpretation does not conflict with the principal's known wishes.[12]

Alternatively phrased, the statutory reference to best interests encompasses the values and preferences of the principal.[13] If a designated agent is making a good-faith assessment of the principal's wishes, as gleaned from the express or apparent concerns of the principal, that agent's decision about life-sustaining medical intervention ought to be upheld. This conclusion is inapplicable only in a few jurisdictions (like Missouri) where clear-cut prior expressions have been made an absolute prerequisite to withdrawal of life-sustaining care of an incompetent patient.[14] In the vast majority of locales, though, a designated health-care agent need only act consistently with the known wishes, values, and preferences of the principal. Clear and convincing evidence of the principal's precise instructions is not then essential.

All the preceding material suggests that application of an advance directive will not always be easy. The imprecision endemic to advance instructions will hamper fulfillment of the declarant's wishes. Nonetheless, the key object is implementation of those wishes. The starting point, and perhaps best index of an incompetent patient's wishes, is the document itself. But because the document will sometimes be vague or uninformative, further interpretive guides will be necessary.

Where language of an advance directive is fuzzy or ambiguous, consideration of the background and circumstances of the directive's adoption is appropriate in order to discern a declarant's actual desires. This is what occurred in a recent Florida case. In *Browning v. Herbert*,[15] an elderly woman had executed a written directive indicating that she wanted life-prolonging procedures suspended if she should reach a terminal condition and death was "imminent." A year later, she suffered a massive stroke and was reduced to a barely conscious (but not vegetative) state. She could survive for up to a year in that debilitated status. The question was whether death was imminent within the meaning of her directive. Looking to the nature and purposes of the entire directive, the court determined that death was imminent within the intendment of the patient.

A similar task has to be undertaken with regard to all imprecise language within an advance directive. Suppose an advance directive employs a term like "heroic means" or "extraordinary treatment" in defining unwanted medical intervention. Was the underlying concern with *expensive* machinery which might deplete the estate? Was the concern *intrusive* machinery which might disturb the comfort of the patient? Or did the declarant intend to dispense with any life-preserving medical intervention once the patient has reached an extremely incapacitated state? If the latter, what incapacitated status did the declarant consider as warranting the withholding of such intervention? In all cases of imprecision, the advance directive's history and background can be examined to try and determine the directive maker's actual intent.

Obviously, a variety of tools might be employed in the effort to fathom a directive's actual intent. One index would be the declarant's statements preceding or contemporaneous with the preparation of the directive. These statements could have come in any of an infinite variety of contexts, from casual chats with friends to pointed discussions with any persons consulted in the preparation of the directive. Each statement must be considered "for what it is worth."[16] That is, a casual, passing remark may carry less force than a considered consultation with a prospective health-care agent or medical care provider.

A declarant's expressions subsequent to the advance directive must also be considered. An advance directive may predate its ultimate implementation by a considerable period. During that period, the maker may have occasion to elaborate on the meaning of the original document, or even to supplement it. Those elaborations or clarifications can prove helpful in discerning the advance directive's intended meaning.

Consideration of a declarant's post-directive statements may even, in rare instances, curtail reliance on the advance directive document. A person's values or perspectives may change over time, and the declarant may have altered or contradicted the original directive, even without formally revoking it. Statutes relating both to living wills and durable powers of attorney commonly recognize this possibility by providing for revocation of the relevant directive by any expression "evidencing an intent to revoke the document."[17]

In other words, revocation of an advance directive can occur without the formality usually demanded for the original creation of the document. This liberal approach to revocation is grounded on the common policy favoring preservation of life. Legislators apparently anticipated a situation where a declarant would repudiate his or her original life-relinquishing inclinations upon being confronted with real life-threatening prospects. Though allowance of informal revocation might tempt some of the declarant's family to invent conversations, the strong public policy favoring preservation of life warrants the risk involved. My objection is to those jurisdictions which allow revocation regardless of the patient's mental condition when "revoking," a topic to which I will soon turn.[18]

As part of the background and circumstances to be examined in gleaning the meaning of an advance directive, should the health-care agent or other decision maker look to the declarant's prior behavior and lifestyle? The answer is that there is some limited utility in resort to such evidence. A person's general lifestyle does not usually provide a pointed or reliable index regarding medical preferences during a dying process.[19] A vigorous and independent person who previously disdained medical intervention may still wish to cling to life at its fringe.

On the other hand, the behavioral patterns of the individual may provide some guidance in interpretation of an advance directive. If the declarant has indicated that dignity and quality of life are important considerations in shaping his or her medical fate, then certain strong dispositions expressed in lifestyle and behavior may help form an understanding of what was undignified in the eyes of the declarant. A person's prior attitude toward family and loved ones might also be examined in deciding whether the suffering of such third parties is a relevant consideration in shaping the declarant's terminal care.[20] Finally, the personal values of the declarant may inform interpretation of terms used in the directive. For example, a devout Catholic who uses the term "extraordinary means" may well intend to adopt the definition of that term found in church doctrine.

JUSTIFIED AND UNJUSTIFIED DEVIATIONS FROM THE TERMS OF AN ADVANCE DIRECTIVE

Even an elaborately drafted advance directive—to say nothing of the sparse, short forms frequently used—cannot anticipate the multitude of conditions and variables that may accompany an eventual dying process. One consequence is that a health-care agent (or other administrator of a directive) will sometimes be justified in deviating from the literal terms of a directive. The question is when such deviations are warranted.

A. Unforeseen Developments

One justification for overriding the terms of an advance directive is changed circumstances from those anticipated by the declarant. This excuse would not be acceptable in the context of a regular will disposing of property, where finality and certainty are deemed preeminent values. Despite occasional injustices, an un-revoked will is enforced according to its terms even in the face of a showing that the expectations or desires of a testator had changed. (A testator's legacy to her trusted son Bob is not vitiated by a demonstration that Bob turned out to be a bum who stole money from his mother, or even by a showing that the testator wanted to disinherit Bob though she neglected to revise her will.) The fact that human life is in issue in administering an advance directive compels a more flexible approach, including some consideration of changed circumstances.

An illustration of a warranted deviation from a directive comes when technological developments give a new cast to the medical situation being confronted.

Suppose, for example, that a directive specifies that treatment for an incurable, degenerative disease be withdrawn when a certain point of deterioration has been reached. Later, that point is reached, but in the interim a drug has been discovered which promises a significant remission. If the declarant's object was to forego treatment only in the face of an irremediable dying process, the development of this drug would furnish a possible basis to override the letter of the advance directive.

Or suppose an advance directive calls for cessation of life-preserving care if the patient should be "continuously unconscious for a period of one week."[21] If the declarant's intent was to permit accurate diagnosis of a permanently unconscious state, and it will now take more than one week to make an accurate medical assessment, the relevant decision makers are clearly warranted in overriding the precise instruction. In these instances, the letter of the advance directive is overridden, in light of unforeseen developments, in order to fulfill the advance directive's spirit.

A changed circumstance might take the form of a negative development impelling deviation from a prior instruction to maintain life-sustaining care. For example, a directive may have dictated administration of a particular medication which had previously produced, or was expected to produce, a therapeutic benefit. If post-competence developments in the patient's condition demonstrate that the medication is no longer achieving the expected benefits, withdrawal of the medication would be consistent with the spirit of the advance directive.[22]

It's not always easy to reconcile tensions between the letter and the supposed "spirit" of an advance directive. Suppose that the patient has been definitively diagnosed as being in a permanently vegitative state (PVS), a state in which the directive unequivocally calls for cessation of medical intervention (consisting at this point of a respirator and artificial nutrition). But Cousin Joe from Des Moines has phoned and said that he wants a chance to take a last farewell from the patient. This will take a couple of days. The patient knew Cousin Joe, and liked him, but had no particular attachment to him. Should the health-care agent delay the instructed demise of the patient in order to accommodate Cousin Joe?

On the one hand, the patient liked Cousin Joe and *might* have favored accommodating him if the patient had anticipated such a circumstance. And the patient will never sense or suffer from the extended survival period. On the other hand, the directive explicitly deems permanent unconsciousness to be a demeaning state and the document does not articulate the interests of relatives as a concern. If I were the health-care agent, I think I would express regrets to Cousin Joe and I would instruct the attending medical staff to pull the respirator plug. But I couldn't fault an agent who chose to accommodate Cousin Joe.

In the last hypothetical, the decision makers must fill a gap in the instructions resulting from an unanticipated circumstance (Cousin Joe's desire to make a parting).[23] It is entirely appropriate to turn to the underlying objects or spirit of the directive and to seek to further those objects. In this particular instance, it's simply not clear whether the contemplated action (delay to accommodate Cousin Joe), while inconsistent with the letter of the directive, is consistent with its spirit. Since one clear object of the directive is to salvage the patient's self-defined dignity, and that dignity is inconsistent with PVS, my inclination is to adhere to that discernible object and uphold the letter of the directive.

Other sources have recognized that the literal terms of an advance directive should not always govern. For example, the 1983 President's Commission for the Study of Ethical Problems in Medicine suggested that deviation from the terms of a directive might be grounded on a "finding that the patient did not adequately envision and consider the particular situation within which the actual medical decision must be made."[24] This position is sound in its implicit recognition that unforeseen developments can make a provision within an advance directive inconsistent with the declarant's objectives (i.e., inconsistent with the spirit of the document). The New Jersey Bioethics Commission's 1990 report also expresses understanding that changed circumstances (such as therapeutic advances) might warrant noncompliance with the terms of an advance directive.[25] That report recognizes that ostensibly clear language can become ambiguous when applied to unforeseen developments.

B. Conflicts with the Patient's Current Best Interests

A strong temptation to deviate from an advance directive will arise where the declarant's instructions conflict with the current interests of the now incompetent patient. This situation should not occur very frequently. Most people desire to cling to life so long as there is a modicum of benefit to continued existence. Only in case of extreme neurological and physical impairment do they really seek removal of life-sustaining medical support.[26] Nonetheless, there will be instances when advance directives prescribe courses which are in tension with an incompetent patient's ostensible well being or immediate best interests.[27]

An advance directive might seek to preserve the declarant's personal vision of dignity (as a vital, fully functional human being) by directing that life support be withheld whenever the person becomes permanently mentally incompetent and is relegated to a nursing home.[28] Such an instruction might be based either on the specter of dependence on others or on the declarant's wish to avoid emotional and financial burdens to attending family during a protracted dying process.[29] Such an instruction—if implemented—could prompt withholding of antibiotics and cause the ensuing demise of an incompetent patient ostensibly enjoying existence but stricken with pneumonia. The patient admitted to the nursing home may be mentally impaired and incompetent yet still be alert, retaining awareness of the environment and apparently enjoying the impaired existence.

Further examples of possible dissonance between an advance directive and a now incompetent patient's immediate interests (meaning immediate well-being) will be presented in chapter 6. In that chapter, I address the moral implications of an agent's acting counter to the current well-being of a now helpless being. (I conclude there that implementation of prior instructions counter to current well-being is not intrinsically immoral.) At this juncture, the question is whether a health-care agent is entitled to use the patient's current well-being as a justification for not implementing the terms of an advance directive.

As noted, there will be considerable temptation to override an advance directive calling for the demise of a helpless patient (the new nursing-home resident) contrary to the patient's immediate well-being (the patient is still aware and getting some satisfaction from existence). The agent (or other decision maker) who succumbs to that temptation may seek to invoke the notion that the declarant did not sufficiently envision or consider the consequences. Recall the suggestion of the President's Commission that deviation from an advance directive might be grounded on "a finding that the patient did not adequately envision and consider the particular situation within which the actual medical decision must be made." That standard deserves some explanation and refinement.

In some instances, an agent's decision to override a directive's ostensible instruction may represent a good-faith interpretation of the declarant's intent—a judgment that the declarant simply did not intend to encompass the situation at hand. The declarant who prescribed that medical treatment should be withheld upon subsequent admission to a nursing home may have contemplated a status of either total immobility or acute embarrassment. That declarant may not have intended to cover a period of "pleasant" ambulatory senility or a situation where anticipated embarrassment did not materialize in fact. Then, if the now incompetent patient does not seem to be suffering in the nursing home, the agent would be warranted in ignoring the literal scope of the instruction regarding nontreatment after admission to a nursing home.

There is, however, a variation of the above scenario which must be considered. The decision not to implement the instruction regarding nontreatment in a nursing-home setting might be grounded on the agent's (or medical personnel's) distaste for the instruction. That is, the declarant may have fully intended the literal meaning of the directive, but refusal to implement flows from the conviction that the instruction was imprudent or ill-considered.

The obstacle to following this course does not come from any serious threat of legal liability. Medical staff, surrounding family, and courts are likely to acquiesce in decisions to maintain an apparently happy patient—despite the tension with the terms of an advance directive. The chances are therefore slim that a health-care agent or other decision maker would face the threat of a lawsuit, let alone actual liability, for providing treatment to a pleasantly senile patient or, generally, for acting according to the contemporaneous well-being of a now incompetent patient. In the unlikely event of a legal proceeding, the sympathies of any trier of fact would be with the decision to respect the material, current interests of the patient. Even if the decision maker were found "liable," any "damages" would be assessed with awareness of the benefits to the patient derived from the actual decision.

Nonetheless, I submit that it is not appropriate for decision makers to override advance directives merely because the declarant's expressed preferences do not coincide with current, material best interests.[30] If the declarant did in fact contemplate the situation actually encountered and still provided for a course contrary to material best interests, that course ought to be respected. Self-determination includes a prerogative to make decisions that most people would regard as foolish or unsound. If a person has considered the prospect of "harm" to his or her own future incompetent persona and nonetheless makes certain personal values predominant, that decision should ordinarily be respected.

I agree, however, with commentators who say that steps should be taken to examine the circumstances surrounding the formulation of an advance directive that appears to subordinate the perceptible current interests of a now incompetent patient. As noted, future-oriented autonomy entails projections, and a problematic decision can no longer be reconsidered by the now incompetent person. It is therefore sensible to ground implementation of a "problematic" life-and-death decision on a determination of whether the declarant really intended the problematic result ostensibly prescribed by the directive. But where good-faith examination discloses that the maker of an advance directive deliberately dictated the result in issue, that directive ought to be upheld.

Indeed, I only reluctantly endorse a limited prerogative to avoid the ostensible terms of an advance directive (in favor of a now incompetent patient's current well-being) conditioned upon a good-faith judgment that the declarant did not really intend to encompass the situation actually confronted. The high stakes involved— the life of an incompetent human being—warrant this limited prerogative. And the reality probably is that some people sign an advance directive without really contemplating some of the graver consequences and dilemmas. When those grave dilemmas occur (such as a clear conflict between a directive and current best interests), I favor allowing the decision makers to make a good-faith inquiry about the directive maker's contemplation of the dilemma confronted. Yet this authorization to avoid an apparent instruction might be misused.

The standard suggested by the President's Commission—involving the "adequacy" of a declarant's consideration of a directive's application—is fraught with danger of manipulation.[31] An agent (or other decision maker) may always contend that the declarant did not "adequately" envision the consequences. The standard supplies an opening for overriding idiosyncratic preferences of the declarant that prove distasteful to the eventual decision makers.

An adequacy of contemplation standard thus threatens to undermine any confidence that idiosyncratic preferences will be followed. One of the benefits of an advance directive is the comfort it can supply to the individual while that person is still competent. That comfort flows from confidence that the advance directive has regulated the future care of the individual in a fashion consistent with personal preferences and values. If eventual decision makers abuse their authority and readily circumvent advance directives, much of the value of such instruments will be lost.

There is only a fine line between saying that a declarant did not contemplate or intend to include the situation at hand (in rejecting care) and saying that the declarant's instruction was ill considered. The former involves interpretation of the directive's meaning, with the conclusion that the declarant simply did not intend the literal scope of the directive's language. The latter involves overriding the declarant's preferences because they are not congruent with the immediate well-being of the now incompetent patient and are, therefore, distasteful to decision makers. I suggest that deviation from the apparent terms of a directive is warranted only upon a good-faith judgment that the declarant did not intend to reject treatment in the situation at hand—whether his or her ostensible well-being would be sacrificed or not.[32]

C. Expressions of Incompetent Patients

By definition, an advance directive represents an autonomous expression of will which becomes effective only after the declarant has lost legal capacity to make the medical decisions at hand. It may seem strange, then, to utilize an incompetent patient's utterances in administering an advance directive. Nonetheless, there is an appropriate role for such expressions. The challenge is to define the bounds of that role.

The starting point of analysis is recognition that incompetency may cover a wide range of mental incapacity. While some patients may be barely aware of their environment and totally unable to comprehend information, others may have some understanding of data relating to their medical condition and proposed treatment (even if they are incapable of making a considered judgment about the data). Utterances from the former class may be incoherent ravings while the latter class may be making meaningful communication. The appropriate response to incompetent patients' utterances depends, in part, on where the patient fits within the range of incompetency.

Some living-will statutes fail to make an appropriate differentiation among incompetent patients. The offending statutes provide that the declarant may revoke a directive "at any time and in any manner, without regard to the declarant's mental or physical condition."[33] This apparently means that any statement countering a living will or contradicting a previous instruction will effectively revoke such instructions, no matter how deteriorated the declarant's mental condition at the time of this "revocation." (Following such a revocation, the declarant would presumably revert to the status of an incompetent patient who had left no prior instructions as to the matter in issue, and the general rules governing the handling of such patients would then prevail.[34] There would be no possibility of the patient issuing further, binding instructions since the patient would lack the requisite mental capacity.)

This extreme statutory receptivity toward revocation of a prior directive is problematic at best. As several commentators have noted,[35] the extreme deference to incompetents' expressions tends to subvert notions of self-determination. A carefully considered advance directive can, in theory, be undermined by the babble of a gravely demented patient. And potential for the manipulation of a demented patient is patent. The decision makers surrounding the patient (perhaps uncomfortable with the substance of a living will) can simply keep asking the patient whether he or she renounces the document until an affirmative response is attained.[36]

A variation on this theme appeared in a recent New York case. There, the now incompetent patient had appointed her daughter as health-care agent. The disgruntled son, apparently upset at the daughter's inclinations regarding care, sought to obtain the mother's "revocation" of the proxy appointment. He recorded a phone conversation with the incompetent patient, using leading questions to elicit one or two word responses. The son then petitioned for removal of his sister as health-care agent. The ploy failed. The judge recognized that the incompetent mother had not comprehended the conversation, and he rejected the petition.[37] Still, the incident underscores the vulnerability of incompetent patients to manipulation of their utterances.

The motivation behind the liberal revocation provisions in living-will statutes is easy to understand. There is a natural revulsion toward removing life-preserving care from a person who is articulating a wish to live.[38] This is so even when the patient is confused and uncomprehending of the real significance of the utterances. At the same time, giving determinative force to incompetent declarations, no matter how demented the patient, seems excessive.

The impropriety of giving force to the expressions of severely demented patients becomes more evident when we consider such a patient calling for death via the removal of life support. Not infrequently, such a patient will ask to be allowed to die or will consistently struggle to remove life-preserving intervention (such as artificial feeding tubes). Many sources have recognized that interpreting such behavior as meaningful choice is inappropriate.[39] Sometimes, this conclusion is grounded on the ambiguity of nonverbal conduct. Indeed, physical resistance to medical intervention can sometimes be ambiguous—possibly reflecting annoyance, anger, or desire for attention, rather than a deliberate choice to die.[40] But the more convincing explanation for reservations regarding such conduct is that the "choices" of grievously demented patients cannot be regarded as meaningful acts of self-determination. If a nondying patient were at a similar stage of mental incapacity, that person's choices would not be accorded binding force. This would be true with regard to medical choices, such as sterilization, or nonmedical decisions, such as disposition of property. There is no reason to accord greater weight to such expressions for purposes of a life-and-death treatment decision.

All this does not mean that the expressions of demented patients should be ignored. If an incompetent patient has any degree of comprehension and ability to communicate, the patient should be consulted about the proposed course of medical handling and the patient's reactions should be considered.[41] Again, this does not mean that the incompetent patient's responses should necessarily be determinative of the course to be followed but only that those responses should be sought and considered by the relevant care providers and decision makers.[42] There are several rationales for this consultation requirement.

First, it is a mark of human respect and dignity to consult with the incompetent patient, even if that patient is not very comprehending. The incompetent patient is a human being, albeit with reduced capacities. It would be inhumane to simply ignore the will and feelings of the incompetent patient while implementing the medical course fixed by the decision makers (even if this course conforms to the patient's advance directive). Nonconsultation and straight performance of fateful medical procedures constitute manipulation of the patient as though he or she were an inanimate object. Consultation thus has a symbolic significance, reminding staff, observers, and perhaps the patient that a human life is at stake.

In addition, the patient may have enough mental capacity to respond with assent to the proposed course.[43] Simple assent, without the capacity for full understanding and mental deliberation, is not informed consent or a genuine exercise of autonomy. But the consultative effort involved in attaining assent recognizes the patient's humanity, and the assent may assuage the patient and ease the ensuing course of treatment in some degree.[44]

The expressions of an incompetent patient can also furnish important insights into the emotional and physical feelings of the patient—insights which are relevant to the implementation of advance directives. The thrust of an advance directive may be to dictate omission of life-sustaining intervention where the burdens of continued existence in a debilitated, incompetent state exceed the benefits. The expressions of the incompetent patient are, in turn, one index of either the burdens (pain, suffering, and indignity) or benefits (emotional satisfaction) being experienced.[45] Even when a patient is totally incapable of making deliberate decisions, the patient may be capable of expressing feelings. If those feelings can be discerned and understood, they can be useful in the administration of an advance directive.

An additional reason for consulting with the incompetent patient and for paying heed to the incompetent's expressions is to assess prospective physical resistance to proposed medical procedures. The patient's resistance may necessitate physical restraints or heavy sedation. Depending on the nature of the medical procedure, the restraints may even be prolonged or repeated in nature. (Resistance to artificial nutrition tubes, frequent blood transfusions, or dialysis attachment provide examples.) Particularly in the case of an incapacitated patient who cannot comprehend the reasons for the treatment, restraints may provoke frustration and anger. The consequence of continued medical intervention in such circumstances would then be prolonged maintenance in an inhumane status—perhaps in a fashion inconsistent with the terms of an advance directive.

The expressions of the incompetent patient may therefore be important both to assessing in advance the patient's reactions to proposed medical intervention and to assessing the patient's feelings and status while undergoing actual restraints. The specter of prolonged or repeated restraint or sedation also helps explain the purpose of seeking assent from a mentally incompetent patient. That assent may diminish the chances that a resisting patient will be relegated to an undignified status during the dying process.

A final possible rationale for consultation with an incompetent patient would be to secure clues as to what the patient would choose if the patient were competent. Resort to such a rationale might occur, for example, where an advance directive is vague and the decision makers are seeking to determine what the declarant would have wanted in the current medical circumstances. This object (to discern what the patient would have wanted, if competent) has been cited in decisions of the Washington State Supreme Court relating to the handling of incompetent patients.[46] That court suggested that current expressions of an incompetent patient might furnish "a strong indicator of the treatment she would choose if competent to do so."[47] However, the same court cautioned that the weight attributed to the incompetent's expressions must depend on the extent to which the patient understands the issue at hand.

This last admonition is consistent with the diminished role of choice in the context of incompetent patients. If the incompetent patient has a substantial understanding of the circumstances, and the patient's "choice" corresponds to the patient's values as consistently held while competent, perhaps there is a meaningful autonomy element in the response obtained.[48] However, if the patient is so demented as not to understand or appreciate the nature and consequences of the choices involved, it is an illusion to talk in terms of autonomy and self-determination. Giving dominion to the deranged expressions of such persons would make a mockery of self-determination when the expressions override a carefully considered advance directive.

In sum, the expressions of an incompetent patient can sometimes be useful guides in shaping administration of a dying process in accord with an advance directive. Their utility, however, varies markedly according to the mental capacity of the patient and the ability of decision makers to accurately interpret the expressions. Statutory provisions which give substantive force to all incompetent expressions inconsistent with prior directives (as by treating them as effective revocations of a living will), are clearly overbroad. The ravings of a deeply demented patient ought not be permitted to override an advance directive. At most, an understanding (even if not deliberately considered) expression by an incompetent patient ought to suspend implementation of an advance directive which conflicts with the expression.[49] That is, in order to suspend the force of an advance directive calling for withdrawal of life support, a life-affirming expression must come from an incompetent patient who at least understands the concept of death. Even then, the force of such an expression probably ought to continue only so long as the position is being communicated by the patient. Thereafter, a considered and clear advance directive ought to govern.

THIRD PARTY OPPOSITION: FAMILY, PHYSICIANS', OR HOSPITALS' OBJECTIONS

To this point in the discussion, the difficulty of interpreting terse or vague language has posed the main obstacle to effective administration of an advance directive. Another obstacle materializes when one of the parties surrounding an incompetent patient—whether family member, physician, or institutional administrator—objects to implementation of a directive's instructions.

Appointment of a health-care agent is one technique for dealing with this hazard. The hope is that the agent will serve as an advocate to secure fulfillment of the declarant's wishes. But in many instances there will be no designated agent. Or the designated agent himself or herself may wonder how to deal with opposition from one of the above sources. Various mechanisms or techniques for enforcement of an advance directive will be discussed in chapter 7. Here, I address the legal status of the parties' objections to implementation of the declarant's apparent instructions.

A. Family Members' Opposition

There are indications that physicians sometimes fail to adhere to advance directives because of opposition by family members surrounding the moribund, incompetent patient.[50] This tendency is not surprising in light of the strong practical disincentives for an attending physician to contest a surrounding family's instructions. The family represent a potentially vocal and disruptive element. They pose a threat of legal recourse if a physician terminates life support contrary to the family's wishes. A specter of controversy, time investment, expense, and adverse publicity therefore looms before any physician who contemplates contravening the family. The much easier course is to go along with the family's wishes. (Similar incentives for deference to family wishes exist if it is a health-care agent who is confronted with a family's opposition to implementation of the now incompetent patient's directive.)

Family opposition might be grounded on either of two bases. One basis would be a family's contention that they understand the patient's real wishes—even if the family interpretation conflicts with the ostensible meaning of the advance directive. In such instances, acquiescence in the family position might be appropriate. As the previous material indicated, compliance with the incompetent patient's actual preferences may sometimes entail deviation from the apparent meaning of an advance directive. The family may be making a good-faith and plausible interpretation of the patient's actual intentions.

Another possible scenario exists. The family's opposition to fulfilling a directive's terms may stem from reasons other than good-faith interpretation of the patient's wishes. For example, the family may simply be emotionally unable to cope with the prospective death and may therefore seek to prevent it. Or the family may be seeking to substitute their view of the patient's best interests for what they deem the patient's aberrational or ill-considered instructions.

Under the second scenario—in which the family want to counter the patient's wishes because of their own preferences—the appropriate course for medical staff (and for a health-care agent, if present) is clear. The patient's wishes are supposed to prevail. If a health-care agent is present and determines that the advance directive dictates cessation of life support, and that determination appears accurate, medical personnel ought to follow that course. Life support should be withdrawn in accord with the directive. If there is no designated health-care agent, physicians should not simply acquiesce in the distorted position pushed by the family. The medical staff (or hospital administration) ought to petition for judicial appointment of a guardian who will be willing to adhere to the advance directive.

In the real world, the disincentives mentioned above will often come into play. As a practical matter, medical staff, and possibly even health-care agents, will defer to the wishes of the surrounding family. This will particularly be the case if the family seek life extension while the advance directive calls for cessation of life support.

B. Physicians' Opposition

Physicians might raise principled objections to implementing an advance directive. One objection would be that sound medical practice impels nonadherence to the now incompetent patient's wishes. A second objection would be that the physician's conscientious scruples don't permit compliance with the course prescribed in the directive. Sometimes these objections overlap.

A physician's objections might pull in either of two directions. Sometimes, a physician might object because an advance directive calls for cessation of life support at a stage considered premature according to the physician's assessment of good medical practice. Sometimes, a directive will call for continuation of life-preserving intervention to a point deemed inappropriate or futile by the physician or by professional standards. The principles to be presented here apply to both these happenstances.

The first inquiry regards an advance directive which prescribes cessation of medical intervention at a stage deemed premature and inappropriate by an attending physician relying on sound medical practice (i.e., professional standards). For example, a declarant, sensitive to personal notions of dignity, may have mandated cessation of life-preserving medical intervention at any point after admission to a nursing home. Later, although the patient is physically "healthy," mental deterioration prompts the patient's admission to a nursing home. Suppose the declarant (now a nursing-home resident) is stricken with pneumonia. Many physicians would object to withholding medical care from such a salvageable patient,[51] even though the patient is incapable of independent living because of chronic ailments and/or mental incapacity—a status deemed intolerable in the patient's advance directive.

Where the physician's objection to "premature" cessation of life-sustaining care is grounded on the rationale of sound medical practice, the patient's wishes ought ordinarily to prevail. This is so because social norms, as judicially interpreted, establish the primacy of patient self-determination over most conflicting professional preferences.

The primacy of social norms over medical preference has been established in many contexts. The whole doctrine of informed consent imposed duties which many physicians viewed as being in tension with their professional role.[52] Yet the contours of that doctrine were fixed by courts and legislatures despite professional qualms and objections. Similarly, as to the standard of skill required of physicians, the courts and legislatures may choose to accept professional custom and practice as the governing legal norm, but they need not do so.[53]

In short, while professional notions of sound medical practice form an important consideration in shaping the legal bounds of physicians' duties, those professional preferences are not paramount. For example, professional judgment received a rude setback when the federal government fixed regulations limiting abortion counseling in medical facilities receiving federal funding. Despite the bitter complaint that the federal rules violated professional standards, those rules were sustained.[54]

A similar lesson has been applied in the context of rejection of life-sustaining medical care. When patients or their representatives sought to reject such treatment, physicians commonly objected that medical standards outweighed patient self-determination.[55] Patients turned to the courts. The judicial response was that a patient's choice "must be accorded respect even when it conflicts with the advice of the doctor or the values of the medical profession as a whole."[56] Though such ringing declarations often appear in the context of competent patients, a similar order of priorities is likely to prevail with regard to incompetent patients and advance directives. A number of courts have accorded binding force to now incompetent patients' prior expressions despite medical practitioners' opposition.[57] The non-contemporaneous nature of advance medical instructions is unlikely to affect the upholding of patient self-determination over professional qualms.[58]

It is true that many legislative measures relating to advance directives mention "reasonable medical standards" or "accepted medical practice."[59] Most of this statutory language resembles that of the Uniform Rights of the Terminally Ill Act, which provides: "A physician or other health-care provider, whose action under this [Act] is in accord with reasonable medical standards, is not subject to criminal or civil liability, or discipline for unprofessional conduct, with respect to that action."[60] The relevant statutory language generally appears in the provision according physicians immunity for compliance with a statutorily approved advance directive.

At first blush, such expressions might be understood as endorsing physician adherence to good medical practice rather than the contrary terms of an advance directive. But it is unlikely that these statutory provisions will upset the understood priority of patient wishes over professional preferences.

The relevant statutory language about "reasonable medical standards" may simply be aimed at preserving claims of medical malpractice when compliance with patient instructions is undertaken in a technically shoddy fashion. For example, a physician who withdraws life support from a supposedly permanently unconscious patient might be liable for having negligently failed to perform the requisite tests of permanent unconsciousness. The language of some states' immunity provisions tends to support this focus on technical proficiency. Connecticut law states:

> [There shall be] no liability in removal or withholding [life support], provided that . . . the decision to withhold or remove such life support system is based on the best medical judgment of the attending physician in accordance with the usual and customary standards of medical practice. . . . "[61]

Delaware explicitly uses the word "negligence" in its immunity provision. The language reads:

> Physicians or nurses who act in reliance on a document exercised in accordance with this [statute] . . . by withholding medical procedures for an individual who executed such document shall be presumed to be acting in good faith, and unless negligent shall be immune from civil or criminal liability.[62]

In sum, the references to "reasonable medical practice" in immunity provisions were not intended to authorize physicians to impose their professional preferences to the detriment of patient choice expressed in advance directives. Moreover, the constitutional status accorded patient choice might mandate that patient choice prevail over professional hesitations concerning the soundness of the patient's chosen course.

There may be some practical limits to the primacy of patient wishes over professional judgment. A medical practitioner is probably not obligated to practice "bad medicine" or violate his or her professional judgment in order to comply with patient preferences.[63] At the same time, the physician may not simply impose his or her will on the patient. The physician's normal recourse is to withdraw from the case and arrange transfer of the patient's care to medical professionals willing to cooperate with the patient's chosen course.

Modern medicine recognizes a broad role for patient autonomy. While some physicians may object, on grounds of good medical practice, to implementation of certain instructions, other practitioners will see fit to comply. Thus, withdrawal from the case will often be a satisfactory outcome. There will be a fellow physician whose professional judgment differs from that of the original attending physician and who can step in and implement the patient's desired medical handling. Such divergence of opinion about professional and ethical issues is not uncommon. It occurs with regard to abortion. It occurs with regard to artificial nutrition. And it may occur with regard to the "premature" stage at which an incompetent patient may be permitted to die. While some physicians may be unwilling to withhold antibiotics from a "healthy" but gravely demented nursing-home resident, other physicians may have no qualms about respecting the patient's advance directive which dictates such a course. In short, the fact that some segments of the medical profession might regard a practice as ethically problematic should not preclude implementation of a patient's desire to follow the problematic practice. (The principal legal boundary on respecting patient choice would be the criminal law, with its constraints against assisted suicide and active euthanasia.)

There may be instances, however, when the advance directive's prescribed course is so problematic—from the perspective of medical judgment or ethics— that few if any practitioners will be willing to cooperate. Transfer of the patient to a cooperating physician may then not be a viable option. The proper resolution of this situation is still unclear.

One option might be to take the patient home, at least if the patient can be made comfortable in that setting. Another option might be litigation to try and force the resisting physician to follow the advance directive. That step would entail considerable expense and effort, and the legal resolution is far from certain. (Courts may be reluctant to compel conduct by physicians which is uniformly regarded as medically unsound. At the same time, modern medicine acknowledges the importance of patient choice, and the patient's self-determination interest might be ruled predominant.) As a practical matter, I suspect that many practitioners will simply impose their preferences by continuing life support in the face of an advance directive which dictates what the practitioner deems "premature" withdrawal of medical intervention.

Suppose the physician's objection to premature withdrawal is based on a strongly felt, personal moral judgment. In other words, on occasion a physician who objects to implementation of an advance directive may rely on personal conscience rather than just professional judgment or sound medical practice. Will such physicians be required to act in violation of their scruples?

Ordinarily, the tension between professional conscience and patient wishes is resolved—as in the case of tension with professional judgment—by respect for both physician and patient interests. That is, a patient (or person acting on behalf of the patient) cannot normally force a health-care professional to violate personal scruples. However, the objecting physician is expected to act to transfer the patient's care to fellow professionals who can, in good conscience, implement the advance directive.

Solicitude for physicians' conscientious objections first surfaced in the context of abortion and sterilization services. In the 1970s, numerous states adopted statutes providing that medical personnel cannot be coerced into providing abortion or sterilization services in violation of their moral scruples.[64]

Similar solicitude for professional conscience has been shown in the context of termination of life-sustaining medical intervention. Cases express unwillingness to compel a physician to violate moral precepts (in order to fulfill a patient's wishes), at least where transfer of care to another health-care provider can be accomplished.[65] Living-will statutes in many states take a similar approach. A physician is not required to follow a medical course violative of his or her conscience, but the physician is expected to seek transfer of the patient to another health-care provider. The main divergence among these statutes relates to the degree of effort the physician must make in arranging a transfer.[66]

Superficially, this legal framework seems to work a commonsense accommodation of patient and professional interests. The patient is entitled to shape the degree of medical intervention into a dying process, even when the decision was made far in advance of implementation and even if the choice is idiosyncratic. Health-care providers are not required to sacrifice their personal or professional scruples. Their alternative is to withdraw from the case while assisting the patient's representatives in finding a provider who can cooperate in implementing the advance directive. So long as a cooperating provider can be found, providers' individual scruples won't prevent implementation of patient choices.

Transfer of the incompetent patient's care to a cooperating physician may be feasible. Sometimes it merely entails referral to another physician within the same institution. Sometimes, though, complications disturb the nice theoretical structure just outlined.

The moribund patient may have developed an attachment to the particular health-care provider, so that transfer to an alternative provider entails a significant emotional price. Or the incident may occur in a relatively isolated geographical area so that transfer to a distant alternative provider imposes a significant burden upon surrounding family and loved ones continuing a deathwatch. Or a particular case may have generated so much publicity that alternative providers are reluctant to get involved. What happens when one of these complications prevents smooth transfer of the patient to alternative medical hands? Does the patient's interest yield, or does the health-care provider's?

If a health-care provider's personal scruples conflict with a declarant's chosen course, and transfer of the patient is not feasible, the provider can probably be compelled to violate his or her conscience. While states have often chosen to respect professional conscience, no constitutional or moral imperative requires that result when there is a conflict with patient choice. This conclusion is drawn by analogy from other contexts in which important public policies have been found to override the conscientious scruples of service providers. An example is enforcement of bans on race or gender discrimination despite the discriminator's conscientious belief in the discriminatory practice.[67] A patient's interest in obtaining medical treatment consistent with an advance directive probably occupies a comparable value status relative to professional conscience.

The little judicial precedent available suggests that a health-care provider can be compelled to violate his or her conscience when an alternative arrangement to accommodate the patient cannot feasibly be made.[68] This has been the case, for example, where the patient has developed a strong emotional bond to personnel within a particular institution,[69] where transfer of the patient would entail hardship for the surrounding family,[70] or where no alternative setting could be found.[71] In effect, the physician is being required, as a condition of medical licensure, to extend a full range of services to anyone accepted as a patient (where withdrawal and transfer is not feasible).[72] This does not seem like an unreasonable burden, at least within the range of medical conduct upheld as legal under the criminal law and not uniformly deemed ethically intolerable by the medical profession as a whole.

The same framework applies when a physician's objection to honoring an advance directive is grounded on a conviction that the requested treatment is medically inappropriate or "futile." (Start thinking about an advance directive which dictates continued life support even as to a permanently unconscious status and about an attending physician who feels that life support in such an instance is pointless.) Often, a claim of medical futility or pointlessness is really one of professional judgment about sound medical practice. Therefore, the same theoretical structure applies as applied to a physician's objection to premature withdrawal of life support. This means that while a physician can not ordinarily be forced to provide care which that physician deems medically unsound or futile, there is an obligation to assist in transfer of the patient to a physician who will implement the patient's chosen course. The patient's autonomy interest is acknowledged and accommodated.[73]

This topic of futile or pointless medical intervention is complex, and it warrants more detailed explanation. Some commentators do assert a physician's prerogative to refuse to provide treatment which is futile, meaning that it carries not even a modicum of benefit to the patient.[74] To the extent the assertion implies a medical prerogative to simply ignore or override a patient's preference for continuance of life-sustaining care, the assertion seems much too simplistic. As several other sources have noted, the concept of futility must differentiate between medical means which will have no physiological effect and means which are believed by the physician to carry no benefit for the patient (even though the means are life-extending).[75] When life-preserving techniques are in issue—as in the case of life support for a permanently unconscious patient—the issue is not technical capacity but values (i.e., is continued life support warranted?).[76]

The answer to that question involves patients' perceptions of the value of gravely debilitated existence and social judgments about allocation of resources, not just medical judgment. Medical professionals are not peculiarly qualified to weigh the interests involved. "[D]eciding whether the life of a severely ill person is worth saving—whether a patient's state of existence is sufficiently good to justify further medical treatment—is not a question that doctors are uniquely, or even specially, qualified to answer."[77]

In short, complex value judgments underlie any contention that life-extending medical intervention is futile. The underlying question is the dispensability of a human life, and the relevant standard for that judgment is a societal issue to be resolved by courts and legislatures after consideration of many perspectives, including those of the medical profession. A medical judgment that an intervention is pointless is relevant but not determinative. Even some *medical* sources agree that medical judgment cannot be paramount in fixing the parameters of the duty of life-preservation. The Society of Critical Care Medicine, for example, recognizes that it is appropriate for a physician to provide service which is meaningful to the patient even though it has "no reasonable medical benefit."[78]

An illustration of the possible tension between physicians' preferences and patients' advance instructions occurred in a 1991 case.[79] A Minnesota hospital sought court appointment of a guardian for an eighty-seven-year-old woman immersed in a permanent vegetative state. The hospital's ultimate object was to secure authorization to end life support (a respirator) because it supposedly constituted "inappropriate medical treatment that is not in the patient's medical interests."[80] The family insisted that treatment should continue because the patient would have wanted continued life support. Their appraisal was based on the patient's prior religious convictions and on alleged prior statements.

Assuming there was a firm basis for the family's contention that the now incompetent patient would have wanted continued life support,[81] the petition for appointment of a new guardian should have been (and was) dismissed. The relevant principles have been presented. The physicians' assertion that continued respirator maintenance would be futile is a claim based on professional judgment about sound medical practice. Physicians ordinarily cannot be forced to practice bad medicine, but their judgment cannot be imposed upon patients' preferences.[82] This means that the attending physician and hospital could not simply override the patient's wishes. They could turn over care to more cooperative physicians but, in the absence of such cooperative physicians, the original attending physicians would be obligated to continue medical maintenance.[83]

There might be rare instances when professional judgment (such as that asserted by the doctors in the Minnesota hospital) is reinforced because the patient's prescribed course is so inhumane as to be beyond the bounds of acceptable professional behavior. (In chapter 6, I speculate about a situation where the now incompetent patient has dictated maximum life support but is later suffering agonizingly and irremediably while begging that life support be withdrawn.) If the patient's prescribed course is inhumane according to widely accepted standards, physician resistance will probably be upheld and allowed to overcome the patient's advance directive.[84]

This possible exception for inhumane treatment does not apply to an advance directive which prescribes medical maintenance in a permanently vegetative state (PVS). It is true that most people regard permanent unconsciousness as a distasteful and undesirable prospect. This is readily understandable, given the horrible void of a permanently vegetative state. Nancy Cruzan's atten... physician testified about her "alternating constipation and diarrhea, stomach troubles, eye problems, rashes, bleeding gums, contorted limbs, seizures and vomiting."[85] But PVS is not yet considered so utterly degrading that continued life support is widely regarded as inhumane. The thousands of PVS patients being maintained[86] undermines any notion that medical maintenance in a PVS is currently considered so inhumane as to be beyond the bounds of acceptable medical practice. (However, it is conceivable that societal norms will eventually evolve to the point that preservation in a PVS is widely considered inhumane.)

The result in the Minnesota case might be different under somewhat different facts. If the patient had never indicated a wish to be preserved in a PVS, and if there were no religious beliefs or other indices that she would have wanted such a course, the family's effort to continue life support might conceivably be supplanted. This displacement of the family's preference would be grounded not on medical futility but on a judgment that the permanently unconscious patient's best interests dictate withdrawal of life support. The standard of best interests is generally used where a now incompetent patient has never expressed personal preferences with regard to life-sustaining medical intervention.[87] Under this standard, a decision maker on behalf of the patient is supposed to decide whether the burdens of potential existence with treatment outweigh the potential benefits.

It may legitimately be asked why a permanently unconscious patient's best interests lie in termination of life support, given that the patient is insensate and is not suffering. The answer is that best interests can include dignity. And the vast majority of people, considering what they want for their own prospective medical handling, regard permanent unconsciousness as an undignified and unwanted status. (People may also be influenced by the perception that care of PVS patients poses an emotional and economic burden on others.) If the vast majority of people would regard termination of life support as being in their own best interests as PVS patients, and the particular patient has never given reason to think that he or she deviates from that perspective, then removal of life support seems most consistent with the best interests of that patient.

In short, the day may soon come when—in the absence of prior instructions to the contrary—decision makers on behalf of permanently unconscious patients will be expected to permit such patients to expire. Such a result will be based on a societal perception that the vast majority of persons would want that result for themselves and that it would coincide with humane and dignified medical handling. That was the instinctive judgment of the New Jersey Supreme Court in 1976 in *Quinlan*. Increasing empirical data confirms that the *Quinlan* court's intuition was correct. Accordingly, courts continue to uphold guardians' decisions to remove PVS patients from life support.[88]

The United States is currently at a juncture where withdrawal of life support from a PVS patient is regarded as a permissible course, consistent with the patient's best interests. Such withdrawal will eventually be the expected course (in the absence of prior patient expressions to the contrary or other indicia of patient will).[89] Again, this position is anchored in the perception that most people define their own best interests in such a fashion and that a permanently unconscious patient has no significant interest in medical maintenance.

In the recent Minnesota case, the family was contending that the patient either expressed or would have expressed a preference for continued life support. They properly sought to ground their assessment of best interests in the values and preferences of the patient herself. Therefore, their decision on behalf of the incompetent patient should prevail over the physicians' judgment about the pointlessness of continued care.[90]

In the Minnesota case, no issue arose about the financing of the disputed care. As in *Cruzan*, public sources were willing to foot the bill. In other instances, however, implementation of an advance directive may raise serious concerns about the allocation of expensive and/or scarce medical resources.[91] Those concerns are legitimate and must ultimately be confronted. Society is and will continue to be unwilling to fund all critical care for all patients. But those resource-allocation issues should be resolved by social judgment—as reflected in considered regulatory and legislative determinations—and not by individual practitioners' judgments that public funds might better be expended elsewhere rather than in the "futile" care sought by a particular advance directive.[92]

C. Institutional Conscience

A hospital may resist implementation of an advance directive on the ground that *its* moral precepts (as opposed to the precepts of staff members) would be offended. In recent years, that claim has most commonly been raised in cases where removal of artificial nutrition was sought by or on behalf of a patient.[93] Is there such a thing as institutional conscience? If there is, does it override a patient's desires regarding medical treatment?

The notion of institutional conscience has aroused some controversy. A few commentators contend that an inanimate object like a hospital can have no conscience. From their perspective, only persons, not bricks and mortar, can have conscientious scruples.[94] By contrast, other observers assert that the development of separate missions or philosophies by health-care-provider institutions "may serve an important purpose in our morally pluralistic society."[95]

My sentiments lie with those who believe that institutions not only can but should have cognizable moral positions. It is true that institutions can't experience the shame or anguish that accompanies an individual's compelled betrayal of conscience.[96] But the institution's founders, owners, board of directors, administrators, and staff could presumably have these feelings. Moral integrity can have a role in determining what goes on within an institution.

On many issues of medical practice, a range of ethical postures is possible. Within that spectrum, it seems desirable that institutions take ethical stands and seek high moral ground. Suppose, for example, the issue were experimentation on human or animal subjects, and the institution took a stricter moral position than required by government regulations. Most people, whether they agree with the particular institutional policy or not, would acknowledge that institutional moral integrity is a meaningful concept in these instances.

Recognition of the concept of institutional conscience does not mean that the institution's interest must always prevail. An institution which believes that AIDS patients are sinners and don't deserve treatment may not necessarily be entitled to turn away AIDS patients. There are many instances when an institutional policy—including positions taken on religious or philosophical grounds—can be overridden by strong public policies. To cite an example, employers or schools which conscientiously believe in their discriminatory policies can be compelled to cease gender or race discrimination. Antidiscrimination laws have been upheld despite the discriminators' deeply held beliefs. But while government may choose to override institutional conscience, it may also decide to recognize and accommodate that conscience.

In the context of health-care providers, both courts and legislatures have generally expressed sympathy with the concept of institutional conscience, especially in the private sector. The first expression of that sympathy came in the 1970s when health care providers were exempted from performing abortions or sterilizations in violation of their conscientious scruples. That relief came both from legislatures[97] and courts.[98]

In the late 1980s and the 1990s, the issue became institutional objections to patients' and guardians' requests for withdrawal of life-preserving treatment. On that issue, there has been limited responsiveness to claims of institutional conscience. The judicial inclination has been to seek an accommodation of both patients' and institutional interests. If it is feasible to transfer a patient to an alternative setting, that step must be taken rather than forcing an institution to provide objectionable care.[99] Transfer to a health-care provider which can conscientiously follow the patient's preferred course both allows the patient ultimately to control the degree of medical intervention and permits the original host institution to maintain its moral integrity. (The original host institution is expected to assist in securing transfer to another health-care provider.)

As in the case of an attending physician with conscientious objections, transfer of a patient from an objecting institution is not always practicable. Publicity attached to a case may deter other institutions from getting involved. Or nearby institutions may share the same scruples as the host institution. Or the patient may have an emotional attachment to particular personnel. Or inconvenience to surrounding family may impede transfer of the patient to another locale.

In the event that transfer cannot practicably be accomplished, an institution will probably be required to cooperate in implementation of the controversial advance directive. This has been the result, for example, where institutions did not give the patient (or family) advance notice about the institution's conscience-based policy. [100]

The implications are plain for health-care agents or others seeking implementation of a "problematic" advance directive. As long as the host institution had served notice about its conscientious policy (such as refusal to remove artificial nutrition), and as long as the moral policy is genuine (as opposed to a contrivance to get rid of an unwanted patient), that policy is entitled to respect. Some effort will have to be made to move the patient to a more responsive setting (or to demonstrate hardship to the patient) before the institution can be compelled to provide the controversial service in violation of its conscience. The health-care agent can expect the institution to take "reasonable steps" to assist in the search for an alternative setting.

6

The Moral Boundaries of Shaping
Post-Competence Medical Care

AN ADVANCE DIRECTIVE seeks to impose a person's own values on a future dying process. A declarant's personal conception of self-respect in dying might be grounded on religious precepts, personal philosophy, or a personal vision of dignity in the dying process. This personal conception of dignity might or might not coincide with the immediate well-being of the incompetent patient at the later moment for implementation of the advance directive.

It is easy to envision instances of extreme dissonance between an advance directive and the perceptible interests of a later incompetent patient. For example, in chapter 4 I mentioned the advance directive of a declarant so sensitive to helplessness that she dictated cessation of life-sustaining intervention beginning at the moment of admission to a nursing home. That declarant might later become mentally impaired and incompetent but remain alert, retaining significant awareness of the environment and ostensibly enjoying existence in a nursing home. If such a person later contracts pneumonia, contemporaneous patient interests would dictate medical intervention, while the advance directive prescribes that the patient should be permitted to die.

In a converse fashion, contemporaneous interests might favor allowing a patient to die while the advance directive prescribes maintaining life-preserving intervention. A person who is a "vitalist," who believes that life is so sacred as to demand preservation to the last possible moment, may issue an advance directive requesting continuation of all life-preserving treatment no matter how dismal the patient's ultimate condition. Subsequently, as a mentally incapacitated patient stricken with terminal cancer, that person might experience unbearable, unremitting pain.[1] Continuing all possible medical intervention would then conflict with the incompetent patient's contemporaneous interests, which impel withdrawal of life-preserving machinery.[2]

These examples test the limits of future-oriented autonomy. In each, a person has issued an advance directive which defines a personal concept of dignity and self-respect, including the upholding of certain personal values. That directive now appears to conflict with the contemporaneous interests of the incompetent persona.[3]

A conflict between personal choice and immediate well-being would not impede effectuation of choice if the person were competent. For a competent person exercising contemporaneous autonomy, personal choice regarding medical treatment need not coincide with material best interests. The respect accorded contemporaneous autonomy extends to personal decisions which deviate from mainstream conceptions of wisdom or best interests. A competent patient may refuse a medical procedure that would leave her in a debilitated state (e.g., an amputation) even though most reasonable people would choose otherwise. Autonomy in contemporaneous medical decision making thus embodies a prerogative to impose personal values and preferences whether they are "sound" or not. Does a similar prerogative attach to prospective autonomy—decisions aimed at post-competence medical handling?[4]

As explained in chapter 2, prospective autonomy is different in some respects from contemporaneous personal choice. That chapter canvassed the problems—including a multiplicity of variables, multiple combinations of variables, medical uncertainty, and declarants' limited perspective—which handicap prospective autonomy. While those problems certainly complicate the task of a declarant seeking to control a future, incompetent dying process, they don't nullify the concept of advance directives. Chapter 2 outlined the rationale for advance directives, a rationale widely accepted in contemporary America. Both courts and legislatures have recognized and even expressed strong sympathy with the principle of advance directives. Yet these sources have not settled the potential conflict between an advance directive and contemporaneous patient well-being.

The cases decided to date do not really resolve the conflict between advance instructions and contemporaneous best interests. There are decisions which speak in fairly absolute terms of a person's "right to avoid circumstances in which the individual himself would feel that efforts to sustain his life demean or degrade his humanity."[5] But these cases do not involve situations in which the previously competent patient's vision of dignity clashes with that patient's subsequent perceptible interests. A few decisions suggest that a previously competent patient's clear directive prevails against a subsequent guardian's appraisal of the incompetent patient's best interests.[6] Yet these judicial expressions occur in cases in which the incompetent patient had reached a permanently unconscious or stuporous state. As such, the cases do not address any real conflict between a prior directive and the perceptible interests of the incompetent patient.[7]

In addition to the above judicial expressions, DPOA-HC laws in many states purport to give a health-care agent the authority to make the same range of decisions that the principal could make if competent.[8] It is a truism that a competent patient would be entitled to reject life-sustaining medical intervention or to consent to nontherapeutic medical procedures even if such a decision did not conform to the apparent well-being of the patient. Thus, in theory, these statutes confer authority on an agent to implement an advance directive which conflicts with the immediate well-being of the incompetent persona. However, the theoretical scope of these statutory measures has not been tested.

The above-cited legal authorities suggest that a person's clear-cut advance directive can prevail over that person's subsequent well-being. Even if that is a legally tolerable course, is it moral to override the immediate well-being of a helpless, incompetent being? At least two concerns have surfaced in the discussions to date.

The first issue involves the moral stature of future-oriented autonomy. It pertains to definition of an incompetent patient's interests and the status of previously declared values whose importance can no longer be appreciated by the now incompetent patient. Via an advance directive, a declarant is seeking to effectuate personal perceptions of self-respect and dignity. Yet at the moment for implementation of those personal values, the incompetent patient may not sense or appreciate the fulfillment of those values. Do that patient's interests encompass elements which can no longer be sensed by the patient (such as nonadherence to the patient's previously articulated conception of a dignified existence)? If the patient can no longer sense invasions of the patient's values, aren't the patient's interests confined to the contemporaneous benefits and burdens being experienced?

Assuming that a person can have interests in having previously important values and choices respected, what about the contemporaneous interests of the incompetent persona who has succeeded the formerly competent patient? Doesn't withdrawal of life-preserving medical support grievously harm a pleasantly senile patient? The possibility of "harming" a helpless, incompetent patient by withdrawing a life-preserving treatment leads to an additional moral contention. The idea is that a person may lose moral authority to dictate the fate of a later, incompetent persona if the later persona is so changed as to have a different "personal identity."

A continuous personal identity supposedly requires some measure of psychological continuity, either through continued memories or beliefs. In the context of death, dying, and advance directives, a competent declarant might become so demented and lacking in psychological continuity as to be considered a new person for moral purposes. If so, it is arguable that one person, the maker of the directive, cannot morally harm or dictate the death of another person—namely, the demented, new persona.[9] In other words, "self-determination" no longer prevails because the original "self" no longer exists. From this perspective, an advance directive might lose its moral stature if, at the moment for implementation, it conflicts with the contemporaneous interests of the incompetent persona.

The remainder of this chapter offers my resolution of the tension between prospective autonomy (as found in an advance medical directive) and an incompetent patient's immediate well-being. First, I present five "scenarios" intended to exemplify the kinds of dilemmas which might arise. Then, I describe and critique the major positions favoring solicitude for immediate patient interests as opposed to previously expressed preferences. Finally, I offer my own resolution of the five scenarios—a resolution giving considerable scope to the declarant's autonomy interest, even to the detriment of immediate patient well-being.

SCENARIOS RAISING CONFLICT AMONG AN INCOMPETENT PATIENT'S INTERESTS

Several examples may help crystallize the potential tension between an advance directive and the contemporaneous interests of an incompetent patient. In the following scenarios, assume that all patients were fifty years old at the time of making an advance directive and that the critical medical decisions are confronted five years later. Assume also that no evidence exists that the patient changed his or her mind or wavered in resolve between preparation of the advance directive and losing competence.

Scenario 1: Person A, a Jehovah's Witness, prescribes in an advance directive that blood transfusions should not be administered regardless of the life-saving potential of such medical intervention. She is aware of the life and death implications of this religiously motivated instruction. Later, A becomes prematurely senile and incompetent. Still later, the senile patient develops bleeding ulcers which demand blood transfusions. With a blood transfusion, she will survive and continue to live as a "pleasantly senile" person for a number of years. The senile A no longer has recollection of, or interest in, religion; however, she remained an avid Jehovah's Witness up until the time of incompetency. Should the attending physician administer a life-saving blood transfusion?

Scenario 2: Person B believes both that life should be preserved to the maximum extent possible and that suffering is preordained and carries redemptive value in an afterlife. B prepares an advance directive in which all possible life-extending medical intervention is requested and all pain relief is rejected. At the time of the preparation of the directive, B has a conversation with a physician in which the physician explicitly warns him that many terminal illnesses entail excruciating pain. Despite that admonition, B directs that all means to preserve life be utilized and that analgesics be omitted. Subsequently, B suffers from cancer, which both affects his brain, rendering him incompetent, and causes him to suffer excruciating pain. Further medical treatment such as radiation or chemotherapy will extend B's life but will not itself relieve the pain or cause any remission in which competence would return. Should the attending physician sedate the patient, or cease the life-prolonging medical intervention, or both?

Scenario 3: Person C is an individual with chronic heart problems. Physicians have informed C that at some stage he will need a heart transplant in order to survive. C prepares an advance directive stating that if he becomes incompetent and survival becomes dependent on a heart transplant, then such a transplant should be rejected because of its expense. C prefers to leave a substantial monetary legacy to his children. Later, C becomes prematurely senile and incompetent. Still later,

C's heart deteriorates and a heart transplant becomes necessary to preserve C's life. With the transplant, C will very likely continue to live for three to five years. Without it, C will die within a few months. The transplant will cost $100,000 and is not covered by any insurance or government benefit program. C's estate totals $100,000. Should a life-extending heart transplant be performed?

Scenario 4: Person D is a health-care professional sensitive to society's needs for organ and tissue donations. In her advance directive, D provides that if she should become incompetent but remain physically healthy, then she wishes to donate a kidney and bone marrow to needy recipients. Later, D is afflicted with Alzheimer's disease and reaches a point of profound dementia. Needy recipients for kidney and bone-marrow transplants have been located. The prospective transplant operations will pose only a slight risk to D and entail only mild pain. At the same time, the now incompetent D has no recollection of her prior instruction and no appreciation of the altruism involved in donating an organ or tissue. She will derive no contemporaneous gain from the contemplated operations. Should the transplants be performed in accord with D's advance directive?

Scenario 5: Person E is a sociology professor known for her intellectual sharpness. E takes enormous pride in that intellectual acuity. E drafts an advance directive prescribing that if she should become mentally impaired and incompetent to the point where she can no longer read and comprehend a sociology text, then all life-preserving medical intervention should be withheld. When reminded by her spouse about the potential for happiness in an incompetent state, E replies that she deems significant mental dysfunction to be degrading and personally distasteful. For her, such a debilitated existence is a fate worse than death. Later, E suffers a serious stroke which renders her permanently incompetent and incapable of reading or performing intellectual tasks. E is also unable to swallow and is therefore dependent on artificial nutrition. At the same time, E does not appear to be in any pain and seems to derive some pleasure from listening to music. Should the life preserving nasogastric tube be continued?

In each of the above situations, people have issued advance directives which effectuate their personal values and concepts of dignity. Yet implementation of those prior instructions conflict in some measure with the contemporaneous interests or well-being of the incompetent persona. Can the advance directive prevail? Does prospective autonomy encompass the prerogative to impact negatively on the incompetent persona?

DEFINING THE INTERESTS OF INCOMPETENT PATIENTS

Law Professors Rebecca Dresser and John Robertson have been prime spokespersons for a position which denigrates reliance on advance instructions. They assert that it is wrong to use advance instructions as a guide to managing the medical treatment of a helpless, incompetent patient.[10] Their basic premise is that the autonomy interests reflected in a person's prior choices become "meaningless" once the incompetent patient can no longer understand and appreciate the violation of those choices. That is, the patient's previously cherished ideas about dignity, religion, or altruism lose importance when their nonimplementation cannot be sensed. For Dresser and Robertson, an incompetent patient "lacks interests in privacy, dignity, and other values that presuppose some conscious appreciation of those concerns."[11]

Professors Dresser and Robertson go even further. They do not just discount the significance of autonomy interests once violation of such interests can no longer be appreciated. They also speculate that if incompetent patients could miraculously be given momentary competence to decide their fate, those patients would focus on their current material interests and not any prior abstract, philosophical, or dignity-related concerns.[12]

A concomitant precept for Dresser and Robertson is that a helpless, incompetent patient's contemporaneous interests (in a debilitated status) ought to be the predominant guide to care so long as the patient retains any significant interest in continued life (which to them includes any patient with the capacity to interact with his or her environment). Dresser and Robertson focus on the current welfare of the incompetent patient. For them, that focus demonstrates moral concern for the debilitated human being. By contrast, it would be morally wrong to allow "meaningless" prior values to prevail over the patient's current interests in continued life.[13]

The Dresser-Robertson position would certainly obviate some hard problems associated with advance directives. Unclear, ill-considered, or deviant instructions could simply be ignored. Health-care providers would be following a humane course by acting according to the contemporaneous, perceptible interests of an incompetent patient. However, the Dresser-Robertson approach seems critically flawed.

The most fundamental flaw is the thesis that incompetent patients are not harmed by rejections of their prior directives. This thesis certainly does not conform to common perspectives and ways of thinking. For instance, if a dying, incompetent Jehovah's Witness receives a blood transfusion in contravention of a prior instruction (in a vain attempt to prompt a remission), we tend to say that the person's religious values have been affected and that this constitutes harm to the patient. If a person dictates in an irrevocable trust that funds be expended in a particular way and the trustee absconds with those funds after the person's incompetency, we tend to say that the now incompetent and unaware grantor has been injured by this breach of faith (as have the intended beneficiaries). If a person expresses a desire to receive all possible life-preserving intervention, yet a life-sustaining ventilator is subsequently withdrawn in order to save another patient, then we tend to see an impingement of the patient's self-determination even if the patient was comatose at the moment of the deed.[14]

There are other examples of societal respect for the unsensed interests of incompetent persons. Assume that a permanently unconscious patient has left no instructions about medical intervention, and assume that he has no surrounding family or friends. What prevents the medical staff from carving up the patient in order to harvest nonvital organs or tissue for the benefit of others? What prevents the conduct of nontherapeutic medical experiments on the insensate being? The obstacle is social respect for the intrinsic dignity interests of persons, even when violations of those interests cannot be felt by the affected individual.[15] Society can and does attribute dignity interests to incompetent persons despite their incapacity to sense or appreciate breaches of those interests.

Attribution of some significance to abstract, unappreciated values of incompetent patients does not resolve the issue at hand. The question remains whether these abstract interests (as articulated in an advance directive) can prevail in the critical context of life-preserving medical intervention, especially when the immediate well-being of the helpless patient would seem to dictate life preservation. If the answer is positive, and I think it is, the key lies in understanding the integral link between prospective autonomy and the success of a person's life.

The late Professor Nancy K. Rhoden was an articulate advocate of the moral force of prospective autonomy in the death-and-dying context.[16] Professor Rhoden argued that the advance instructions of a competent person have considerable moral force, even if that person reaches an incompetent state in which failure to honor prior wishes cannot be felt or appreciated. For Rhoden, it is highly "humane" and respectful of human dignity to give force to future-oriented decisions, even at the expense of some contemporaneous interests of a now incompetent persona. She comments:

> The competent person's primacy derives from his status as moral agent [autonomous individual]. Moral agency is inherently future directed, and the future may . . . encompass one's incompetency. Prior directives are the tools for projecting one's moral and spiritual values into the future. These values seem to me worthy of respect even when they conflict with the subsequent, purely physical, interests of an incompetent.[17]

Rhoden further states:

> Viewing the patient only in the present divides her from her history, her values and her relationships—from all those things that made her a moral agent. . . . If a person has stated, "treat me, when incompetent, as if my competent values still hold," respect for persons demands that we do so.[18]

Professor James F. Childress adds: "The principle of respect for persons, which supports respect for the autonomous patient's choices, also supports reliance on the nonautonomous person's prior autonomous directives."[19]

Is all this convincing? Or is the Dresser-Robertson position more appropriate in emphasizing the contemporaneous, material interests of the incompetent patient? Does that position reflect a morally correct focus on the helpless patient's immediate interests? Just because people want others to treat them in post-competency as if they had their prior sense of dignity intact does not necessarily mean that society should promote such a "delusion." In other words, the moral foundation for allowing persons to impose choices about dignity and personal values upon a future incompetent persona needs elaboration.

A starting point in examining the moral foundation is to note the importance people commonly attach to prospective control over the dying process. It is apparent that many people care mightily about their post-competence medical handling, and they hope (if not expect) to shape their own fates in the face of potentially fatal afflictions. The hundreds of thousands of requests for advance directive forms provide one index of public interest. The 1991 Danforth Act, federal legislation requiring health-care institutions to inform patients about advance directives, provides another index of the perceived importance of advance directives.

Why do people care so much about controlling a post-competence dying process? Beyond noting the fact of widespread interest, it is useful to understand the rationale which moves people in this direction. Of course, a variety of motives may impel people to try and direct their post-competence medical fate. In part, the concern may be avoidance of the suffering sometimes incurred during a fatal affliction. But I suggest that the central concern is maintenance of a personal conception of dignity and self-respect, which includes shaping of a dying process consistent with one's character and values.

Post-competence maintenance of dignity and character may be important to avoid feelings of embarrassment or humiliation.[20] But avoidance of unpleasant emotions is not the sole or even dominant object. In significant part, a person's control over a post-competence dying process is an effort to mold other people's posthumous recollections of the person's character and values. This desire to shape recollections is grounded on common recognition of a tie between human dignity and a personal image projected to others. And because of a perceived tie between dignity and lifetime image, individual self-fulfillment and self-respect are seen as dependent not just on dominion over important decisions while the person is still competent and acutely aware but on dominion over a lifetime image.

The self-realization value of autonomy is commonly seen, then, as encompassing control of medical intervention in the intimate matter of dying, even at post-competence stages. A person views control over the post-competence dying process as part of an effort to shape the subsequent images and recollections of his or her life. Those images include both the self-image which the person may hold while still mentally aware and the post-competence images which surrounding people and survivors may hold.

People understand that a lifetime image can be critically affected by the portion of existence involving their incompetent persona. Professor Ronald Dworkin has observed that "it seems essential to someone's control of his whole life that he be able to dictate what will happen to him when he becomes incompetent."[21] This is so because the nature of how one is remembered is considered important to the success of one's life and survivors' recollections are affected by the lingering impressions of the moribund persona.[22] The ultimate specter is a protracted period of demeaning debilitation or of burden (emotional and/or economic) being imposed on surrounding loved ones. Justice Stevens, dissenting in *Cruzan*, recognized the important interest in not having memories sullied by a protracted and undignified dying process. He remarked: "Nancy's interest in life . . . includes an interest in how she will be thought of after her death by those whose opinions matter to her. . . . How she dies will affect how that life is remembered."[23]

The advance instructions actually issued by people tend to confirm a preoccupation with shaping lifetime recollections and framing a lifetime image consistent with a declarant's character. A common goal is to avoid a debilitated status which the declarant regards as undignified or demeaning. Living wills and other advance instructions frequently focus on avoiding existence in a degraded state. For example, the cases dealing with the prior expressions of patients in a permanently vegetative state (PVS) reflect that focus. Courts hearing such cases understand and empathize with people's distaste for the utter helplessness, the wasted bodily status, and the devitalized personality associated with PVS.[24]

Another common object of a person's advance instructions is to avoid emotional and financial burdens to attending family during the dying process.[25] In *Cruzan*, Justice Brennan noted the understandable wish of people to prevent "a prolonged and anguished vigil" for surrounding family.[26] Public surveys disclose that many persons wish to avoid future medical maintenance in the event of total and permanent dependence on others.[27] Such predilections might be grounded either on a wish to avoid what is perceived as a helpless, undignified state or on a concern for the surrounding persons burdened by the future patient's care.

This common solicitude for family interests reflects understanding that the recollections a person leaves behind are shaped by more than the visual images of the deteriorated, incompetent persona. A person's altruistic nature and concern for the interests of family and others are also part of the character and recollections which the individual cultivates. That character influences the human relationships one has with others, human relationships which form part of a person's individual image and legacy. A person who has nurtured certain relationships during competency may seek to advance those relationships even during post-competency, perhaps by an advance directive which dictates that the emotional and financial interests of surrounding family be considered in shaping the person's post-competence medical handling.[28] Implementation of such an instruction helps an individual perpetuate a relationship which he or she has sought to cultivate as part of a lifetime character. It honors an autonomous person's effort to build a life image and legacy.

A similar phenomenon occurs with regard to a person's dedication to religious or philosophical beliefs or to other personal ideals. Adherence to those ideals is part of an individual's personal integrity and character.[29] Implementation of those ideals at a post-competence stage of life carries forward the person's character and affects other people's recollections of that character.

From all the above, it is clear that respect for prospective autonomy (as reflected in an advance medical directive) honors the same kind of values applicable to autonomy generally. Self-determination in shaping medical intervention during any naturally occurring dying process upholds personal priorities and thus honors human capacity for choice. When that self-determination is upheld at a post-competence stage of existence, society honors the *fulfillment* of human capacity for choice as represented in each person's shaping of his or her lifetime priorities and character.[30] In prescribing post-competence care, every declarant seeks to preserve a personal vision of dignity, to imprint his or her own character on this critical juncture, and to continue personal ideals.

Even given the important autonomy interests at stake, can those interests prevail when arrayed against the immediate well being of a helpless, incompetent persona? We know that autonomy in the death-and-dying context is so valued by society that it is upheld against many competing interests. As noted in chapter 1, competent persons may reject life-sustaining intervention even when they are salvageable to healthful existences. This means that society waives any interest in the patient's productive capacity in order to uphold self-determination. Moreover, a choice to reject life support will be upheld even if the decision impacts negatively on other persons. A patient may reject life support in contravention of strong physician preferences to continue treatment. A patient may choose to reject life support and expire even if terrible grief will be caused to surrounding loved ones. A parent may even reject life support when the ensuing death will adversely affect a dependent minor.[31]

A similar priority of interests is likely to prevail in extension of the self-determination prerogative to the setting of post-competence medical decisions. Competing interests (such as medical preferences about sound medical practice) will not likely be permitted to override prior patient choice. Courts already view implementation of the prior instructions of a now incompetent patient as fulfillment of a "right" to self-determination. To ignore such instructions would relegate the patient to the status of an object whose fate is determined by others rather than of a human who has shaped his or her own fate.

The moral foundation for upholding prospective medical autonomy seems sound. In effect, society is saying that people have "earned" the right to shape their post-competence care and thus to shape recollections of each individual's lifetime. Each person, while competent, cultivates and nurtures a particular vision of body and soul, thereby fulfilling the potential of human autonomy. By preserving the body and developing the character associated with it, a person earns the moral prerogative of shaping the post-competence images and recollections other persons will have of the previously competent individual.[32] (By the way, there are burdens, not just privileges, associated with being the lifetime master of a particular body. When an incompetent patient is languishing in a hospital, the assets accumulated during the competent phase of existence are being dispensed to cover costs of care.) The bottom line, though, is that a competent person justifiably views control over a post-competence dying process as part of the earned prerogative to shape the subsequent images and recollections of his or her life.

A competent person's prerogative of shaping post-competence developments is recognized in numerous situations. I've already referred to the judicial acceptance of advance medical instructions. A similar solicitude for prospective autonomy underlies the disposition of property by will, contracts for post-competence care (e.g., nursing-home residency), and requests regarding disposal of a cadaver. Society conceivably could choose to intervene and direct the allocation of wealth upon a person's death, but it chooses, rather, to afford people wide discretion in the distribution of their property. In part, this choice reflects a utilitarian concern for the encouragement of wealth accumulation; but in part, it also reflects a moral judgment that people have earned a right to dispose of their property. That prerogative is important to people partly because they seek to shape the images and memories which will survive their competency and their lives.

People's expectations that future-oriented decisions will be respected upon incompetency are not grounded simply on personal preferences or aspirations. Social structures and conventions have also supplied a foundation for such expectations. Even before the development of legislative mechanisms for promoting control of post-competence medical intervention, society demonstrated considerable respect for individuals' future-oriented autonomy. Irrevocable trusts and durable powers of attorney furnished legal mechanisms for persons to prospectively control the post-competence disposition of property. Conventional wills served as a vehicle for disposition of property after death. Contract law allowed for post-competence implementation of a person's preferences in such matters as care setting and disability insurance. Additionally, families commonly honored a person's prior requests regarding burial or other disposition of his or her cadaver, including a subsequent gift of anatomical parts.[33]

In these respects, as well as others, society commonly upheld a person's future-oriented decisions even when the person no longer had capacity to appreciate violations of those personal values or preferences. Professors Dresser and Robertson would distinguish death-and-dying decisions from other exercises of future-oriented autonomy on the basis of the serious, negative consequences involved, such as the death of an incompetent patient when an advance decision dictates the withdrawal of life-preserving medical intervention. A maker of an advance directive can thus be materially harmed by being allowed to die while still possessing significant interests in life. According to Dresser and Robertson, this is unlike the maker of a will who is dead and therefore cannot be affected by implementation of an ill-considered or unwise disposition of property.[34]

I doubt that the potential for inflicting serious "harm" to one's future interests provides a sufficient basis to distinguish advance medical directives. First, if one recognizes the continuing, prospective autonomy interests of the moribund patient, implementation of an advance directive is not inflicting net harm to that patient. Second, accepted forms of future-oriented autonomy also have the capacity to harm a future, incompetent persona. A person can bind oneself to disadvantageous contracts and dispose of wealth in a fashion which negatively impacts on a future, incompetent persona. The latter could be accomplished by outright gifts, by irrevocable trusts, or perhaps by durable powers of attorney. In all these instances—as in the instance of shaping medical intervention in a dying process—respect for a person's competent prospective decisions is morally justified by respect for the person and the lifetime image being cultivated.

The above depiction of the common importance attached to abstract interests, such as dignity and altruism, in a post-competence state underlines another flaw in the Dresser-Robertson thesis. Specifically, they claim that if persons could miraculously regain momentary cognition in order to make an informed decision in their present state of incompetency, they would act according to their contemporaneous interests (apparent benefits and burdens) rather than their prior values. However, it is impossible to test the premise and no reason can be seen to accept it a priori.

There is no reason to assume that a person's values and priorities would change while the person is in a permanently incapacitated status. If a person previously cared about the indignity of a severely deteriorated status, or if a person cared about the emotional and financial well-being of surrounding family, those deeply rooted values would presumably persist.[35] Those values were felt deeply enough that the individual, when competent, knowingly used them to dictate her or his death-and-dying process. Experience shows that competent persons commonly issue instructions that they not be maintained in a permanently unconscious state even though they are aware that they will not sense or experience the degradation of such a state. This can best be explained by people's acute concern about how they will be remembered and the distasteful image which may be left behind. In short, the Dresser-Robertson premise regarding noncontinuity of a person's priorities seems dubious at best.

PERSONAL IDENTITY AND THE STATUS OF AN INCOMPETENT PERSONA

Some commentators suggest that a person can lose "personal identity" via loss of the memory and character which distinguish an individual.[36] From this perspective, an incompetent persona may be, in effect, a different person from the being who previously formulated an advance directive. The declarant, then, would arguably have no moral right to "harm" the incompetent persona by directing the withholding of life-sustaining medical treatment. Harm would be inflicted at least so long as the incompetent persona's pain and suffering did not make life so torturous as to be considered a fate worse than death.

The notion of personal identity seems to be of limited utility. No source employing this concept defines the degree of memory loss or character change that would make an incompetent persona a "new" person. Even if an administrable standard were defined, it would probably have limited practical application. In many instances, an incompetent persona retains a significant measure of long-term memory of a prior, competent status, thereby retaining his or her original personal identity. If an incompetent persona is so severely demented as to have lost all or almost all memories, the resulting being (a new personal identity) would have very limited contemporaneous interests. This is true, for example, for the incompetent persona who is in a permanently vegetative or barely conscious state and lacks relational or interactional capacity.[37]

Professors Allen E. Buchanan and Dan W. Brock use the limited interests of a severely demented patient to partially finesse the personal identity dilemma. They argue that a persona so severely demented as to lose basic cognitive or interactive capacity is no longer a "person" with cognizable moral interests. Thus, a competent person can dictate the fate of a future persona in a persistent vegetative state because that latter persona is not, for Buchanan and Brock, a person with equal moral status.[38] For them, such a nonperson has radically truncated interests. However, if a profoundly demented persona is still aware, that persona does have cognizable interests. For example, if a demented persona is still subject to pain, Buchanan and Brock would question the moral status of a prior directive which would produce a painful death. Similarly, Buchanan and Brock would probably deem it morally necessary to protect a profoundly demented person with clear capacity for pleasurable sensations from a prior directive dictating termination of care.[39]

This last situation does suggest an instance when the personal identity argument seems most troubling. A person has total or almost total loss of memory (perhaps an individual with advanced Alzheimer's disease) yet is aware and capable of experiencing pleasure. From the perspective of memory, at least, it is as if the original declarant had miraculously undergone a brain transplant. Is the declarant entitled to dictate the medical fate of this new persona?

I would argue that the answer is yes—that a declarant ought to be permitted to control medical intervention via an advance directive regardless of the degree of memory retained by the incompetent persona. From a legal perspective, "although each individual goes through many stages and transformations of varying significance in the passages of a lifetime, the individual nevertheless remains ultimately and essentially the same person from cradle to grave."[40] In other words, the life span of each person's embodiment is a unitary event even if the persona associated with the embodiment becomes so severely demented that he or she retains no recollection of the prior competent persona. Along these lines, Professor

Dworkin asserts that "the competent and demented stages of life are steps in a single life, . . . [and] the competent and demented selves are parts of the same person."[41] Under this vision of a person's singular lifetime, the fates of various personas that may emerge over time are inextricably entwined.

This judgment about a single, unified life conforms to the way people see their own lives, as shown by the effort to employ advance directives. Someone who makes a prior directive sees herself or himself as the unified subject of a human life. Such people see their concern for their bodies, their goals, or their families as transcending their (future) incapacity.[42] For most persons, then, it is self-evident that they ought to be given prospective dominion over post-competence matters such as medical intervention, property dispositions, residency locus, organ donations, autopsy, and funeral arrangements.

The notion of a single integrated existence encompassing both competence and post-competence stages also conforms to the way others view a person's life. A person is remembered as one being, even if that being undergoes radical changes during a lifetime. The incompetent persona is viewed by surrounding persons as a reflection or extension of the former self, still embodying the values and beliefs previously associated with the now incompetent person. Thus, we still think of the incompetent individual as a Catholic, Jew, or whatever faith he or she previously professed. Similarly, that person is perceived as maintaining a character (self-centered, altruistic, or whatever) even if that character is no longer discernible. In short, the concept of a unitary existence—with a competent and post-competent being viewed as having a single personal identity—conforms both with how people see themselves and how others see them.

The moral foundation for permitting a competent person to control the fate of a later, incompetent persona has already been presented. The competent person nurtured and developed the body, character, and relationships later associated with the incompetent persona. The competent person thus *earned* a certain prerogative to direct the fate of the succeeding, incompetent persona as that fate impacts on the recollections of a person's integrated lifetime. As noted, the competent person has lifetime burdens as well as privileges. That person's accumulated assets will fund all care provided to the later, incompetent persona.

The incompetent patient, no matter how demented, is still a human being and possesses certain immediate interests. The demented persona may not only have physical sensations but might even be in an ostensibly pleasant emotional state. While I have argued that an advance directive has considerable moral status and ought usually to prevail, there is a question about limits. To what extent should prospective autonomy interests yield to the contemporaneous interests of the incompetent patient or to the interests of others?

My response to this question comes via resolution of the scenarios previously outlined. For me, the key element in circumscribing autonomy is the concept of humane conduct toward an incompetent being. There are boundaries to what basic humanity permits people to do to themselves. Just as society limits what a competent person can do to his or her competent self, there is a limit on what a person can dictate for his or her future, incompetent persona. In the next section I will explain how this notion of humane treatment impacts on actual medical situations.

RESOLUTION OF THE SCENARIOS

As already suggested in chapter 5 in dealing with administration of advance directives, an ostensible clash between advance instructions and contemporaneous patient interests will seldom require judicial resolution. As a practical matter, the health-care agent or other decision makers will tend to "interpret" an advance directive to accord with the clear-cut contemporaneous interests of the patient. It is legitimate for administrators of an advance directive to examine whether the declarant really contemplated and intended to encompass the situation now confronted. And when obvious harm to the now incompetent patient is threatened by implementation of a directive, the decision makers may well find that the declarant did not envision the situation that has now unfolded.

Even if the advance directive's administrators are knowingly misinterpreting or distorting the declarant's (perhaps idiosyncratic) wishes, a decision to favor the perceptible, contemporaneous interests of a now incompetent patient will seldom be challenged or overturned. Medical staff, surrounding family, and courts are likely to acquiesce in decisions to maintain an ostensibly happy patient or to allow a severely anguished patient to die, regardless of the apparent intention of the directive.[43]

Even if administrators of an advance directive are, as a practical matter, often guided by clear-cut contemporaneous interests of an incompetent patient, a question remains regarding what *should* be the result. Should the declarant's considered wishes be derogated to the immediate interests of the patient?

Commentators have expressed diverse views on the subject. A few simply assert that prior choices, if specific, must prevail over contemporaneous patient interests.[44] By contrast, Professor Dresser argues that an advance directive should not be followed if the incompetent patient has any significant interest in continued life—meaning a capacity to interact with the environment.[45] As we know, she accords little status to prior expressions. Even commentators who generally respect advance directives tend to draw a line in situations when the directive calls for withholding life-preserving medical intervention from an apparently content, though demented, patient. Professors Rhoden, Buchanan, Brock, Nancy M.P. King, and Sanford H. Kadish seem to agree that an advance directive should not be implemented if to do so would terminate a life that "clearly contains more pleasure and enjoyment than suffering and pain."[46]

The commentators' restraint regarding advance directive implementation appears to flow from two considerations. First, future-oriented autonomy may have somewhat less force than contemporaneous autonomy. With contemporaneous self-determination, one can be sure that an effort is made to dissuade the competent patient from a foolish choice, allowing the competent patient to continue to reassess the competing personal interests right up to the moment of implementation of a terminal decision. By contrast, an advance directive is based on projections and speculation about prospective interests, and it may not be clear how much the declarant actually considered the situational conflict now confronted by the decision makers. In particular, it may be difficult to determine how much the declarant was confronted and challenged concerning any morally problematic instructions issued. Second, there seems to be a moral compunction or instinctive revulsion about allowing a helpless, ostensibly content individual to die—even when the decision is grounded on that individual's own prior direction.

My own position would be to implement, in most instances, a considered, future-oriented determination even at the expense of an incompetent patient's contemporaneous interests. As noted, advance directives have moral stature because a person's self-determination and self-realization goals naturally include a strong interest in shaping future images and recollections. Because those recollections become embodied in, and associated with, an incompetent persona, thus affecting other people's lifetime memories of the unitary person, the person's prior autonomous decisions deserve respect.

Moreover, there is no intrinsic bar to competent decisions which may entail future harm. A person can give away one's wealth, subject to rules involving fraud against creditors, even though that act might cause substantial hardship to a future incompetent persona. Self-determination includes a prerogative to make decisions which most people would regard as foolish or unsound. Once a person has made a considered judgment, even an imprudent future-oriented decision should ordinarily be respected.

It is acceptable that special steps be taken to examine the circumstances surrounding the formulation of an advance directive that appears to subordinate the perceptible contemporaneous interests of an incompetent patient. As noted, future-oriented autonomy entails projections, and a problematic decision can no longer be reconsidered by the now incompetent person. Therefore, it is sensible to require that implementation of a "problematic" life and death decision be predicated on an examination of whether the maker of the advance directive really considered and intended the problematic result ostensibly dictated.

This means that the ultimate decision makers should at least inquire whether the directive maker was aware of the problematic consequences now being faced. For example, did the vitalist declarant realize that excruciating pain might be encountered during an extended dying process? Did the future-oriented person seeking to avoid indignity realize that the incompetent persona might derive some pleasure from a debilitated existence? Such inquiries are legitimate. But when good-faith examination discloses that the maker of an advance directive knowingly dictated the result in issue, then that directive ought ordinarily to be upheld.

With regard to the scenarios presented above, I take the position that the advance directives should be implemented in each instance. I'll address each case to indicate where I think constraints might properly come into play.

Scenario 1 (the Jehovah's Witness who has prospectively rejected all blood transfusions): A person's autonomy should include the prerogative to choose religious precepts that govern the competence and post-competence portions of a lifetime. This is so whether or not violations of those religious precepts will be sensed or felt by the person. The premise is, as already explained, that persons may be harmed by disrespect for their values and self-defined dignity even if that disrespect is not sensed or appreciated. If prospective autonomy is a meaningful concept, as I think it is, then the injury to autonomy interests from disregarding the advance directive outweighs the harm to the incompetent persona. The result is similar to that of the competent Jehovah's Witness who rejects a life-saving blood transfusion.

The fact that the critical moment comes years after the original directive should not matter so long as the directive reflects a deliberate judgment and so long as there is no indication that the person's values changed while still competent. The situation here is different from that of parents who are legally precluded from imposing religious precepts on immature minors in a fashion that will seriously harm the incompetent minor. Here, a mature adult has adopted a religious tenet with the understanding that the decision may subsequently disadvantage her own material interests as an incompetent persona.

Scenario 2 (the vitalist patient in excruciating pain): If a person has made a considered decision that, for purposes of future medical intervention, sanctity-of-life principles should prevail over distaste for suffering, then that choice ought to be respected. It is certainly a heartrending spectacle to contemplate the helpless, anguished patient being sustained in reliance on prior instructions. There will be a great temptation to find that the patient did not sufficiently anticipate or appreciate the prospective pain and, therefore, ought to be spared the consequences of an "imprudent" directive.

Yet, when the advance directive seems considered and unambiguous, it is not immoral to hold the patient to the bargain. Respect for autonomy justifies such a result. People may have strong philosophical or religious beliefs in both the sanctity of life and the meaning of suffering. Those beliefs can form a legitimate part of the personal character and self-image which an individual may seek to project during a lifetime, including the post-competence dying process.

A possible rationale for nonimplementation of an advance directive might arise where an incompetent patient has reached such a degraded and undignified status that it is simply inhumane to allow a patient's prior directive to dictate prolongation of that status. For example, B (who left an advance directive dictating all possible intervention) may not only be groaning in agony but also thrashing to the point at which continuous physical restraint is necessary to keep his life-preserving medical intervention in place. Is not the specter of this helpless, agonized, and tethered human being enough to conclude that basic humanity demands some relief despite the patient's carefully considered advance directive? Have we not reached the moral boundary of autonomy? Just as a self-determination prerogative cannot morally encompass self-mutilation or consent to slavery, can we not say that the prospective imposition of an utterly degrading status on an incompetent patient is simply beyond tolerable bounds?

My answer is yes. There are limits to what even I can stomach under the rubric of autonomy. However, a few caveats should be imposed on a boundary to future-oriented autonomy governed by intrinsic human dignity.

First, the criterion ought to be intrinsic human dignity as understood by a clear majority of the population. The fact that a guardian's subjective version of human dignity will be offended by adherence to advance instructions ought not be determinative. This caveat has application to B's case in scenario 2. Many people would not be offended by continued administration of life-preserving treatment, in accord with the patient's prior instructions, despite the incompetent patient's significant suffering. Many people would acquiesce in a person's prerogative to design a dying process consistent with personal views about the nature and value of suffering. Only when actual suffering reaches the level most people would label intrinsically inhumane should the patient's directive be overridden.

Second, the directive should be breached only to the minimum extent necessary to avoid inhumane handling. In scenario 2, for example, B ought to be given analgesics (in contravention of the directive), but the life-sustaining intervention should be continued in accord with the directive. In this way, the patient's intrinsic human dignity is preserved as consistently as possible with the patient's advance instructions.

Another wrinkle might be added to the scenario if B, the now incompetent patient, were not only in obvious distress but also verbally begging to have the life-preserving medical intervention withdrawn (contrary to his advance instructions). I touched on the matter of contemporaneous expressions in chapter 5. There, I explained that declarations by a currently incompetent patient can be given only limited force. That force depends on the degree of dementia involved. (While some patients may be barely conscious and totally unable to comprehend, others may have some degree of understanding of their conditions.)

If B understands his situation and comprehends the prospect of death, the pleading for cessation of medical care warrants consideration. At the very least, the expressions are an index of the patient's degree of suffering. At some point, extreme suffering may convince the relevant decision makers that continued intervention is inhumane.

Contemporaneous expressions will also influence those decision makers whose natural inclination is to follow the incompetent patient's clear-cut current interests. The previously vitalist patient's current requests to be allowed to die may then reinforce the decision makers' determination to override the advance directive prescribing prolongation of the tortured existence. The decision makers may see the patient's utterances as confirmation of their choice to act according to that patient's contemporaneous interests.

As the patient is incompetent, the expressions cannot be regarded as acts of genuine self-determination. Nonetheless, an aware (though legally incompetent) patient may be able to give assent to a proposed course of medical handling, and that assent is entitled to some recognition.[47] By contrast, the utterances of a gravely demented patient can reflect neither self-determination nor assent. Such deranged utterances certainly cannot be permitted to override a clear advance directive. If the patient is severely demented, reliance on the verbal "revocation" of a vitalist advance directive is inappropriate.[48]

Even when the incompetent persona is aware and has some comprehension, ascribing binding force to contemporaneous utterances is problematic. Suppose the patient had been a devout Catholic who always believed in the reception of last rites. He or she, however, is now an incompetent persona with some, but limited, understanding of the issue and is declining last rites. Should we follow the incompetent's current wishes, or should we adhere to the advance directive? Unambiguous, competently made instructions should prevail so long as the treatment dictated for the incompetent persona is not fundamentally inhumane. Receipt of the last rites would not be widely perceived as inhumane.

Another obstacle to implementation of B's directive might be posed by attending physicians or other health-care providers. They might be contending either that continued medical intervention is "futile," because the patient's condition is so dismal as not to benefit the patient, or that continued treatment conflicts with the providers' personal scruples.

This issue was touched on in chapter 5, which deals with administration of advance directives. The proper resolution is to uphold the patient's advance instructions (here calling for continued life support) despite the tension with the physicians' views of sound medical practice or medical ethics. This is not to say that health-care providers will be compelled to furnish care they deem medically or ethically inappropriate. Accommodation of all interests is sought by transfer of the patient's care to another professional who is willing to cooperate with the patient's chosen course.[49] This disposition is particularly appropriate when preservation of life is the patient's chosen course.

In some instances, professional scruples might be reinforced by a determination that the patient's previously prescribed course is so inhumane (in application) as to be beyond the bounds of acceptable medical behavior. That is, a universally accepted professional standard of conduct might prohibit implementation of the patient's wishes. A court would be reluctant to order compliance with such a problematic instruction. Even though courts, as agents of society as a whole, are not compelled to accept medical norms, the impetus is strong to adopt a universally respected professional norm. And without judicial intervention it would be difficult to find medical professionals to implement the disputed directive.

Another practical constraint is the availability of resources to finance B's protracted medical struggle. There is no constitutional obligation or societal inclination to finance all beneficial medical services. The impetus to fund a medical service is even less for care which is torturous to the incompetent patient and inappropriate from the perspective of some medical staff. Health-care providers may prove unwilling to provide this latter type of care to the impecunious "vitalist" patient.

Scenario 3 (the expensive heart transplant): If C were still competent, there would be little question that the patient would be entitled to reject a heart transplant for the sake of preserving a fiscal stake for his or her descendants. The patient would then be permitted to die despite the possibility of preserving a clearly meaningful existence for a number of years. Should C's altruistic nature and impulses be denied merely because the critical personal decision was made years before the moment for its implementation? Should the contemporaneous interests of the now incompetent persona impel life-preservation?

For the same reasons future-oriented autonomy permits a person to impose his or her religious precepts on a subsequent incompetent persona, a person's articulated, altruistic principles should prevail.[50] A person should be able to shape the collective memory of that person's lifetime, including recollections of the person's character and principles. Continued respect for those principles are part of the contemporaneous interests of the now incompetent patient.[51]

Professor Yale Kamisar posed to me a hypothetical variation on this scenario. Suppose, he suggested, C's descendants (the people whose economic stake C sought to protect) renounce their economic interest. In other words, suppose C's family prefers to preserve his incompetent existence even if it costs them a $100,000 legacy. They are therefore telling the attending physician to ignore C's advance directive and to perform the life-extending surgery.

This is a tough dilemma. The very beneficiaries of C's altruism are seeking to waive their interest in favor of extending his life. As a practical matter, many physicians would probably follow their instructions.

Yet, the whole point of prospective autonomy is to allow a declarant to fix priorities in a post-competence dying process. C made the considered judgment that he would prefer death rather than expensive preservation of his debilitated existence. The concept of advance directives would be endangered by acquiescence in the family's reordering of C's priorities. After all, many declarants prescribe a post-competence course in order to spare their loved ones burdens and suffering. If those loved ones can simply renounce their interest and thereby alter the declarant's wishes, that altruistic type of advance directive would have little force.

Of course, my response might be different if circumstances had markedly changed subsequent to the preparation of the advance directive. Suppose, for example, the family show that the economic status of the children (the economic beneficiaries of C's demise) had substantially changed over time. They no longer need the $100,000 nearly to the degree they did when C's advance directive was issued. If the economic circumstances changed *after* C's incompetence, the family's argument seems strong. C himself might well have preferred life-saving surgery in light of the family's diminished economic need. If the changed circumstances occurred before C became incompetent, but he did not alter his advance directive, the picture is more murky. Arguably, C's failure to alter his directive means that his assessment of the importance of the $100,000 legacy did not change.

Scenario 4 (harvesting an organ and tissue): Like the advance directive in scenario 3, D's advance directive to donate a kidney and bone marrow upon death is grounded in altruism. In this case, her solicitude is directed toward some future unknown organ recipients rather than known family members. Also, the altruistic gesture takes the form of authorizing removal of an organ or tissue rather than mere rejection of life-sustaining medical intervention.

Use of a prospective organ donation to fulfill an altruistic impulse is consistent with the previously expressed notion that a person's body is associated with a single, unitary existence. That is, the competent declarant tends to see the kidney (or bone marrow) as his or her own. The credit for altruism is registered in recollections about the unitary person even though the incompetent persona may not sense satisfaction from the altruism involved or from the approbation engendered. D will be remembered as the generous donor of the life-saving organ and tissue. Thus, the advance directive ought to be implemented even though the operation involved will have no therapeutic value for the now incompetent patient.

In the hypothetical case as presented, the harvesting operations would pose slight risk and create only mild pain for the incompetent persona. Suppose, though, that the incompetent patient is debilitated to a point at which the operation would pose a significant mortal risk for that patient.

One reaction is that the prescribed course now resembles suicide more than the rejection of life-sustaining medical intervention in the face of a naturally occurring dying process. This person is initiating a course of conduct involving a bodily invasion which will place his or her life in jeopardy. It may well be that health-care professionals would refuse to cooperate with such a venture even if the patient were competent. If that is the case (i.e., the patient's prescribed course would not be followed even if the patient were competent) then a fortiori that course need not be followed for the now incompetent patient.

Assume again that D's risk is slight and the pain modest. Suppose now the incompetent persona does not assent to the operations so she will have to be restrained and forced to undergo the procedures. In other words, implementation of the course prescribed in the advance directive will subject the incompetent persona to a measure of indignity. How does this element get factored in?

If good-faith investigation discloses that the declarant never considered the possible degradation of the incompetent persona, that fact might provide a rationale for deviation from the prescribed course. At least if the declarant was extremely sensitive to bodily restraint, a good-faith judgment might be that D would have altered her resolve in the face of the indignity of restraint. But if good-faith investigation discloses that the declarant probably would want the transplant performed (regardless of the implications for the incompetent persona), then the advance directive should be implemented.

Just as an advance directive can prescribe the withdrawal of life support and arguably "harm" an incompetent persona, a directive should be able to dictate a course which subjects the incompetent persona to a measure of indignity. The limit to this principle has been discussed above in the context of scenario 2. At some point the course prescribed by the advance directive becomes so intrinsically inhumane that decision makers may justly refuse to fulfill the directive. But that point would not be reached in the present scenario so long as the restraint of the incompetent persona would only be temporary.[52]

Scenario 5 (the demented professor): For E, maintaining a dignified image was crucial. Similar to her, some people wish to preserve for posterity their images as vital, active, and acute individuals. Part of the self-respect and dignity that they value is grounded on avoiding a deteriorated status which they regard as degrading.

A declarant's concern about deterioration may reflect apprehensions of frustration, embarrassment, or humiliation of being viewed in a state of incompetency. If that is the rationale for the original instructions, and if the feared emotions don't materialize (as best the decision makers can tell), then there might be a legitimate basis to override E's advance directive. But such apprehensions might not be the core of the declarant's concern. Previously active and vital people may seek to avoid an undignified status (such as permanent unconsciousness or extreme dementia) even if they understand that there will be no emotional suffering in the debilitated state. In part, their concern may be to avoid mental anguish or burdens for surviving relatives who must cope with the debilitated individual. Or, the person may simply view a life image (and the personal investment in cultivating that image) as being debased by a gravely deteriorated period of existence.

In principle, this aspiration to maintain dignity deserves as much respect as the religious or altruistic motivations discussed in previous scenarios. Indeed, religious precepts, concern for survivors' interests, and concern about a dignified image are all part of the self-respect, values, and character which an individual seeks to cultivate in a lifetime.

As a result of strokes, brain trauma, or degenerative neural diseases, many persons reach a point of grave physical and mental debilitation. The names Conroy,

Clark, Dinnerstein, Foody, and O'Connor all represent a court case in which the saga of such a person is recounted. The formerly vigorous person has become a helpless patient, confined to bed, unable to feed himself or herself, and usually incontinent. The patient is conscious, but barely so. It is difficult to determine if the patient is in physical or emotional pain. The patient may occasionally groan, sigh, or smile. The patient may be aware of surrounding people but cannot recognize or communicate with friends or loved ones. The patient has no hope of recovery. The patient is indefinitely sustained by artificial nutrition, by kidney dialysis, or by mechanical ventilation.

In such a situation—when the contemporaneous benefits and burdens of the incompetent patient can no longer be measured with any confidence—the patient's previously articulated, dignity-based instructions ought unquestionably to prevail. The incompetent patient has reached a level of incapacitation which many previously vital persons would view as demeaning. If a person has indicated in an advance directive that such a status is personally distasteful, then that judgment ought to be respected. This is so even if the uncomprehending, deteriorated patient is not perceptibly suffering and has some remaining capacity for pleasure.

Some commentators would draw the line at an incompetent patient whose potential for pleasure and satisfaction seems to clearly outweigh any material detriments (such as perceptible pain and suffering). An illustrative case is the "pleasantly senile" person. This incompetent individual may have lost all short-term memory and may be incapable of functioning intellectually at anything resembling the person's previous level. Nonetheless, the person seems "happy" and capable of deriving certain simple pleasures from life (such as E's listening to music). The commentators' thesis seems to be that it is inhumane or immoral to withhold or withdraw life-preserving medical intervention from such a person, even in reliance on an explicit advance directive. I'm not so sure.

One premise accepted above (in scenario 2) is that certain handling of an incompetent patient might be so intrinsically degrading or undignified as to be inhumane (according to widely shared societal standards). That principle has some relevance to the present context. For example, if the withholding of medical intervention would prompt an agonizing dying process for the ostensibly content, yet incompetent patient, that result might be labeled inhumane and impermissible. In many situations, though, the withholding of life-preserving medical intervention could be accompanied by palliatives to provide a painless dying process.

The further question is whether it is intrinsically immoral to implement an advance directive which calls for withholding life-preserving medical intervention from a gravely deteriorated, previously vital individual when the incompetent persona still has clear capacity for net pleasure or satisfaction from continued existence. From a perspective that values prospective autonomy, it is not immoral for E to seek to preserve an image of vitality—a certain version of self-respect—by dictating the withholding of further medical intervention from his or her incompetent deteriorated persona. This is so even if E's incompetent persona is still capably of deriving some pleasure from existence (such as by listening to music). As long as withholding medical intervention will not impose cruel suffering on the incompetent patient, an unambiguous and considered directive should be upheld.

I'm not sure how often this issue will arise. I would think that most people would not want to prompt the demise of their ostensibly happy future persona. Yet it is not intrinsically immoral for a person to shape future medical intervention in a way which will minimize any period of substantially deteriorated existence. Avoidance of a personally demeaning dying process is, ordinarily, part of the self-realization and self-respect furthered by future-oriented autonomy.

Of course, my moral perspective on E's case may be perverted by an obsessive-compulsive preoccupation with notions of autonomy. If my perspective is indeed aberrational as tested by prevalent social standards, it perhaps ought to be ignored. I concede that if allowing E to die is widely deemed immoral, then that judgment ought to instruct the legal norm governing those responsible for the medical fates of incompetent patients. However, the intrinsic moral nature of withholding life-preserving medical treatment from a contented but severely demented patient is still an open issue. It is a subject for continued public debate informed by medical, legal, and philosophical inputs. For me, giving expansive scope to advance directives, even to the detriment of the ostensible immediate interests of an incompetent persona, is both morally and legally sustainable.

7

Enforcing Advance Directives

THE LEGAL VALIDITY of an advance directive means little if the document is ignored or resisted in practice. To date, a fair amount of informal and anecdotal evidence indicates that living wills are frequently ignored.[1]

The reasons for this phenomenon could be several. Surrounding family members may be moved by their own concerns—often emotional inability to "let go"—or their own perceptions of the incompetent patient's best interests. (And medical staff may be acquiescing in the family's preferred course because the family represent the most vocal and immediate force seeking to influence care.) Or medical staff may be unfamiliar with the binding legal status of an advance directive and therefore may be pushing for their version of good medical practice. Or medical personnel may have ethical qualms about the course laid out in the advance directive. Or the medical staff may be puzzled about the meaning and content of a particular advance directive. (Chapter 4 recounted how some instruction directives can be singularly uninformative.)

Appointment of a health-care agent is a device intended in part to deal with these impediments to fulfillment of advance instructions. An agent is supposed to be familiar with a principal's wishes and dedicated to seeing that they are implemented. However, appointment of an agent is not a panacea. Some declarants will be unable to enlist a suitable agent. In those instances, an instruction directive—without designation of a health-care agent—will be the only document at hand. Moreover, presence of a designated health-care agent provides no guarantee that surrounding family and/or medical personnel will adhere to an advance directive. And an agent encountering such resistance to the principal's instructions may well be unfamiliar with institutional dynamics and may well be unsure how to cope with resistance from medical staff or from the patient's family.

All these scenarios involving deviation from an advance directive suggest that mechanisms for enforcement of such documents will have to be found. To date, no widespread ethic of respect for advance directives has emerged in the medical profession and in health-care institutions. There is no culture which accepts advance directives as a natural and integral part of medical practice.

Educating the lay and medical publics about the advance directive technique may spur some change in attitude. The federal Patient Self-Determination Act of 1991 (PSDA) is aimed at accomplishing that educative task.[2] But education alone is unlikely to impel uniform compliance with advance directives. Inevitably, there will be some need to coerce medical respect for advance instructions. The availability of coercive measures will reinforce the message supplied by the PSDA: that an advance medical directive is a legitimate and important means for a person to try and impose a measure of dignity on his or her dying process.

Experience with advance directives is still too sparse to determine whether effective enforcement machinery is possible. In this chapter, I will consider the primary existing routes for securing implementation of an advance directive in the face of hesitancy or resistance from those parties surrounding the incompetent patient.

All enforcement machinery is dependent on an advocate on behalf of the now incompetent patient. Ordinarily, a designated health-care agent will serve as that advocate. The succeeding descriptions of possible enforcement mechanisms are in large part intended to guide health-care agents in performing their advocacy role. As a preliminary matter, though, I'll address the problem of a declarant who couldn't or didn't name an agent.

In the absence of a health-care agent, deviations from an instruction directive (at least deviations in the direction of extending life) will be difficult to curb. In some such instances, any surrounding family and attending medical staff will reach a mutual understanding to follow a medical course counter to the patient's advance directive. When that occurs, no advocate of the patient's wishes is present to contest that mutual understanding. Only if a dissident family member or a dissident staff person surfaces will there be a voice for adherence to the patient's advance directive. And, as chapter 5 pointed out, dissent will not likely surface so long as the treatment course seems consistent with the incompetent patient's immediate well being.

This advocacy void will surely plague the patient without a health-care agent. Eventually, the void may be filled by patients' advocates employed by health-care institutions or by government-paid guardians on behalf of the institutionalized disabled.[3] Such paid advocates could conceivably monitor care of incompetent patients and could be charged with promoting adherence to an advance directive. But the United States is still a long way from that solution. Not every institution has a patient's advocate. Not every such advocate is schooled about advance directives and their legal framework. And it may well be that no patient's advocate would intervene without being summoned by some party connected to the incompetent patient. Similar problems exist with regard to those few jurisdictions which have special guardians on behalf of the institutionalized disabled.

All this points me to one conclusion with regard to the unrepresented incompetent patient: compliance with an advance directive will be largely dependent on the good will and good faith of surrounding family and medical staff.[4] Coercive mechanisms will seldom impact on those parties because there will be no advocate to initiate action. An important question becomes: how can a declarant, in advance, promote the desired voluntary, good faith compliance with an advance directive?

The most obvious tool is frank discussion with the family and physicians likely to be attending a declarant's dying process. We already established that such discussion is critical for the purpose of explaining the declarant's wishes—as so many advance directives contain only cursory, cryptic instructions. It is now evident that a further purpose can be served by discussions between the declarant, on the one hand, and family and physicians on the other. That purpose is enlisting sympathy for, and willingness to adhere to, the declarant's instructions.

It is very important, then, for a declarant who will not be naming a health-care agent to conduct a serious discussion with the likely attending physician about the contents of the declarant's advance instructions. Beside elucidating the meaning of the directive, the conversation should aim at conveying the declarant's seriousness and deliberateness. The conversation can thus dispel any question about the declarant's determination to have his or her wishes carried out. Beyond that, the declarant should seek assurance from the physician that the latter understands and intends to comply with the directive. While this verbal promise won't be readily enforceable by the subsequently incompetent patient, it at least creates a moral incentive for the physician to comply. The physician will have made an explicit promise to the declarant. A cynic might observe that this promise, plus $1.25, will get the declarant on the subway (in New York City). I have more faith than that in physicians' moral rectitude.

In the best of all possible worlds, a declarant would enter into a written contract with the prospective attending physician. The patient would agree to seek post-competence medical care from the physician and to pay for that care. The physician would agree to adhere to a good-faith interpretation of the declarant's advance instructions. In addition, the physician might agree to a schedule of liquidated damages (preagreed sums) payable to the declarant's estate for any period during which the declarant's wishes are flaunted. Finally, an immunity provision in the contract would reaffirm that the physician will incur no liability for good-faith adherence to the directive.

Why is such a contract confined to "the best of all possible worlds?" The problem is lack of incentive for a physician to enter into such a contract. If the physician has had an enduring relationship with the declarant, that physician will both expect to be the eventual attending physician and to be paid—all without any advance contract. Why should such a physician agree in writing to honor the advance directive and to pay damages for disrespecting the directive? At the moment, there aren't incentives for a physician to enter the advance contract described.

On the other hand, perhaps market forces will someday make the above hypothetical contract a reality. Perhaps physicians will compete for the business of servicing the needs of an increasingly aged population. Physicians might then seek to reassure patients and prospective patients about the caring, sensitive treatment being offered. And the above-described contract might be one element in the effort to communicate the desired solicitude.

Of course, what good is this "contract" if the patient will be incompetent at the critical moments? Who's going to enforce the contract against the nonadhering physician? If there had been a suitable "advocate" at hand, the declarant would have designated that person as a health-care agent and wouldn't particularly have needed the contract.

Again, my only hope is an economic incentive. If the declarant has any descendants or beneficiaries, the declarant's "estate" has a financial interest in the liquidated damages for any violation of the hypothetical contract. So, at the time of making the advance contract, the declarant would provide a copy to all persons connected to the estate and inform the contracting physician about that step. There would then be a financial disincentive to the physician's dishonoring of the advance contract.

This advance contract idea obviously needs fine tuning. Can liquidated damages be fixed so that they at least roughly correspond to projected actual damages? (That is a prerequisite to a valid liquidated-damages clause.) Should we be wary about creating a financial interest (in the beneficiaries of the estate) in having life-sustaining care extended in violation of an advance directive? Is there a hazard that such beneficiaries would intervene in terminal decisions and encourage violations of the declarant's instructions? And, of course, will there be sufficient incentives to induce any physician to enter into such an advance contract? But my starting point was the discouraging conclusion that, in the absence of a health-care agent, declarants will be hard put to assure implementation of their advance directives. The advance contract is simply one suggestion for filling the void. An alternative might be sought in institutions whose protocols require an ethics committee to monitor administration of all advance directives.

So far in this chapter, the assumption has been that a health-care agent (an advocate of the incompetent patient) offers the best hope for securing adherence to an advance directive. How good is that hope? The underlying question is whether a health-care agent has effective means for enforcing an advance directive.

Suppose that an advance directive both designates Pat, the declarant's daughter, as health-care agent and instructs that life-sustaining treatment cease if her father becomes demented to the point of being unable to read and understand a newspaper. Later, the declarant suffers a series of strokes which leave him permanently incompetent, bedridden, and incapable of reading a newspaper.

This incompetent patient is living in a long-term care facility. He is aware of his environment and smiles when given a back rub or when visited by loving family. There is no indication that the patient is in pain. The patient could live for many months in this state.

Now suppose this incompetent patient contracts pneumonia. Without antibiotics, the patient will die of pneumonia within ten days. The patient's son (i.e., the health-care agent's brother) and the attending physician both favor giving the patient antibiotics in order to cure the pneumonia. Both are aware of the patient's advance directive, but both have reasons for continuing care. The son cannot bear the thought of letting the father die while the father still derives some pleasure from existence. The attending physician considers it unsound medical practice to allow a patient in this condition to go untreated.

Pat (the patient's daughter and health-care agent) is determined to follow her father's considered instructions. She is convinced that he is presently in precisely the kind of debilitated state that he wanted to avoid. What mechanisms can Pat, as health-care agent, use to enforce her father's directive?

INTERNAL INSTITUTIONAL ROUTES

Pat should not want to make a federal case out of this controversy. The object is to secure prompt, caring, and careful implementation of her incompetent father's advance instructions. Litigation is an expensive, time-consuming, and exhausting process. (Only a few barracuda populating major law firms *want* to litigate.) Because Pat wants expeditious resolution of her dispute, her first recourse ought to be to gentle (but increasingly not so gentle) persuasion.

The obvious starting point is the attending physician. Armed with the document designating her as health-care agent and any other evidence of her father's wishes, Pat ought to try and persuade that physician to conform care to the advance instructions. If the physician continues to voice concern about sound medical practice, Pat might express interest in consulting with an institutional ethics committee. Or she might mention the possibility of bringing in another practitioner who would be comfortable with the advance directive. The physician will undoubtedly express concern about Pat's brother, who is insisting on full medical treatment. Pat should remind the physician that she is her father's designated agent and charged with responsibility for his post-competence care.

Chances are that this first interchange between Pat and the attending physician will not move the latter. If the physician remains resistant, I can imagine two principal strategies: a confrontation mode and a mediation mode. They could be undertaken together or in succession, starting with confrontation.

The confrontation mode could start with a second conversation with the attending physician and proceed up the supervisory ladder, first to the relevant department head and then to the hospital administrator. The main feature of the confrontation mode is threats. Pat is convinced of the legal and moral soundness of her effort to implement her father's directive; she is determined to accomplish that object. She can seek to convey the seriousness of her effort by warning about the recourse she intends to pursue if her object is thwarted. What exactly are the steps she is threatening?

The first threat is aimed at the pocketbook. In all her conversations with the relevant health-care providers, Pat will insist that no payment will be forthcoming for services which she did not authorize or which would have been obviated if her orders had been followed. Pat is asserting that no payment is due for treatment provided counter to a patient's wishes as expressed in an advance directive and as interpreted by an authorized health-care agent. Her contention has a solid legal foundation. Commentators agree that no payment is due for such unwanted services,[5] and there is legal precedent supporting that contention.[6]

The nonpayment threat is most realistic if the patient's assets are funding the current services and if Pat, as health-care agent, has some control over those payments. If some other source has control of the now incompetent patient's assets, (like, God forbid, Pat's brother), Pat's threat looms hollow. Similarly, if medical services are being financed by a private insurer or government benefit program, Pat's threat carries less clout. She would have a hard time prompting a third-party payor to cease payments for life-sustaining treatment. This would be so either because of the insurer's bureaucratic maze, which likely has to be negotiated, or because of sluggish response from third-party payors. A 1992 anecdote recounts how the Medicare Inspector General's office, reponding to an allegation of $150,000 in unauthorized hospital service, said it did not have resources to even investigate such a piddling abuse.[7] Nonetheless, Pat can, in good conscience, state her intention to contact the relevant third-party payor in order to prompt a refusal to pay for unauthorized services to her father.

Pat's second threat is to turn to outside agencies having some sort of regulatory power over the health-care providers. In some states, for example, the state health department will have regulations obligating providers to recognize and honor advance directives.[8] Pat can threaten to file a complaint about violation of the applicable· regulation.

An alternative (or additional) regulatory channel is the federal Department of Health and Human Services (HHS). That agency administers compliance with federal regulations governing recipients of Medicaid and Medicare funds. (Virtually every hospital receives such funds.) The Patient Self-Determination Act (PSDA) of 1991 requires every funds recipient to "ensure compliance" with state law applicable to advance directives.[9] Pat can justifiably contend that nonadherence to her father's instructions breaches that obligation of compliance with state law. (As discussed in chapter 2, state law generally recognizes and enforces a declarant's prospective-autonomy interests.)

It is unclear whether Pat's threat to resort to HHS will be effective. The ultimate sanction available to that agency is disqualification of the health-care provider from participation in the federal program. The chances of that sanction being used to remedy a complaint about continuation of life-sustaining care are somewhere between zero and nil. Nonetheless, no hospital administrator or medical practitioner relishes having a federal investigator nosing about in response to a complaint. And if Pat's complaint uncovers an offending institutional pattern or practice, there might be some hope of engendering a serious HHS response, short of a termination of funds. So there is at least some chance that the institution will take seriously Pat's warning about resort to HHS.

A threat of invoking an administrative-type remedy might also be leveled at the attending physician. He or she might well be a health-care provider subject to the same PSDA obligation (and same HHS jurisdiction) described above. Moreover, the physician's professional obligation—as is becoming increasingly clear—is either to implement an advance directive or to transfer care to a fellow professional willing to cooperate with the patient's instructions. This means that Pat can threaten to invoke professional discipline against the attending physician who is violating that professional duty. This conclusion is reinforced by statutory provisions in approximately ten states whose living-will statutes explicitly label as "unprofessional conduct" a physician's failure to fulfill obligations such as the duty to honor a directive or transfer care of the patient.[10]

Pat's threat to file a complaint about unprofessional conduct may not move the attending physician very much. First, the channels of professional discipline (proceedings before a state board of medical examiners or other professional body) are notoriously slow and cumbersome. Second, the relevant professional board may not apply very stringent standards for compliance with advance directives. The physician may be given room to maneuver on issues such as the clarity of the patient's instructions, norms of sound medical practice, medical judgment about the patient's prognosis, or solicitude about the incompetent patient's immediate well-being. Third, even if the professional board were to find some violation of professional norms, the sanction imposed would be light. A private letter of reprimand might turn out to be the only penalty imposed.

For all these reasons, the specter of professional discipline might not seem very imposing. Still, no physician wants to have to account for his or her conduct before a group of peers authorized to impose sanctions such as suspension from medical practice. If Pat genuinely believes that the attending physician is not conforming to professional norms or legal obligations, the threat to initiate a disciplinary proceeding seems highly appropriate.

The final step in the confrontation mode is to threaten litigation. In theory, suit might be brought seeking to compel the attending physician to implement the father's advance directive[11] and/or to obtain monetary damages for the physician's failure to implement the directive. The chances of success in this hypothetical suit will be analyzed below. For the moment, I want to comment on the impact of a threat to litigate.

The attending physician knows that litigation is costly, time-consuming, and wearing. He is anxious to avoid litigation. At the same time, he knows that Pat is not likely to sue. Litigation is costly and exhausting for the plaintiff as well as the defendant. If Pat has no control over her father's assets, there is no assurance that she will be reimbursed. Pat is unlikely to invest the time, money, and effort unless she is confident that significant relief will be forthcoming. Therefore, the impact of a litigation threat depends in part on Pat's chances of success in that suit and the likely relief (to be analyzed below).

Even if the chances that Pat really would sue are slim, and even if her chances of substantial monetary relief are not great (issues still open), a threat to sue in this context strikes me as a legitimate tactic. First, Pat's legal claim seems sound. She is indeed entitled to seek enforcement of her father's advance directive. Second, physicians continue to operate under the misapprehension that their main hazard of liability stems from a wrongful-death action for implementing prior instructions.[12] They need to be apprised that money damages can flow from *failure* to implement such instructions.[13] (Interestingly, though, in the instant scenario, Pat's brother might be making noises about a wrongful-death suit at the same time that she is threatening to sue because of continued life support. The attending physician, now certainly in a tizzy, needs sound legal advice.)

Pat might try a mediation strategy rather than launching the confrontation mode. The most likely vehicle for the mediation strategy is the internal Institutional Ethics Committee (IEC), which exists in most hospitals today.[14] The IEC is usually an interdisciplinary body composed of some combination of physicians, administrators, nurses, clergy, a psychiatrist, and a lawyer. Often there will be a lay community representative as well. The articulated function of the IEC will vary from institution to institution. Sometimes, its task is simply to design institutional policy regarding sensitive ethics issues. While that task may include fixing policy about advance directives, it might not include intervention in particular patients' cases. Often, though, the IEC is available to serve a consultative function regarding a dispute surrounding a patient's dying process.

Let's assume that the particular IEC has jurisdiction to provide consultation on particular cases. Whether Pat should indeed turn to that IEC depends on the circumstances in the particular institution.[15] She must first examine the composition of the particular IEC and determine, to the extent possible, whether it has adopted an approach sympathetic to patients' rights. In some instances, the IEC will be captive to institutional interests and will not offer any realistic hope of a favorable response to Pat's position.

In other instances, though, there is hope for constructive IEC input. The IEC might remind the attending physician about the legal prerogatives of patients and their health-care agents. The IEC might reassure the attending physician that compliance with the advance directive is within professional bounds. The IEC might examine the advance directive and confirm Pat's conclusion that its terms apply to the patient's current condition. All these might be constructive inputs encouraging the attending physician and/or hospital administration to facilitate Pat's effort to implement her father's wishes.

In outlining Pat's main options in enforcing her father's advance directive, I've focused on using internal institutional channels to cajole or cudgel the relevant health-care providers. I don't pretend that this will be an easy or assuredly successful route.

A poignant reminder of the difficulties involved appears in an April 1992 op-ed piece in the New York Times.[16] The piece recounts the saga of a veteran physician and his lawyer brother seeking to effectuate their father's prior instructions during the father's bout with terminal cancer. The father, himself a physician, had determined to reject nonpalliative medical intervention. Despite conferences with medical personnel and hospital administrators, and despite pointed reminders about possible legal recourse, the sons' efforts proved unavailing. Vigorous, unwanted diagnostic and therapeutic procedures continued for two weeks until the father was moved to a hospice for his final hours.

The op-ed piece graphically illustrates how daunting and frustrating it can be to cope with busy physicians and an institutional bureaucracy. The author, the physician son, wonders how lay persons will fare where two experienced professionals failed.

I still recommend pursuing internal institutional channels, at least as a starting point. Perhaps the brothers in the op-ed piece would have had more success if they had been armed with a written instruction directive. Perhaps the lawyer in the story could have been clearer or firmer about the external options that the brothers intended to pursue. In any event, internal channels seem to offer the best hope of expeditiously securing the desired object: compliance with the declarant's instructions. Litigation should be regarded only as an ultimate resort.

SUING THE HELL OUT OF THEM

In our litigious society, the notion of suing for enforcement of an advance directive automatically strikes a responsive chord. If the attending medical personnel and/or host institution are resisting implementation of her father's advance directive, why shouldn't Pat "sue the hell out of them"?

The theoretical framework for liability of the health-care providers certainly exists.[17] One possible source of liability is contract law. When a physician undertakes care of a patient, an implied contract is created. One of the implied terms of that contract is that the patient is entitled to shape medical intervention. That prerogative can be exercised in a prospective fashion by use of an advance directive. A physician thus arguably breaches an implied contract by contravening the terms of an advance directive. Under contract-remedies doctrine, a breaching party is liable for the foreseeable damages flowing from the breach. In a typical case, those damages may include the patient's medical expenses for unwanted treatment and the patient's pain and suffering associated with that unwanted treatment.[18]

Tort law also provides a potential legal handle. Under the doctrine of informed consent, a physician ordinarily commits a battery by administering unauthorized medical treatment. While an exception might apply for emergency treatment, that exception would not apply where, as here, the patient's advance directive rejects the care in question. A tortfeasor physician would be potentially liable for all proximate damages caused by unauthorized treatment (including associated medical expenses and, perhaps, pain and suffering). A possibility even exists that surrounding family could recover for *their* pain and suffering during the physician's prolongation of existence counter to an advance directive.

The common-law claims grounded in contract and tort law would be reinforced in the few states whose living-will statutes provide for "civil liability" as a statutory remedy for violation of a physician's duties.[19] (Usually, the physician's duty is to comply with an advance directive or secure transfer of the patient's care to a cooperative professional.) While the extent of the "civil liability" is not specified in those statutes, recoverable damages probably mirror those available pursuant to the common law.[20]

In the vast majority of states, however, living-will statutes will not be helpful in imposing liability on health-care providers for noncooperation with an advance directive. This is not surprising given the background for adoption of these legislative measures. A key object of living-will statutes was to insulate physicians against liability for voluntary implementation of living wills.[21] Much less exertion went into designing sanctions for noncompliance with such documents. In approximately twenty-two states, no penalty at all is prescribed for such noncompliance.[22] In most of the remaining states, the sole sanction suggested is "professional discipline"—a recourse whose flaws have already been mentioned.

If the noncooperating institution is government owned, the federal Constitution might provide a legal handle for liability. I argued in chapters 1 and 2 that a patient's autonomy to shape medical intervention in a dying process is a fundamental aspect of liberty. If that is so, a public institution which knowingly violates a clear-cut advance directive should be liable in damages for committing a constitutional tort.[23]

At this point, Pat's supporters are probably salivating with enthusiasm to file suit. She ostensibly has at least two, and possibly four, causes of action: in contract, in tort, in constitutional tort, and (in a few locales) under a living-will type statute.

I hate to be a spoilsport, but I have to dampen that enthusiasm somewhat. First, a reminder about the practical disincentives to suit. Litigation is expensive, both because of attorneys' fees and court costs. In the kind of suit under discussion, experts will have to be recruited and their fees paid. Litigation is time-consuming, even when a case involving a dying patient is given accelerated consideration. Both sides need a modicum of time to prepare their cases, and postponements are common to accommodate one side or another or the court. (There will be multiple sides because the institution and health-care professionals may have separate representation and a guardian ad litem may be appointed on behalf of the incompetent patient.) Litigation concerning a helpless, dying patient also draws media attention.

Pat can expect to see her name prominently displayed in the local papers, if not broadcast over the local airwaves. All these practical elements might dissuade Pat from filing suit.

Even if Pat has the temerity to face the above practical obstacles, she can anticipate a variety of defenses on behalf of the defendant health-care providers. The defendants may be contending that the advance instructions are unclear and that the patient's wishes are therefore too murky to justify removal of life support. They may be contending that "reasonable medical standards" dictate continued treatment and that they are entitled to adhere to such professional standards.[24] The defendants may be contending that the advance directive in issue exceeds the permissible bounds of the state's living-will law.[25] The hospital may be contending that it made reasonable efforts to transfer care to a cooperating professional but that such efforts proved futile.[26] These defendants' claims raise debatable issues. Pat and her attorney may ultimately succeed in refuting or overcoming the claims, but their existence means that an eventual favorable outcome is far from assured.

Let's assume for the moment that Pat overcomes all the hurdles listed, both practical and doctrinal. She wins the lawsuit. What has she accomplished? Did she secure for her father a death conforming to his conception of dignity as expressed in his advance directive? Did she succeed in socking it to the recalcitrant physician and hospital in terms of money damages?

As to the first question (Did Pat's father achieve a death consistent with his vision of dignity?), the answer is maybe. The suit to compel respect for his advance directive would have continued for weeks, if not months. If Pat won at the trial court level, the defendants might have appealed. Appeals would postpone the final disposition for more months. It's quite possible that her father would die in the interim, having received the unwanted medical intervention. On the other hand, it's conceivable that Pat would win a quick victory at the trial court level and that the defendants would choose not to appeal. At least after a few weeks of litigation, Pat would have secured either defendants' adherence to her father's instructions or transfer of care to a cooperating health-care provider. (Of course, the physicians may have administered antibiotics pending the outcome of the litigation, with the result that Pat's father would have survived at least one bout with pneumonia.)

As to the second question (Did Pat sock it to the defendants for money damages?), the answer is probably no. The one clearly compensable item of damages is medical expenses associated with the unwanted medical treatment. Depending on the period Pat's father survived with treatment, and depending on the nature of the treatment, those expenses might be considerable. However, in many instances third-party payors will have financed the relevant care. Those payors are subrogated to Pat's potential award for medical expenses. Thus, the sums actually recovered by Pat (or her father's estate) would turn out to be only those amounts not covered by third-party payors.

Pat's attorneys' fees might be a compensable item if incurred in an effort, while her father was still alive, to compel compliance with her father's advance directive.[27] Similarly, fees paid to expert witnesses and other costs associated with such an injunctive proceeding might be compensable. However, in a litigation aimed at securing monetary damages, counsel fees connected with *that* litigation are not ordinarily recoverable.

The really juicy potential item of damages is pain and suffering. Juries are capable of awarding very large sums as compensation for mental anguish, and that item is theoretically recoverable here.[28] Unfortunately, in the context of a patient like Pat's father, there are significant obstacles to recovery of pain and suffering damages.

The first obstacle is a practical one: establishing that pain and suffering in fact occurred. In many instances, an incompetent patient will not be perceptibly suffering during a period when life-sustaining treatment is continued counter to advance instructions. This is certainly so for a patient who is comatose or only semiconscious during the period in question. It may also be so for patients who are still conscious and aware. Pat's father, for example, may not have experienced significant embarrassment and humiliation from his debilitated existence—even if apprehension of those feelings had partially motivated his advance directive.

The second obstacle is a theoretical one involving judicial reluctance to impose damages for "wrongful life." A damage suit on behalf of Pat's father contends, in effect, that he should have been allowed to die and that defendants owe damages for keeping him alive and causing him pain and suffering. The strong judicial presumption, however, is that life is worthwhile and valuable. There is understandable judicial reluctance to endorse the assessment by Pat's father that he would have been better off dead.[29] Such judicial endorsement might be inferred from a damage award for pain and suffering, for the defendants will contend both that they conferred a benefit upon Pat's father by extending his life and that the value of any enjoyment or satisfaction derived from his extended life ought to be set off against the pain and suffering experienced. Because courts are sensitive to the notion that they should not be evaluating the emotional benefits and detriments of a life, they will continue to drag their feet in assessing damages for pain and suffering in this context.[30]

It is true that Pat's father—not any judge—initially made the decision (expressed in his advance directive) that death would be preferable to a debilitated life without further capacity to read. His autonomy interest entitled him to make that judgment and to resist medical efforts to coerce continued treatment. But recognition of that autonomy right does not necessarily demand award of monetary damages for continued existence when any such award impliedly assigns a low monetary value to that continued life. That Pat's father considered life without reading so distasteful as to warrant dying does not mean that a court must ignore the value or benefit derived from his continued existence.

The final obstacle is a likely tendency by triers of fact (judges and juries) to sympathize with the health-care providers' perspective in cases like those of Pat's father. Defendants will point out that they strove to preserve the life of an aware, functioning human being (albeit in contravention of that human being's advance directive). There will be enough empathy with this position to prevent assessment of mammoth damage awards.

To sum up, and to paraphrase James Joyce, the way of the health-care agent is hard. The first recourse is to institutional channels, and those channels are likely to prove difficult and frustrating. Pat, as health-care agent, will need extraordinary determination to convince the resisting health-care providers to implement her father's advance directive. This is especially so here because Pat's brother is on hand contending that his father should not be permitted to die. The second recourse, to an IEC, might prove successful. But that will depend on the nature and composition of the particular IEC. Moreover, even if the IEC responds sympathetically, its advice will not bind the relevant health-care providers. They might continue to resist.

The ultimate recourse, litigation, might prove successful. But it is more likely to prove expensive, exhausting, and frustrating to Pat.

8

New Jersey's Model Legislation

MOST READERS should stop at this point. The central mission of this book has been completed. I have presented advance directives from all the salient angles: historical foundation, legal framework, format, content, interpretation, and enforcement. My insights have all been communicated.

This last chapter is intended for people interested in reforming current state legislation governing advance directives. (This group might include not just legislators but many physicians, health-care providers of all sorts, lawyers who deal with issues of death and dying, and lay people who care deeply about society's response to medical technology's capacity to sustain a prolonged, debilitated moribund existence.) The need for some reform has already been explained. Chapter 3 noted a variety of common statutory defects which may handicap people's ability to exercise full control over post-competence medical intervention.

This chapter's focus is New Jersey because that state's new legislation—the Advance Directives for Health Care Act adopted in July 1991[1]—comes as close as any existing legislation to meeting the criticisms articulated in chapter 3. In some respects, the New Jersey legislation (hereinafter the A.D. Act) can serve as a useful model for new legislation or for reform of existing legislation in other states.

The succeeding part of this chapter highlights the ways in which the A.D. Act surpasses the bulk of prior legislation treating advance directives. As will be shown, the A.D. Act provides expansive scope for the autonomy of competent persons to shape post-competence medical intervention. In addition, the New Jersey Bioethics Commission has provided informative material aimed at assisting the public in understanding and using advance directives. These sources (the A.D. Act and the Commission's booklet) offer sensitive guidance not only for persons preparing advance directives but also for health-care agents, medical personnel, and other decision makers ultimately charged with implementing an advance directive. At the same time, the A.D. Act is not perfect. The last section of this chapter comments on a few question marks which, to my mind, might mar what is, on the whole, a very sound piece of legislation. But first, the kudos.

ADVANTAGES OF NEW JERSEY'S ADVANCE DIRECTIVE ACT

A. An Integrated Statute

Many states have more than one statute relating to advance directives. Often this means a living-will type statute along with a durable-power-of-attorney-for-health-care (DPOA-HC) type statute. These separate measures can easily be a source of confusion and uncertainty. They sometimes give conflicting signals as to the scope of a health-care agent's authority, or they cause confusion about the relationship between a living will and a document appointing an agent.[2]

By contrast, the A.D. Act takes a comprehensive, integrated approach. It provides both for an instruction directive (a living-will type document) and a proxy directive (designation of a health-care agent). The Act encourages an "integrated" document, combining both elements. But it recognizes that some persons will rely solely on an instruction directive and others solely on a proxy directive.

The Act's melding of the two major approaches to advance directives should minimize the tension and confusion that sometimes flows from separate statutes. In addition, explanatory material circulated by the New Jersey Bioethics Commission helpfully offers a variety of options to a declarant.[3] Forms are provided for a proxy directive, for an instruction directive, and for a combined instrument. The same booklet succinctly explains the advantages and disadvantages of each format.

In a few states, most notably New York, the primary legislative input comes in the form of a broad DPOA-HC type measure (without a living-will type law).[4] A person is permitted to designate an agent who may be empowered to make "any and all health care decisions on the principal's behalf that the principal could make."[5] By enabling a health-care agent to make the same decisions that the principal could have made if competent, such measures may avoid the limitations concerning "terminal condition" and artificial nutrition often found in living-will statutes. A broad DPOA-HC statute thus offers wide scope to a person's prospective autonomy interest in shaping post-competence medical handling.

The question arises: should legislative intervention in this area be confined to authorization of proxy directives, as was done in New York? The New York State Task Force on Life and the Law, which developed New York's legislation, specifically considered, and ultimately rejected, the idea of combining, in one law, provisions relating to substantive instructions and those relating to a health-care agent.[6] Statutory attention to instruction directives was deemed superfluous since the New York courts had already recognized prior instructions as evidence of an incompetent patient's wishes which govern the decisions of a designated health-care agent.[7] The Task Force believed that further professional education of health-care providers concerning the force of a living will (or other evidence of a patient's prior expressions) was all that would be necessary for the successful utilization of advance instructions.[8] A proxy directive was seen as "a better, more effective vehicle" than an instruction directive (living will), because the latter supposedly would require that the declarant anticipate a wide range of medical contingencies.[9]

My perspective is that exclusive statutory focus on proxy directives (as in New York) undervalues the utility and importance of instruction directives in achieving results truly consistent with a declarant's wishes. It is true that nothing prevents use of instruction directives in a jurisdiction which provides statutorily only for a proxy directive. Indeed, such laws require the agent to implement the principal's wishes and thus contemplate the existence of some substantive instructions. Nonetheless, the A.D. Act's comprehensive approach—combining in one law provisions regarding substantive instructions and proxy designation—seems preferable.

Equal statutory focus on substantive instructions should promote public and professional awareness of the importance and status of a written instruction directive. This awareness is particularly important for people who cannot recruit a suitable person to serve as a health-care agent (as is the case, for example, for some isolated elderly people).

The A.D. Act clarifies the effect of an instruction directive as a means to effectuate personal preferences in the absence of a designated health-care agent. One section makes an instruction directive "legally operative" upon an attending physician and any other decision maker responsible for an incompetent patient. All such decision makers are directed to uphold the specific terms of an instruction directive and to "exercise reasonable judgment" to implement the intent and spirit of the directive when its terms do not provide clear-cut guidance regarding the incompetent patient's current condition.[10] This provision eliminates any doubt about the validity and binding force of a written instruction directive (a living-will type instrument).

B. Expansive Scope of Prospective Autonomy

In chapter 3, I criticized provisions found in many living-will laws (and some DPOA-HC statutes) confining the substantive content of an advance directive. I mentioned, among other things, limitations relating to terminal condition, artificial nutrition, and pregnancy. To my mind, New Jersey does it better. Although the language of the A.D. Act is still subject to judicial interpretation, my reading is that the Act overcomes all the common pitfalls and gives extremely expansive scope to a declarant's self-determination prerogative.

The most important New Jersey improvement relates to the "terminal condition" limitation—the notion in some living-will laws that life-sustaining care can only be withdrawn when an incompetent patient is facing unpreventable death within a short period of time. Such a limitation is plainly inconsistent with many declarants' desires to avoid indefinite medical maintenance in a gravely debilitated condition. Many people view a gravely debilitated, protracted dying process as intolerable—perhaps because of the indignity or frustration of utter helplessness and dependence, or because of distress over the image and recollections to be left with survivors, or because of the emotional toll on loved ones, or because of depletion of a potential legacy. Such apprehensions are not confined to permanent unconsciousness; they apply as well to medical prolongation of a severely debilitated state such as a barely conscious condition provoked by a severe stroke or other brain trauma.

The new A.D. Act appears to respond sympathetically to the dignity-related concerns of persons intent on avoiding a protracted, debilitated dying process. Section 67(a) addresses the circumstances in which life-sustaining medical intervention may be withdrawn pursuant to an advance directive. Three subsections of Section 67(a) mitigate the harsh effects of the terminal condition precondition found in some living-will statutes.[11]

Subsection (2) speaks to permanent unconsciousness and authorizes cessation of life-sustaining medical intervention (in accord with an advance directive) for a patient in that status. Subsection (3) speaks to a declarant whose instructions refer to a "terminal condition." That term is broadly defined as "the terminal stage of an irreversibly fatal illness, disease, or condition."[12] The Act explains that there is no specific life expectancy limitation intended. A prognosis of six months or less (absent the contemplated life-sustaining medical intervention) is deemed a terminal condition, but that period is given as a guideline only.[13] In other words, the A.D. Act does not confine a "terminal condition" to the very last stage of a fatal illness, when death is fairly imminent.

Subsection (4) of Section 67(a) goes even further. It authorizes cessation of life-sustaining treatment (consistent with an advance directive) when the patient has reached a "serious irreversible condition" and "the likely burdens associated with the medical intervention . . . may reasonably be judged to outweigh the likely benefits . . . or imposition of the medical intervention on an unwilling patient would be inhumane."

Subsection (4) is the key provision for purposes of advance directives which seek to cover nonprolongation of a gravely debilitated (but conscious) state unwanted by the declarant. For that purpose, it is important to establish that the "burdens" mentioned in Section 67(a)(4) can include dignity concerns (such as dysfunction, helplessness, and dependence) as well as other values and preferences of the patient—in addition to pain and suffering, which would customarily be considered burdens.[14] Examination of the language and background of the A.D. Act indicates that the term *burdens* was indeed intended to have such an expansive meaning.

The A.D. Act and the report of the New Jersey Bioethics Commission that preceded the Act's passage are replete with indications that an advance directive can encompass a person's full range of values and preferences. Section 61(f) of the Act enjoins any designated health-care agent to make the same decision the patient would have made under the circumstances now confronted.[15] The report stresses both that a critical goal of the advance directive is to assure respect for a declarant's wishes and that those wishes should embody the patient's own concept of important considerations in shaping medical handling.[16] "The patient possesses knowledge of his or her own personal values and goals without which the risks, benefits, and burdens of proposed treatment options, and therefore the patient's true wishes and best interests, cannot be meaningfully evaluated."[17]

Even where no instruction directive exists, or where the principal's instructions are not clear, the health-care agent is admonished to act in a manner consistent with the intent and spirit of the patient's wishes as best they can be discerned. The governing standard becomes "best interests" of the now incompetent patient; best interests, in turn, are to be assessed in accord with the patient's wishes.[18] "The authority . . . to act in the patient's best interests rests on the understanding that such a judgment will in fact be grounded in and consistent with the available evidence of the patient's own values and objectives."[19] The report explains that the Act seeks to further the patient's well-being, which is "grounded in the patient's own values and objectives."[20] In short, the statutory language and background offer ample support for the proposition that the "burdens" in Section 67(a)(4) include a declarant's predilections regarding indignity and other personal values.

An expansive interpretation of the burdens to be considered in administering advance directives pursuant to Section 67(a)(4) would also be consistent with the A.D. Act's express object of preserving relevant constitutional rights. Section 67(c) explicitly disclaims legislative intent to abridge any right to refuse treatment under either the New Jersey or federal constitutions. In New Jersey, In re *Peter*[21] indicates that a person is entitled to shape post-competence medical handling according to personal values without limitation to customary notions of burden such as physical pain. That prerogative likely enjoys constitutional status pursuant to either the New Jersey or federal constitutions.[22]

The New Jersey Supreme Court has declared that an incompetent patient enjoys the "same right to autonomy in medical decisions as a competent patient."[23] This apparently means that a person may use an advance directive to direct future medical intervention to the same extent that a competent person can direct contemporaneous medical care. A competent person, in turn, is entitled to bring considerations of dignity and other personal concerns into play in shaping medical intervention in a dying process.[24]

A broad reading of Section 67(a)(4)—one which permits an advance directive to reject life-sustaining care even when a patient is preservable indefinitely and not perceptibly suffering—is essential. I previously noted that many declarants seek to avoid maintenance in a gravely debilitated condition which they regard as demeaning or undignified. If burdens, for purposes of Section 67(a)(4), were confined to pain and suffering, then rarely would a debilitated patient attain the relief from indignity often being sought via an advance directive. As many commentators have noted, it is extremely difficult to assess the degree of emotional or physical suffering of a severely demented patient.[25] A health-care agent can more easily and accurately implement an advance directive grounded on the principal's delineation of a severely debilitated status which the principal deems subjectively intolerable.

The sample advance directives prepared by the New Jersey Bioethics Commission are sensitive to the possible desire to avoid the "burden" of prolonged medical maintenance in a gravely debilitated condition. One of the options offered to a declarant is to decline treatment for an irreversible illness or condition which is not necessarily fatal. The option is aimed at a future condition in which the patient is experiencing "severe and progressive physical or mental deterioration and/or permanent loss of capacities and faculties" valued highly by the patient.[26] The form document suggests to the principal that he or she use the blank space provided to describe "the faculties or capacities which, if irretrievably lost, would lead you [the declarant] to accept death rather than continue living."[27] The clear implication is that the subjectively distasteful nature of a gravely debilitated existence (as outlined in an advance directive) is to be considered as part of the burdens to be assessed by the agent administering the advance directive.[28] In short, there is cause for optimism that the A.D. Act, in application, will fully uphold a declarant's prospective autonomy.

Another area in which the A.D. Act affords flexibility is with regard to artificial nutrition. The living-will laws of some states differentiate between artificial nutrition and conventional medical treatment. I previously considered and rejected the arguments supporting this differentiation—notions that removal of artificial nutrition "causes" a patient's death in some unique way or conveys a negative symbolic message about human caring. The New Jersey legislature confronted these arguments, ultimately rejecting them in the A.D. Act's final version.

In the New Jersey Bioethics Commission's draft bill proposing an advance directive law, as originally adopted by the New Jersey Senate,[29] a distinction was maintained between artificial nutrition and other medical treatment. Section 16 of the bill significantly circumscribed the conditions in which artificial nutrition might be withdrawn pursuant to an advance directive. The incompetent patient would have to be in a terminal condition (the end stage of an irreversible dying process).[30] In addition, the patient would have had to explicitly authorize removal of nutrition, and the implementation decision by an agent would have to be reviewed by an institutional ethics committee (or other review body) prior to implementation. The Commission's report justified the special treatment of artificial nutrition, as opposed to conventional medical intervention, on grounds of "social policy."[31] The report mentioned "respect for and protection of human life, and the preservation of public confidence in the caring role of health care professionals."[32]

The final A.D. Act rejects the original bill's policy which differentiates artificial nutrition from conventional medical technology. The original Section 16, restricting cessation of artificial nutrition, is stricken. Section 55, as amended, explicitly includes "artificially provided fluids and nutrition" within the broad definition of life-sustaining treatment which can be withheld pursuant to an advance directive, even without explicit authorization.

Despite the New Jersey Bioethics Commission's original suggestion that "respect for . . . human life" and "preservation of public confidence in the caring role of health care professionals" might warrant special status for artificial nutrition, the A.D. Act's final approach seems sound. Numerous medical and legal sources have considered and rejected the asserted distinctiveness of artificial nutrition. For example, the President's Commission for the Study of Ethical Problems in Medicine, the New York State Task Force on Life and the Law, the New York Academy of Medicine, and the Hastings Center Task Force on Death and Dying all found no logical distinction between cessation of artificial nutrition and cessation of other life-sustaining technology.[33] New Jersey's final approach thus coincides with popular perspectives, with uniform judicial reaction and with the expressions of numerous medical organizations.

Another concession to declarants' autonomy comes in the A.D. Act's handling of pregnancy. Sections 56 and 58(a)(5) provide that a female declarant may, but need not, include special instructions with regard to the impact of pregnancy on instructions for life support. New Jersey thus avoids the unconstitutional approach present in states which purport to suspend the effect of a female's advance directive during the entire period of pregnancy. The A.D. Act leaves the issue of life support during pregnancy entirely in the female declarant's hands. No mention is made of fetal interests, even those of a third trimester fetus.

The thorniest autonomy issue is advance instructions which conflict with an incompetent patient's contemporaneous well-being, and this issue is not definitively resolved by the A.D. Act. I argued in chapter 6 that a considered advance directive ought to be upheld even to the detriment of some current interests of an incompetent patient. It is at least arguable that the A.D. Act adopts that approach—anticipating implementation of advance directives despite tension with a patient's current material interests.

The A.D. Act's whole focus is on respect for a declarant's wishes. It contemplates that an advance directive will be implemented according to its terms if it provides "clear direction" or "clear and unambiguous guidance under the circumstances."[34] "Best interests" of the incompetent patient are mentioned as a default standard to be used only when the actual wishes of the declarant cannot be determined by the persons applying an advance directive.[35] The clear implication is that the declarant's expressed preferences govern even if in tension with immediate well-being.

There is additional support for the proposition that a declarant's competently expressed preferences govern. Best interests, for purposes of the A.D. Act, probably encompass a patient's personal preferences (including dignity-related concerns and altruistic values) as well as physical well-being. The Bioethics Commission report accompanying the relevant bill stated: "[T]he authority . . . to act in the patient's best interests rests on the understanding that such a judgment will in fact be grounded in and consistent with the available evidence of the patient's own values and objectives."[36]

Finally, the Act confers authority to withdraw life-sustaining treatment (consistent with a directive) for a chronically debilitated patient suffering from a "serious irreversible illness or condition [where] the likely risks and burdens associated with the medical intervention . . . may reasonably be judged to outweigh the likely benefits."[37] So long as the burdens mentioned include offense to the patient's personal values and preferences, the A.D. Act apparently allows the declarant's self-determination interest to prevail. I already argued that burdens under the Act do include such personal-value considerations. Recall also that New Jersey courts declare both that an incompetent patient retains the *same* autonomy right as a competent patient and that a competent patient clearly may reject treatment which most people would consider prudent.

The only doubt about the dominance of self-determination over immediate patient well-being stems from some cryptic phrases in the background report to the A.D. Act prepared by the New Jersey Bioethics Commission. In discussing the circumstances in which the administrator of an advance directive might deviate from the terms of the directive, that report notes, in passing, that the administrator should be "most attentive" to whether the directive is "contrary to the patient's best interests."[38] The comment is not clarified. At another juncture, the report suggests that a directive could be interpreted in a fashion inconsistent with its terms "to protect patient well being."[39] Both comments probably refer to instances when unanticipated changes in medical technology (or other unforeseen circumstances) make the literal terms of the declarant's directive inconsistent with the patient's current best interests. In that event, the terms of the advance directive can be ignored in order to achieve a result consistent with the spirit of the document as a whole.[40] This is not the same as saying that a declarant's clearly expressed preferences can be overridden whenever they are not congruent with material "best interests" of the patient in the narrow sense of that term.

C. Guidance to Administrators of Advance Directives

Provisions within the A.D. Act anticipate many of the difficulties associated with application of an advance directive, and they offer sufficient flexibility for sensible administration. Take, for example, the vagueness that plagues many short-form advance directives. The A.D. Act acknowledges that an advance directive's language will not always be clear and may not even be the declarant's final and definitive expression. A health-care agent is enjoined to "give priority" to an instruction directive.[41] But the agent is also authorized to consider other evidence of the now incompetent patient's wishes, including statements of the declarant outside the advance directive itself.[42] Administrators of an advance directive are generally enjoined to follow the "intent and spirit" of directives that do not furnish clear-cut instructions.[43] In light of the frequent imprecision of advance directives, referral of decision makers to additional indices of the declarant's intentions is probably constructive.

The A.D. Act also seems sufficiently flexible to permit a health-care agent or other administrator to deviate from the terms of an advance directive when appropriate. For example, although the Act normally contemplates that a directive's "clear direction" will be followed, it also urges a health-care agent to "make the health care decision the patient would have made."[44]

This ought to furnish sufficient authorization to deviate from a directive's language where changed circumstances make the literal text inconsistent with the declarant's discernible objectives. The background report accompanying the New Jersey Bioethics Commission's draft bill expresses an understanding that changed circumstances (such as therapeutic advances) might warrant noncompliance with the terms of an advance directive.[45] The report recognizes that ostensibly clear language can become ambiguous when applied to unforeseen circumstances.[46]

The A.D. Act also appears to address sensibly the difficult issue of post-competence expressions by a declarant. Section 63(b) requires a health-care agent to discuss treatment options with the incompetent patient "to a reasonable extent" and to "take the patient's expressed wishes into account in the decision making process." This statutory enjoinder to consult with an incompetent patient makes sense for reasons already explained in chapter 5. Consultation has a symbolic function in recognizing the patient's human status. It also has an instrumental value in furnishing insights into the emotional and physical feelings of such patients, feelings which are important in the administration of an advance directive.

All this does not mean that an incompetent patient's expressions should be determinative of the medical course to be followed. I argued in chapter 5 that an incompetent patient's input ought to be sought and considered but not necessarily followed in administration. The first portion of Section 63(b), dictating that decision makers "take the patient's expressed wishes into account," is consistent with that approach. An additional paragraph in Section 63(b) goes further and compels adherence to certain expressions by the incompetent patient. The relevant language provides:

> [I]f a patient who lacks decision making capacity clearly expresses or manifests the contemporaneous wish that medically appropriate measures utilized to sustain life be provided, that wish shall take precedence over any contrary decision of the health care representative and any contrary statement in the patient's instruction directive.

The motivation behind this provision is understandable and admirable. There is a natural revulsion toward removing life-preserving care from a person who is articulating a wish to continue living.[47] At the same time, according determinative and continuing force to incompetent declarations, no matter how demented the patient, is excessive. (Certainly, it would be inappropriate to give such status to the deranged utterances of a patient expressing a wish to die.) Giving deference to the expression of a gravely demented patient (in preference to a carefully considered advance directive) could subvert self-determination. The potential for the manipulation of a demented patient is patent. Decision makers on behalf of the patient, if uncomfortable with the substance of the advance directive, could simply keep asking the patient whether he or she renounces the original instruction until an affirmative response is attained.

It is possible to interpret Section 63(b) in a fashion that makes it consistent with common sense and with respect for a declarant's self-determination. An utterance from a gravely demented patient should not be regarded as a "clear" expression for purposes of Section 63(b). Only if a patient comprehends the concept of death and the significance of his or her life-affirming utterance should such an utterance override a clear and considered advance directive.

Even in the latter situation, the effectiveness or "precedence" of contemporaneous expressions (over a conflicting advance directive) should continue only as long as the life-affirming position is being communicated by the patient. Afterward, a clear and apparently considered advance directive should regain its effective status. In effect, an advance directive renouncing life support should only be "suspended" by an incompetent patient's life-affirming expression.

As to problems of administration faced when health-care providers pose conscientious objections to implementing an advance directive, the A.D. Act breaks little new ground. New Jersey has adopted the same basic structure prevailing under most living-will legislation. That is, professional conscience is recognized, but professionals with conscientious objections are expected to assist in arranging transfer of responsibility to more accommodating health-care professionals.

A.D. Act Sections 62(b) and 62(c) authorize individual health-care professionals to invoke "sincerely held personal or professional convictions" in order to decline to participate in withdrawal of life-sustaining measures pursuant to an advance directive. An objecting physician is required to act to transfer the patient's care to fellow professionals who can cooperate in good conscience with the course prescribed in the advance directive. Although the Act doesn't articulate a "reasonable efforts" standard, that is probably the scope of the transfer duty imposed on the objecting physician.

The A.D. Act does not resolve the question of what happens when transfer of the patient cannot be accomplished even after reasonable efforts. The physician cannot simply withdraw from the case, leaving the patient to fend for himself or herself.[48] At the same time, the Act itself does not require a physician to implement a personally repugnant course in the event that transfer cannot be arranged. The background report accompanying the original bill underlying the A.D. Act indicates that "judicial intervention" may then become necessary.[49] It does not suggest what the result of such intervention should be. I argued in chapter 5 that the tension might well be judicially resolved in favor of the patient's autonomy interest. That is, a patient's interest in controlling medical care by means of an advance directive might well override an individual health-care provider's scruples where transfer cannot practicably be arranged.

As to institutional health-care providers, the A.D. Act deviates somewhat from the prevailing pattern. In most states, institutional conscience is recognized, and the objecting institution is expected to assist in securing transfer of the problematic patient to a more accommodating institution. While A.D. Act Section 54(d) acknowledges the importance of the "ethical integrity" of health-care institutions, only a "private, religiously-affiliated health care institution" is accorded a right to refuse participation in withdrawal of life-sustaining measures.[50] Private nonsectarian institutions are not entitled to invoke institutional conscience in order to refuse implementation of "offensive" advance directives.

The explanation is plain for excluding nonsectarian institutions from a right to conscientious objection in this context. Drafters of the legislation were apprehensive that recognition of such a right would "risk unduly diminishing the number of institutional settings in which patients and families can properly expect their rights and wishes to prevail."[51] The concern was that institutions would manufacture "moral" policies either in order to shun difficult cases that had engendered or might engender unwelcome publicity or in order to avoid economic costs associated with certain types of moribund patients.[52] The conscience-based concerns of sectarian institutions would, by contrast, presumably be bona fide. Moreover, a claim based on religious conscience would be reinforced by the Constitution's Free Exercise Clause.

The statutory differentiation between religiously affiliated and nonsectarian health-care institutions parallels a distinction intimated by the New Jersey Supreme Court in the abortion context. In *Doe v. Bridgeton Hospital*,[53] the New Jersey Supreme Court required three private, nonsectarian hospitals to permit elective abortions despite the moral objections of the hospitals' boards of directors. The court ruled that hospitals are "quasi-public" institutions and therefore subject to certain public-service obligations despite their conscientious scruples.[54] As in the case of Section 65(b) of the A.D. Act, the court was apprehensive that adequate health-care facilities would not be available to meet the needs and preferences of the consumer population.

The apprehension concerning availability of health-care providers willing to implement controversial or idiosyncratic advance directives is understandable.

Families seeking to transfer patients from objecting institutions have often encountered widespread institutional refusal to accept a transfer patient for the purpose of implementing an advance directive. Nonetheless, it is by no means clear that a total exclusion of conscience claims by private, nonsectarian institutions is a necessary measure.

New York's recent legislation concerning health-care agents takes a different approach. There, a private hospital is entitled to formulate and implement a policy against cooperating with terminal decisions if the policy is based on "religious beliefs or sincerely held moral convictions central to the facility's operating principles."[55] In addition, patients and family must be informed in advance about the policy, and the hospital must seek to transfer the patient in the event of conflict. If transfer to a more accommodating facility is not arranged, the objecting hospital must either honor the health-care agent's decision or "seek judicial relief."[56]

Experience under the New York model should help determine whether the A.D. Act's nonrecognition of institutional conscience in the private, nonsectarian sector is excessively accommodating to patients' interests. That is, if private New York institutions do not use the available exemption in a fashion which overly impedes the honoring of advance instructions, it will indicate that New Jersey's approach was unnecessarily broad.

I would issue another caveat with regard to the A.D. Act provisions relating to professional conscience. Section 65(c) mentions that nothing in the A.D. Act requires a health-care institution to act contrary to "accepted medical standards." This provision recalls the discussion in chapter 5 of professional refusals to provide "medically futile" care which might be requested in an advance directive. In that discussion, I warned that medical judgments that life-extending care is futile and expendable ought rarely to prevail in the face of an advance directive prescribing continued medical intervention. I would hope that Section 65(c) of the A.D. Act would not be interpreted as generally elevating professional judgment over patient self-determination.

The success or failure of the A.D. Act will offer an important clue to the fate of advance directives. The New Jersey legislation provides a comprehensive and forward-looking approach to advance directives. It ought to promote the effective use and administration of such instruments and thus help persons shape the contours of medical intervention in order to secure a modicum of dignity in the dying process.

I'll end with the same warning given in the Introduction. The stakes are high in the effort to shape a humane approach to medical technology's capacity to prolong patients far beyond previous bounds. Pressures are mounting to employ new responses (such as assisted suicide and active euthanasia) to people's apprehensions about dying in a prolonged, debilitated status. The advance directive is supposed to be an important tool in achieving a death with a modicum of dignity without resort to those radical responses. Failure of this tool, and a failure of medicine and law to shape medical intervention in the dying process in a fashion consistent with what most people would want, would assure that assisted suicide and/or active euthanasia will proliferate. In short, a lot depends on the sensitive promotion, interpretation, and administration of advance medical directives. This book was aimed at advancing those objects.

Advance Directive for Health Care

There may come a time when I am unable, due to mental incapacity, to make my own health-care decisions. In order to provide the guidance and authority needed to make decisions on my behalf:

> I, Norman L. Cantor, hereby declare my instructions and wishes for my future health care. This advance directive for health care shall take effect in the event I become unable to make my own health-care decisions, as determined by the physician who has primary responsibility for my care and my designated health-care representative. I direct that this document become part of my permanent medical records. My two current physicians, —— and ——, have been provided with copies of this document.

Part One: Designation of a Health-Care Representative

I hereby designate:

> Name
> Address
> Telephone

as my health-care representative to make any and all health-care decisions for me, including decisions to accept or to refuse any treatment, service, or procedure used to diagnose or treat my physical or mental condition, and decisions to provide, withhold or withdraw life-sustaining measures. I authorize my representative to secure all medical records and take all steps, including litigation or transfer from one locale to another, which she may deem appropriate in implementing this directive.

I have discussed the terms of this designation with my health-care representative, and she has willingly agreed to accept the responsibility for acting on my behalf.

If the person I have designated above is unable, unwilling, or unavailable to act as my health-care representative, I hereby designate the following person to act as my health-care representative, in the order of priority stated:

1. Name
   Address
   Telephone

2. Name
   Address
   Telephone

Part Two: Instructions for Care

I direct my representative to make decisions on my behalf in accordance with my wishes as stated in this document or as otherwise known to her. In the event my wishes are not clear, or if a situation arises I did not anticipate, my health-care representative is authorized to make decisions in my best interests, as defined in this document.

I direct that the central guideline shaping my medical handling be my best interests, including consideration of pain and suffering and all the dignity-related factors mentioned in this document. This means that if, in the course of my medical care, the burdens of continued life with treatment become greater than the benefits I experience, or if my condition is demeaning (as I've defined it below), life-sustaining measures are to be withheld or discontinued.

Before I turn to instructions relating to particular types of circumstances, I mention certain guidelines which apply to all post-competence decisions on my behalf. First, while my instructions call for withholding of life-preserving medical care in various situations, palliative care is always to be provided. That is, pain relievers or sedatives should be provided to relieve intractable pain or extreme emotional upset insofar as the need for such palliative agents can be discerned. Also, I would always expect to be maintained in a clean, sheltered, and comfortable environment. Nursing care aimed at providing a clean and dignified environment should therefore always be furnished.

Second, medical treatment to be rejected may include all forms of medical intervention whether complex, like respirators, or simplistic, like blood transfusions or antibiotics. Artificial nutrition and hydration are also included. Different treatments may entail different consequences and side effects (e.g., the long-term dependence on a dialysis machine) so that differentiations among types of treatment may have to be made in the course of actual decision making. Yet there is no intention here to categorize certain treatments as ordinary and others as extraordinary for purposes of shaping my medical future. Best interests will have to be assessed on a case-by-case basis with regard to my specific condition and various proposed treatments.

I now turn to the circumstances in which life-sustaining medical intervention should be foregone. If there should come a time when I become permanently unconscious, and it is determined by my attending physician and at least one additional physician with appropriate expertise who has personally examined me, that I have irreversibly lost consciousness, I direct that life-sustaining measures be withheld or discontinued.

I realize that there may come a time when I am diagnosed as having an incurable and irreversible illness, disease, or condition which may or may not be terminal. My condition may cause me to experience a permanent loss of capacities and faculties I value highly. My best interests and my dignity are to be the general guidelines in shaping medical intervention in such instances. I direct that those guidelines be administered in accord with the following considerations.

1. *Physical Pain.* To the extent that analgesics still leave significant physical pain or produce prolonged stupor, this should be deemed a significant factor adverse to my best interests.

2. *Indignity.* There are certain conditions which for me, an independent person who has been extremely active in both intellectual and physical pursuits, would be demeaning and degrading. I understand that in my state of incompetency I may not feel or sense the humiliation or degradation with which I am concerned. Nonetheless, it is important to me, as a currently autonomous being, to shape my medical future in accord with my conception of dignity. It is important to me to be remembered as a person possessing certain characteristics, whose absence I consider undignified or demeaning. I direct that medical intervention be guided by my conception of personal dignity described herein. In other words, my best interests as an incompetent person should be judged with the following elements of indignity in mind.

A major element of indignity for me is helplessness. If, for example, I permanently lose the capacity to feed myself, this is a significant blow to my dignity. Inability to dress or bathe myself should also be considered a significant blow to my dignity. Similarly, if I lose control of my bodily evacuations so that I must be diapered or otherwise attended, this constitutes a significant blow to my dignity.

Another aspect of helplessness is physical restraint. It may be that in my incompetence I will physically resist administration of medical treatment or otherwise act out so as to necessitate physical restraint in order to protect myself or others. Such conduct may be purely instinctive without any awareness or reason behind the actions. Nonetheless, it is demeaning to be trussed up or physically restrained for significant periods. If prolonged or repeated restraint (or, alternatively, prolonged or repeated sedation reducing me to a stupor) is necessary, this involuntary restraint is to be considered a significant blow to my dignity.

3. *Mental Deterioration.* By definition, this advance directive is relevant only when I have lost competence to make my own medical decisions. While it is difficult for me to conceive of life without such mental capacity, I understand that persons lacking such capacity can still derive enjoyment and benefit from their existences. Therefore, while the prospect of mental incompetence is troubling to

me, that fact, by itself, should not be deemed a basis for withholding or withdrawing medical treatment.

At the same time, there is a level of severe mental dysfunction which for me is demeaning and repugnant. For example, permanent inability to recognize and/or interact with my relatives or friends would, by itself, constitute an intolerable, demeaning status. Along these lines, incapacity to read and understand a newspaper or magazine would reflect a level of mental dysfunction very troubling to me. If I am permanently reduced to such a level of dysfunction, this would at least constitute a significant blow to my dignity, to be considered along with the other elements of indignity and burden mentioned in this document. Thus, for example, if my mental deterioration reaches this level, and I am also physically immobilized or afflicted by other significant elements of indignity, I would want cessation of life-sustaining medical intervention.

4. *Physical Disability*. I have always been a vigorous person. Thus, it is hard to imagine existence without capacity to engage in physical pursuits. Nonetheless, I consider myself resilient enough and life-affirming enough to adjust to a significant degree of physical disability, including even blindness or inability to walk. Consequently, physical incapacity by itself should not be regarded in my case as a demeaning or degrading state.

While severe physical disabilities would not by themselves be a basis for ending life-preserving care, such disabilities in combination with extreme mental deterioration or other significant blow or blows to my dignity might well prompt a determination that my best interests dictate the cessation of medical intervention in the face of a potentially life-threatening disease or condition. This last statement refers to the conditions which I have described above as depriving me of dignity (such as incontinence or inability to feed myself). I reiterate that such extreme incapacities should be considered significant blows to my dignity.

My degree of actual or prospective physical disability should be considered in conjunction with my level of mental dysfunction. That is, if my mental deterioration deprives me of the ability to cope with whatever physical disabilities are involved, that fact should be included in calculating my best interests.

5. *Chronic and Degenerative Disease*. I am aware that there are a number of incurable diseases and conditions which gradually and insidiously cause physical and/or mental deterioration over a prolonged period, before eventually leading to death. Alzheimer's disease and ALS (Lou Gehrig's disease) provide two examples known to me. If my incompetence coincides with such an affliction, I direct that medical intervention be shaped in accord with the formula outlined above. This instruction means that when irreversible deterioration has reached a point which can be defined as demeaning by my standards, life-preserving medical care should not be continued. I understand that as a consequence death may be permitted much earlier than it would ensue if medical intervention were maintained until the most advanced stages of the disease process. My wish is to avoid those stages of the

dying process in which my existence has become demeaning according to the standards described in this document.

At any point when my condition is demeaning, my wish is that life-preserving medical treatment be withheld or withdrawn. Again, this instruction applies to all forms of treatment, whether simplistic or complex, and includes artificial nutrition where normal alimentary processes have been incapacitated (whether by the underlying degenerative disease or by any other pathology which has developed). This instruction also applies to preventive measures (such as antibiotics) and measures capable of curing intervening diseases (such as pneumonia). However, in making a determination whether to employ preventive and curative measures once my condition is demeaning, my agent should consider any pain or discomfort or indignity associated with a nonintervention course; that is, consideration should be given to whether these negative consequences of withholding preventive or curative measures would make the dying process inhumane.

Part Three: Signature and Witnesses

By writing this advance directive, I inform those who may become entrusted with my health care of my wishes and intend to ease the burdens of decision making which this responsibility may impose. I understand the purpose and effect of this document and sign it knowingly, voluntarily, and after careful deliberation.

Signed this _____ day of _____, 19____ .
Signature _____

I declare that the person who signed this document did so in my presence, that he is personally known to me, and that he appears to be of sound mind and free of duress or undue influence. I am eighteen years of age or older, and I am not designated by this or any other document as the person's health-care representative nor as an alternate health-care representative.

1. witness _____
   address _____
   city _____ state _____
   signature _____

2. witness _____
   address _____
   city _____ state _____
   signature _____

Form Health-Care Power of Attorney

The following form is based on a form first prepared by Charles Sabatino for the American Bar Association and the American Association of Retired Persons. It has been adapted by Elizabeth Patterson, and her version is printed at 42 So. Car. L. Rev. 582–87. I have revised her version.

HEALTH-CARE POWER OF ATTORNEY

1. *DESIGNATION OF HEALTH-CARE AGENT*

I, _____, hereby appoint:
(Principal)

_____
(Agent's name)

_____
(Address)
Home Telephone: _____ Work Telephone: _____
as my Agent to make health- and personal-care decisions for me, as authorized in this document, during any period of mental incompetence which I may undergo.

2. *AGENT'S POWERS AND DUTIES*

I grant to my Agent full authority to make decisions for me regarding my health care. In exercising this authority, my Agent shall follow my desires as stated in this document or as otherwise expressed by me or known to my Agent.

In making any decision, my Agent shall attempt to discuss the proposed decision with me to determine my desires if I am able to communicate in any way. In the event my wishes as previously expressed are unclear, my Agent shall make a choice for me based upon what my Agent believes to be in my best interests as expressed by me in this document or elsewhere. My Agent's authority to interpret my desires is intended to be as broad as possible, except for any limitations I may state below.

Accordingly, unless specifically limited by Section H below, my Agent is authorized as follows:

A. To consent, refuse, or withdraw consent to any and all types of medical care, treatment, surgical procedures, diagnostic procedures, medication, and the use of mechanical or other procedures that affect any bodily function, including, but not limited to, artificial respiration, nutritional support and hydration, and cardiopulmonary resuscitation;

B. To authorize, or refuse to authorize, any medication or procedure intended to relieve pain, even though such use may lead to physical damage, addiction, or hasten the moment of, but not intentionally cause, my death;

C. To authorize my admission to or discharge from, even against medical advice, any hospital, nursing-care facility, or similar facility or service;

D. To take any other action necessary to making, documenting, and assuring implementation of decisions concerning my health care, including, but not limited to: the granting of any waiver or release from liability required by any hospital, physician, or other health-care provider; the signing of any documents relating to refusals of treatment or the leaving of a facility against medical advice; and the pursuing of any legal action, in my name and at the expense of my estate, either to force compliance with my wishes, as determined by my Agent, or to seek actual or punitive damages for the failure to comply;

E. To have access to medical records and information to the same extent that I am entitled to, including the right to disclose the contents to others;

F. To contract on my behalf for placement in a health-care or nursing-care facility, or for health-care related services, without incurring personal financial liability for the contract;

G. To hire and fire medical, social-service, and other support personnel responsible for my care;

H. The powers granted above do not include the following powers or are subject to the following rules or limitations:

_____

_____

_____

3. *ORGAN DONATION* (INITIAL ONLY ONE)

My Agent may _____ or may not _____ consent to the donation of all or any of my tissue or organs for purposes of transplantation.

4. *STATEMENT OF DESIRES AND SPECIAL PROVISIONS*

With respect to any life-sustaining treatment, I direct the following: (INITIAL WHICHEVER OF THE FOLLOWING THREE PARAGRAPHS REFLECTS

YOUR WISHES. IN PARAGRAPH D YOU MAY ADD TO WHICHEVER
PARAGRAPH YOU CHECKED OR YOU MAY PROVIDE INSTRUCTIONS
IN YOUR OWN WORDS IF YOU WISH.)

(A). _____ GRANT OF DISCRETION TO AGENT. I do not want my
life to be prolonged nor do I want life-sustaining treatment to be provided or
continued if my Agent believes the burdens of the treatment outweigh the expected benefits. I want my Agent to consider the relief of suffering, my personal
beliefs, the expense involved, and the quality as well as the possible extension
of my life in making decisions concerning life-sustaining treatment.

OR

(B). _____ DIRECTIVE TO WITHHOLD OR WITHDRAW TREAT-
MENT. I do not want my life to be prolonged, and I do not want life-sustaining
treatment if either:

1. I have a condition that is incurable or irreversible and, without the administration of life-sustaining procedures, is expected to result in death within
   a relatively short period of time; or
2. if I am in a state of permanent unconsciousness.

OR

(C). _____ DIRECTIVE FOR MAXIMUM TREATMENT. I want my
life to be prolonged to the greatest extent possible, within the standards of accepted medical practice and without regard to my condition, the chances I have
for recovery, or the cost of the procedures.

AND/OR

(D). _____DIRECTIVE IN MY OWN WORDS:

_____

_____

_____

_____

5. *STATEMENT OF DESIRES REGARDING TUBE-FEEDING*

With respect to artificial nutrition and hydration, including by means of a nasogastric tube or tube into the stomach, intestines, or veins, I wish to make clear
that (INITIAL ONLY ONE)

(A). _____ I *do not* want to receive these forms of artificial nutrition and
hydration, and they may be withheld or withdrawn under the conditions given
above.

OR

(B). _____ I *do* want to receive these forms of artificial nutrition and hydration.

6. *SUCCESSORS*

If an Agent named by me refuses to serve or becomes otherwise unavailable (or if an Agent is my spouse and is divorced from me or separated from me), I name the following as successors to my Agent, each to act alone and successively, in the order named. The word *Agent* in this document includes a Successor Agent who has assumed authority to act pursuant to this section.

A. First Alternate Agent:

                    _____

        Address: _____

     Telephone: _____

B. Second Alternate Agent:

                    _____

        Address: _____

     Telephone: _____

7. *PROTECTION OF MY AGENT AND THIRD PARTIES WHO RELY ON MY AGENT*

No health-care provider or other person or entity that either reasonably relies upon a person's representation that he or she is the person named as my Agent or relies in good faith on a health-care decision made by my Agent shall be liable to me, my estate, my heirs or assigns, for recognizing the Agent's authority or relying on the decision.

No Agent who in good faith makes a health-care decision pursuant to the authority granted herein shall be liable to me, my estate, or my heirs or assigns, on account of the substance of the decision.

8. *ADMINISTRATIVE PROVISIONS*

A. This power of attorney is intended to be valid in any jurisdiction in which it is presented.

B. My Agent shall not be entitled to compensation for services performed under this Health-Care Power of Attorney, but he or she shall be entitled to reimbursement for all reasonable expenses incurred as a result of carrying out the Health-Care Power of Attorney.

C. The powers delegated under this power of attorney are separable so that the invalidity of one or more powers shall not affect any others.

9. *UNAVAILABILITY OF AGENT*

If at any relevant time the Agent and Successor Agents named herein are unable or unwilling to make decisions concerning my health care, and those decisions are to be made by another surrogate, I direct that the surrogate make all decisions in accord with my directions as stated in this document.

BY SIGNING HERE I INDICATE THAT I UNDERSTAND THE CONTENTS OF THIS DOCUMENT AND THE EFFECT OF THIS GRANT OF POWERS TO MY AGENT.

I sign my name to this Health-Care Power of Attorney on this _____ day of _____, 19____. My current home address is:

_____

_____

Signature: _____

Name: _____

WITNESS STATEMENT

I declare, on the basis of information and belief, that the person who signed or acknowledged this document (the principal) is personally known to me, that he/she acknowledged this Health-Care Power of Attorney in my presence, and that he/she appears to be of sound mind and under no duress, fraud, or undue influence.

Witness No. 1

Signature: _____ Date: _____

Print Name: _____ Telephone: _____

Residence Address: _____

_____

Witness No. 2

Signature: _____ Date: _____

Print Name: _____ Telephone: _____

Residence Address: _____

_____

The New Jersey Bioethics Commission's Combined Advance Directive for Health Care (Combined Proxy and Instruction Directive)

I understand that as a competent adult I have the right to make decisions about my health care. There may come a time when I am unable, due to physical or mental incapacity, to make my own health care decisions. In these circumstances, those caring for me will need direction concerning my care and will turn to someone who knows my values and health care wishes. I understand that those responsible for my care will seek to make health care decisions in my best interests, based upon what they know of my wishes. In order to provide the guidance and authority needed to make decisions on my behalf:

I, _____ hereby declare and make known my instructions and wishes for my future health care. This advance directive for health care shall take effect in the event I become unable to make my own health-care decisions, as determined by the physician who has primary responsibility for my care, and any necessary confirming determinations. I direct that this document become part of my permanent medical records.

In completing Part One of this directive, you will designate an individual you trust to act as your legally recognized health care representative to make health care decisions for you in the event you are unable to make decisions for yourself.

In completing Part Two of this directive, you will provide instructions concerning your health care preferences and wishes to your health care representative and others who will be entrusted with responsibility for your care, such as your physician, family members and friends.

Part One: Designation of a Health Care Representative

A) CHOOSING A HEALTH CARE REPRESENTATIVE:
I hereby designate:

name _____

address _____

city _____ *state* _____

telephone _____

as my health care representative to make any and all health care decisions for me, including decisions to accept or to refuse any treatment, service or procedure used to diagnose or treat my physical or mental condition, and decisions to provide, withhold or withdraw life-sustaining measures. I direct my representative to make decisions on my behalf in accordance with my wishes as stated in this document, or as otherwise known to him or her. In the event my wishes are not clear, or a situation arises I did not anticipate, my health care representative is authorized to make decisions in my best interests, based upon what is known of my wishes.

I have discussed the terms of this designation with my health care representative and he or she has willingly agreed to accept the responsibility for acting on my behalf.

B) ALTERNATE REPRESENTATIVES: If the person I have designated above is unable, unwilling or unavailable to act as my health care representative, I hereby designate the following person(s) to act as my health care representative, in the order of priority stated:

1. *name* _____   2. *name* _____
   address _____   *address* _____
   city _____ *state* _____   *city* _____ *state* _____
   telephone _____   *telephone* _____

Part Two: Instruction Directive

In Part Two, you are asked to provide instructions concerning your future health care. This will require making important and perhaps difficult choices. Before completing your directive, you should discuss these matters with your health care representative, doctor, family members or others who may become responsible for your care.

*In **Sections C and D**, you may state the circumstances in which various forms of medical treatment, including life-sustaining measures, should be provided, withheld or discontinued. If the options and choices below do not fully express your* *wishes, you should use* **Section E,** *and/or attach a statement to this document which would provide those responsible for your care with additional information you think would help them in making decisions about your medical treatment.* **Please familiarize yourself with all sections of Part Two before completing your directive.**

C) GENERAL INSTRUCTIONS. To inform those responsible for my care of my specific wishes, I make the following statement of personal views regarding my health care:

Initial ONE of the following two statements with which you agree:

1. _____ I direct that all medically appropriate measures be provided to sustain my life, regardless of my physical or mental condition.

2. _____ There are circumstances in which I would not want my life to be prolonged by further medical treatment. In these circumstances, life-sustaining measures should not be initiated and if they have been, they should be discontinued. I recognize that this is likely to hasten my death. In the following, I specify the circumstances in which I would choose to forego life-sustaining measures.

If you have initialed statement 2, on the following page please initial each of the statements (a, b, c) *with which you agree:*

a. _____ I realize that there may come a time when I am diagnosed as having an incurable and irreversible illness, disease, or condition. If this occurs, and my attending physician and at least one additional physician who has personally examined me determine that my condition is **terminal,** I direct that life-sustaining measures which would serve only to artificially prolong my dying be withheld or discontinued. I also direct that I be given all medically appropriate care necessary to make me comfortable and to relieve pain.

In the space provided, write in the bracketed phrase with which you agree:

To me, terminal condition means that my physicians have determined that:

____ **[I will die within a few days]** ____ **[I will die within a few weeks]**
____ **[I have a life expectancy of approximately** _____ **or less** *(enter 6 months, or 1 year)]*

b. _____ If there should come a time when I become **permanently unconscious,** and it is determined by my attending physician and at least one additional physician with appropriate expertise who has personally examined me, that I have totally and irreversibly lost consciousness and my capacity for interaction with other people and my surroundings, I direct that life-sustaining measures be withheld or discontinued. I understand that I will not experience pain or discomfort in this condition, and I direct that I be given all medically appropriate care necessary to provide for my personal hygiene and dignity.

c. _____ I realize that there may come a time when I am diagnosed as having an **incurable and irreversible** illness, disease, or condition which may not be terminal. My condition may cause me to experience severe and progressive physical or mental deterioration and/or a permanent loss of capacities and faculties I value highly. If, in the course of my medical care, the burdens of continued life with treatment become greater than the benefits I experience, I direct that life-sustaining measures be withheld or discontinued. I also direct that I be given all medically appropriate care necessary to make me comfortable and to relieve pain.

(Paragraph c. covers a wide range of possible situations in which you may have experienced partial or complete loss of certain mental and physical capacities you value highly. If you wish, in the space provided below you may specify in more detail the conditions in which you would choose to forego life-sustaining measures. You might include a description of the faculties or capacities, which, if irretrievably lost, would lead you to accept death rather than continue living. You may want to express any special concerns you have about particular medical conditions or treatments, or any other considerations which would provide further guidance to those who may become responsible for your care. If necessary, you may attach a separate statement to this document or use Section E to provide additional instructions.)

Examples of conditions which I find unacceptable are:

_____

_____

_____

_____

D) SPECIFIC INSTRUCTIONS: Artificially Provided Fluids and Nutrition; Cardiopulmonary Resuscitation (CPR). _Above you provided general instructions regarding life-sustaining measures. Here you are asked to give specific instructions regarding two types of life-sustaining measures—artificially provided fluids and nutrition and cardiopulmonary resuscitation._

In the space provided, write in the bracketed phrase with which you agree:

1. In the circumstances I initialled on page 3, I also direct that artificially provided fluids and nutrition, such as by feeding tube or intravenous infusion,

[be withheld or withdrawn and that I be allowed to die]
[be provided to the extent medically appropriate]

2. In the circumstances I initialled on page 3, if I should suffer a cardiac arrest, I also direct that cardiopulmonary resuscitation (CPR)

[not be provided and that I be allowed to die]
[be provided to preserve my life, unless medically inappropriate or futile]

3. If neither of the above statements adequately expresses your wishes concerning artificially provided fluids and nutrition or CPR, please explain your wishes below.

E) ADDITIONAL INSTRUCTIONS: *(You should provide any additional information about your health care preferences which is important to you and which may help those concerned with your care to implement your wishes. You may wish to direct your health care representative, family members, or your health care providers to consult with others, or you may wish to direct that your care be provided by a particular physician, hospital, nursing home, or at home. If you are or believe you may become pregnant, you may wish to state specific instructions. If you need more space than is provided here you may attach an additional statement to this directive.)*

F) BRAIN DEATH: *(The State of New Jersey recognizes the irreversible cessation of all functions of the entire brain, including the brain stem (also known as whole brain death), as a legal standard for the declaration of death. However, individuals who cannot accept this standard because of their personal religious beliefs may request that it not be applied in determining their death.)*

Initial the following statement only if it applies to you:

_____ To declare my death on the basis of the whole brain death standard would violate my personal religious beliefs. I therefore wish my death to be declared solely on the basis of the traditional criteria of irreversible cessation of cardio-pulmonary (heartbeat and breathing) function.

G) AFTER DEATH—ANATOMICAL GIFTS: *(It is now possible to transplant human organs and tissue in order to save and improve the lives of others. Organs, tissues and other body parts are also used for therapy, medical research and education. This section allows you to indicate your desire to make an anatomical gift and if so, to provide instructions for any limitations or special uses.)*

Initial the statements which express your wishes:

1. _____ **I wish** to make the following anatomical gift to take effect upon my death:

   A. _____ any needed organs or body parts

   B. _____ only the following organs or parts

   _____

for the purposes of transplantation, therapy, medical research or education, or

   C. _____ my body for anatomical study, if needed.

   D. _____ special limitations, if any;

   _____

If you wish to provide additional instructions, such as indicating your preference that your organs be given to a specific person or institution, or be used for a specific purpose, please do so in the space provided below.

_____
_____
_____

2. _____ **I do not wish** to make an anatomical gift upon my death.

Part Three: Signature and Witnesses

H) COPIES: The original or a copy of this document has been given to the following people *(NOTE: If you have chosen to designate a health care representative, it is important that you provide him or her with a copy of your directive.):*

1. *name* _____   2. *name* _____
   address _____   *address* _____
   city _____ *state* _____   *city* _____ *state* _____
   telephone _____   *telephone* _____

I) SIGNATURE: By writing this advance directive, I inform those who may become entrusted with my health care of my wishes and intend to ease the burdens of decisionmaking which this responsibility may impose. I have discussed the terms of this designation with my health care representative and he or she has willingly agreed to accept the responsibility for acting on my behalf in accordance with this directive. I understand the purpose and effect of this document and sign it knowingly, voluntarily and after careful deliberation.

Signed this _____ **day of** _____, **19**____.

signature _____

address _____

city _____ *state* _____

J) WITNESSES: I declare that the person who signed this document, or asked another to sign this document on his or her behalf, did so in my presence, that he or she is personally known to me, and that he or she appears to be of sound mind and free of duress or undue influence. I am 18 years of age or older, and am not designated by this or any other document as the person's health care representative, nor as an alternate health care representative.

1. *witness* _____

   address _____

   city _____ *state* _____

   signature _____

   date _____

2. *witness* _____

   address _____

   city _____ *state* _____

   signature _____

   date _____

Prepared by the New Jersey Commission on Legal and Ethical Problems in the Delivery of Health Care (New Jersey Bioethics Commission) March 1991.

A Values Profile

I. Introduction

The following questionnaire is designed to guide your medical treatment after you have become incompetent (that is, you are unable to understand the nature and consequences of important medical decisions). The object is to instruct about what level of deterioration would warrant cessation of life-sustaining medical intervention on your behalf. Unless you indicate otherwise, you can assume that comfort care (care intended to keep you clean and comfortable) will always be provided.

Listed below are factors which some people consider important in shaping post-competence medical care. You are asked to give your own reactions to the various factors.

Some people's main concern is that their existence not be prolonged during the last stages of an unavoidable dying process (i.e., when they have been stricken with an incurable fatal condition). If that is your main concern, Section II below gives you a chance to indicate the time span which you consider the "last stage" of an unavoidable dying process.

Some people are more concerned about medical prolongation of their lives—whatever the possible survival period—after they have permanently deteriorated to a condition which they consider personally undignified and intolerable. If that is your main concern, Sections III through VIII below give you a chance to define the conditions which, for you, would be intolerable.

II. A Terminal Condition

In my post-competence state, if I face an incurable condition which, according to medical judgment, will cause my death with or without medical intervention, I want life-sustaining care to cease, as follows:

_____ when I have less than a year to survive

_____ when I have less than six months to survive

_____ when I have less than a month to survive

_____ when I have less than a week to survive

_____ none of the above; I want all life-sustaining care to be continued

_____ none of the above; I want my treatment to depend on my condition, not the remaining life span

III. Pain and Suffering

In my post-competence state, I am concerned about extreme pain to the following extent: (check one)

_____ intolerable; I prefer death

_____ a very negative factor, to be weighed with other factors in determining my best interests

_____ unimportant

My attitude toward pain which can be controlled only by substances which leave me drowsy and confused most of the time:

_____ intolerable

_____ a very negative factor, to be weighed with other factors in determining my best interests

_____ unimportant

IV. Mental Incapacity

In my post-competence state, I am concerned about the level of my mental deterioration to the following extent: (check one)

_____ a very critical factor

_____ important yet not determinative by itself, a factor to be weighed with other factors in determining my best interests

_____ unimportant

My attitude toward a permanently unconscious state, confirmed by up-to-date medical tests, showing no hope of ever regaining consciousness:

_____ intolerable; I prefer death

_____ tolerable

_____ tolerable, so long as insurance or

other nonfamily sources are paying the bills

My reaction to profound dementia to the point where I can no longer recognize
and interact with my loved ones:

_____ intolerable, I prefer death
_____ a very negative factor, to be
weighed with other factors in determining my best interests
_____ tolerable

My reaction to dementia to the point where I can no longer read and understand
written material:

_____ intolerable, I prefer death
_____ a very negative factor, to be
weighed with other factors in determining my best interests
_____ tolerable

V. Physical Immobility

In my post-competence state, I am concerned about physical immobility to
the following extent:

_____ important
_____ unimportant

My reaction to being permanently bedridden:

_____ intolerable; I prefer death
_____ a very negative factor, to be
weighed with other factors in determining my best interests
_____ tolerable

My reaction to being nonambulatory, meaning I can leave my bed but can
only move around in a wheelchair:

_____ intolerable; I prefer death
_____ a very negative factor, to be
weighed with other factors in determining my best interests
_____ tolerable

VI. Physical Helplessness

In my post-competence state, I am concerned about my independence and my ability to tend to my own physical needs to the following extent:

    _____ a very critical factor
    _____ important yet not determinative by itself, a factor to be weighed in determining my best interests
    _____ unimportant

My reaction to being incapable of feeding myself:

    _____ intolerable; I prefer death
    _____ a very negative factor, to be weighed with other factors in determining my best interests
    _____ a somewhat negative factor
    _____ unimportant

My reaction to being incapable of dressing myself:

    _____ intolerable; I prefer death
    _____ a very negative factor, to be weighed with other factors in determining my best interests
    _____ a somewhat negative factor
    _____ unimportant

My reaction to being incontinent:

    _____ intolerable; I prefer death
    _____ a very negative factor, to be weighed with other factors in determining my best interests
    _____ a somewhat negative factor
    _____ unimportant

VII. Interests of Loved Ones

In my post-competence state, the emotional and financial burdens imposed on my loved ones are of concern to the following extent:

    _____ a critical factor
    _____ an important factor, depending on degree of burden
    _____ unimportant

My reaction to emotional strain posed for my spouse or other loved ones surrounding me during my incompetency:

      _____ an important factor
      _____ a somewhat important factor
      _____ irrelevant; they owe it to me

My reaction to a financial burden being imposed on my spouse or other loved ones:

      _____ an important factor
      _____ a somewhat important factor
      _____ irrelevant; they can afford it
      _____ irrelevant; my life is the critical factor

My reaction to my assets being depleted by heavy medical expenses being used for my care:

      _____ an important factor
      _____ somewhat important
      _____ irrelevant; I earned it

VIII. Living Arrangements

I would find any of the following living arrangements intolerable so that, if there were no alternative, I would prefer cessation or withdrawal of life-sustaining medical care:

      _____ living at home, but with need for full-time help
      _____ living permanently in the home of one of my children or other relative
      _____ living permanently in a nursing home or other long-term care facility
      _____ being confined to a hospital with little or no hope of ever leaving

Notes

Introduction

1. See James F. Fries, "Aging, Natural Death, and the Compression of Morbidity," 303 New Eng. J. Med. 130 (1980). There are some predictions that medical science will ultimately prevail and conquer even degenerative ailments. See Silverstein, *The Conquest of Death* 13 (1979); Ellis, "Immortality Made Easy: A Short Guide to Longevity," in *Omni's Future Medical Almanac* 130 (Teresi & Adcroft eds., 1987). The likelihood, however, is that periods of chronic disability will be postponed and compressed, not eliminated entirely as factors in causing death. See Edward L. Schneider & Jacob A. Brody, "Aging, Natural Death, and the Compression of Morbidity: Another View," 309 New Eng. J. Med. 854 (1983); Binstock, "Health Care of the Aging: Trends, Dilemmas, and Prospects for the Year 2,000," in *Aging 2000: Our Health Care Destiny* (Gaity & Samorajski eds., 1985). Dying is unlikely to become outmoded.

2. Congressional Summary, "Losing a Million Minds: Confronting the Tragedy of Alzheimer's Disease and Other Dementias" 16–21 (Office of Technology Assessment 1987).

3. "The ultimate horror [is not] death but the possibility of being maintained in limbo, in a sterile room, by machines controlled by a stranger." In re *Torres*, 357 N.W. 2d 332, 340 (Minn. 1984).

4. See, e.g., John E. Ruark et al., "Initiating and Withdrawing Life Support," 318 New Eng. J. Med. 25, 27 (1988); Sidney H. Wanzer et al., "The Physician's Responsibility Toward Hopelessly Ill Patients," 320 New Eng. J. Med. 844 (1989); Charles L. Sprung, "Changing Attitudes and Practices in Forgoing Life-Sustaining Treatments," 263 JAMA 2211 (1990). Between 85% and 90% of critical-care health professionals acknowledge withholding life-sustaining treatment from patients deemed to have irreversible and terminal disease; see id. at 2213.

5. Appointment of a health-care agent is commonly accomplished by signing a durable power of attorney, pursuant either to a state law relating generally to durable powers of attorney or to a state law specifically providing for a durable power of attorney for health care (DPOA-HC). In this book I will treat a written designation of a health-care agent as a form of advance directive. This is done both because the designation is aimed at controlling post-competence medical handling and because it is frequently accompanied by substantive instructions to the designated agent.

1. The Bounds of Autonomy for Competent Medical Patients

1. Chapter 2 discusses the concept of prospective autonomy and describes the respect it has been accorded.

2. In re *Farrell*, 529 A.2d 404 (N.J. 1987); *State v. McAfee*, 385 S.E.2d 651 (Ga. 1989); *Satz v. Perlmutter*, 362 So. 2d 160 (Fla. Dist. Ct. App. 1978), aff'd, 379 So. 2d 359 (Fla. 1980); *Norwood Hosp. v. Munoz*, 564 N.E.2d 1017 (Mass. 1991); *Fosmire v. Nicoleau*, 551 N.E.2d 77 (N.Y. 1990); *McKay v. Bergstedt*, 801 P.2d 617 (Nev. 1990).

3. See *Farrell*, 529 A.2d at 412; Nancy S. Jecker & Donnie J. Self, "Medical Ethics in

the 21st Century: Respect for Autonomy in Care of the Elderly Patient," 6 J. Crit. Care 46, 46–51 (1991).

4. See Edmund D. Pellegrino & David C. Thomasma, "The Conflict Between Autonomy and Beneficence in Medical Ethics: Proposals for a Resolution," 3 J. Contemp. Health L. & Pol'y 23, 24 (1987); see also Jay Katz, *The Silent World of Doctor and Patient* (1984).

5. See *Schloendorff v. Society of New York Hosp.*, 105 N.E. 92, 93 (N.Y. 1914).

6. See, e.g., *Gray v. Romeo*, 697 F. Supp. 580, 588 (D.R.I. 1988); In re *Estate of Longeway*, 549 N.E.2d 292 (Ill. 1989); *Farrell*, 529 A.2d at 410; In re *Guardianship of Browning*, 568 So. 2d 4 (Fla. 1990); Thomas C. Marks, Jr., & Rebecca C. Morgan, "The Right of the Dying to Refuse Life Prolonging Medical Procedures: the Evolving Importance of State Constitutions," 18 Ohio N.U.L. Rev. 467 (1992).

7. Justice O'Connor raises this possibility in her concurring opinion in *Cruzan v. Director, Missouri Dep't of Health*, 110 S. Ct. 2841, 2858–59 (1990).

8. This last assertion—that an agent would enjoy the same range of decision-making power as a competent patient—is not intuitively self-evident. It is conceivable that a state would have to respect the appointment of an agent and accord that agent decision-making authority but would not have to give the agent as much choice as the competent patient would have. That is, it is conceivable that a state could impose its parens patriae authority (to protect helpless individuals) in order to limit the substantive choices which an agent or proxy can make. This is so because prospective autonomy (as reflected in advance directives) is not precisely the same thing as contemporaneous autonomy. The divergence is discussed in chapters 2 and 6.

9. *Cruzan*, 110 S. Ct. at 2841.

10. The parents' assertion was that even in the absence of autonomous choice by the now incompetent patient, the parents or some other guardian would be constitutionally entitled to make the same decision regarding terminal care that the patient would make if competent. In that fashion, the parents would be exercising Nancy's own constitutional interests. The attribution of autonomy-based rights to an unconscious patient (who has never issued prior, clear-cut instructions) raises fascinating and important constitutional questions. Those questions are beyond the scope of this book. This book treats situations where patients have issued advance instructions and have thereby exercised their autonomy interests.

11. *Cruzan*, 110 S. Ct. at 2852.

12. John A. Robertson, "Cruzan and the Constitutional Status of Nontreatment Decisions For Incompetent Patients," 25 Ga. L. Rev. 1139 (1991); Yale Kamisar, "When Is There a Constitutional "Right to Live?" 25 Ga. L. Rev. 1203 (1991); Thomas A. Eaton & Edward J. Larson, "Experimenting With the "Right to Die" in the Laboratory of the States," 25 Ga. L. Rev. 1253 (1991); James Bopp, Jr., & Daniel Avila, "The Due Process 'Right to Life' in *Cruzan* and its Impact on 'Right-to-Die' Law," 53 U. Pitt. L. Rev. 193 (1991).

13. There are scores of such decisions. See, e.g., the cases cited in note 6; see also Marks & Morgan, supra note 6, at 474.

14. *Cruzan*, 110 S. Ct. at 2852. For pre-Cruzan surveys of the relevant Supreme Court authorities, see Patricia Lerwick, Note, "Withdrawal of Life-Saving Treatment; Patients' Rights—Privacy Rights," 42 Me. L. Rev. 193, 199–208 (1990); Thomas Wm. Mayo, "Constitutionalizing the Right to Die", 49 Md. L. Rev. 1033, 112–25 (1990); Stewart G. Pollock, "Life and Death Decisions: Who Makes Them and By What Standards?" 41 Rutgers L. Rev. 505 (1989).

15. *Cruzan*, 110 S. Ct. at 2857.

16. *Snyder v. Massachusetts*, 291 U.S. 97, 105 (1934).

17. See *Moore v. City of East Cleveland*, 431 U.S. 494, 503 (1977); *Bowers v. Hardwick*, 478 U.S. 186, 192 (1986). See generally Susan R. Martyn & Henry J. Bourguignon, "Coming

to Terms with Death: The *Cruzan* Case," 42 Hastings L.J. 817, 848–50 (1991), regarding the role of history and tradition in defining fundamental liberty interests.

18. *Cruzan*, 110 S. Ct. at 2885. Justice Stevens speaks in terms of a "freedom to conform choices about death to individual conscience." *Id.* Arguably, this language might be read to embrace other forms of choosing death (such as assisted suicide or active euthanasia). I doubt that Justice Stevens intended such an expansive notion. The traditional freedom of conscience in dying to which he refers encompassed rejection of unwanted medical intervention and freedom to withdraw entirely from medical supervision and to die at home. The traditional freedom did not encompass active intervention to shorten natural dying processes. The distinction between a right to reject medical intervention and a right to die is discussed in detail later in this chapter.

19. *Cruzan*, 110 S. Ct. at 2890.

20. *Cruzan*, 110 S. Ct. at 2856–57.

21. For example, see the dissenting opinion of Justice Lynch in *Brophy v. New England Sinai Hosp., Inc.*, 497 N.E.2d 626, 642–44 (Mass. 1986).

22. See Philip G. Peters, Jr., "The State's Interest in the Preservation of Life: From Quinlan to Cruzan," 50 Ohio St. L.J. 891, 897 (1989); Martha A. Matthews, Note, "Suicidal Competence and the Patient's Right to Refuse Lifesaving Treatment," 75 Cal. L. Rev. 707, 719 (1987).

23. "[W]orse than the pain itself, is the frustration, bodily insult and the humiliation of having a stranger or some authority decide contrary to one's own wishes the quality, the nature, the form and the manner of one's own future life." In re *Farrell*, 514 A.2d 1342, 1346 (N.J. Super. Ct. Ch. Div. 1986), aff'd, 529 A.2d 404 (N.J. 1987).

24. See *Satz v. Perlmutter*, 362 So. 2d at 160; *Bouvia v. Superior Court*, 225 Cal. Rptr. 297, 305, 179 Cal. App. 3d 1127 (1986) (speaking to the "ignominy, embarrassment, humiliation, and dehumanizing aspects" felt by the patient in her helpless, debilitated state); see also In re *Conroy*, 486 A.2d 1209, 1249 (N.J. 1985) (Handler, J., concurring).

25. *Cruzan*, 110 S. Ct. at 2852–53.

26. *Cruzan*, 110 S. Ct. at 2855.

.27. See, e.g., polls cited in Justice O'Connor's concurring opinion in *Cruzan*, 110 S. Ct. at 2857 n.1; Times Mirror Center for the People and the Press, *Reflections of the Times: The Right to Die* 6 (1990); Star-Ledger/Eagleton Poll, in the Newark Star-Ledger, Aug. 10, 1988, at A1.

28. See *Bowers v. Hardwick*, 478 U.S. at 190.

29. *Roe v. Wade*, 410 U.S. 113 (1973).

30. See *Planned Parenthood v. Casey*, 112 S. Ct. 2791 (1992).

31. In re *President and Directors of Georgetown College*, 331 F.2d 1010 (D.C. Cir.), cert. den., 377 U.S. 978 (1964) (dissenting opinion).

32. See *McKay v. Bergstedt*, 801 P.2d at 622–23; *Norwood Hosp. v. Munoz*, 564 N.E.2d at 1021; *Guardianship of Browning*, 568 So. 2d at 10; In re *Guardianship of L.W.*, 482 N.W.2d 60, 65 (Wis. 1992); *Guardianship of Doe*, 583 N.E.2d 1263,1267 (Mass. 1992). Other post-*Cruzan* decisions speak of a common-law right to reject life-preserving medical treatment. See *Estate of Longeway*, 549 N.E.2d at 297; *Mack v. Mack*, 618 A.2d 744, 755 (Md. 1993).

33. See, e.g., Leanne J. Fisher, Note, "The Suicide Trap: Bouvia v. Superior Court and the Right to Refuse Medical Treatment," 21 Loy. L.A. L. Rev. 219, 251–52 (1987); C. Everett Koop and Edward R. Grant, "The 'Small Beginnings' of Euthanasia: Examining the Erosion in Legal Prohibitions Against Mercy Killing," 2 Notre Dame J.L. Ethics & Pub. Pol'y 1585 (1986); Stanley S. Herr et al., "No Place to Go: Refusal of Life-Sustaining Treatment by Competent Persons with Physical Disabilities," 8 Issues in L. & Med. 3, 27–33 (1992).

34. *Conroy*, 486 A.2d at 1223. See also *McAfee*, 385 S.E.2d at 652; *Norwood Hosp. v. Munoz*, 564 N.E.2d at 1023; *McKay v. Bergstedt*, 801 P.2d at 623.

35. E.g., David C. Blake, "State Interests in Terminating Medical Treatment," 19:3 Hastings Cent. Rep. 5, 6–7 (May 1989).

36. Thus, government could insist that a patient receive full information about the consequences of a terminal decision, including information about the resources which might be available to ease the patient's plight if life-preserving medical intervention were accepted. See *McKay v. Bergstedt*, 801 P.2d at 621.

37. See, e.g., In re *Rodas*, No. 86PR139, slip op. at 28 (Mesa City Colo. Dist. Ct. 1987). But see Herr, supra note 33, at 4 (arguing that some judges undermine respect for disabled lives in endorsing terminal decisions).

38. See In re *Gardner*, 534 A.2d 947, 955 (Me. 1987); *Fosmire v. Nicoleau*, 551 N.E.2d at 80; *Saunders v. State*, 492 N.Y.S.2d 510, 517 (Sup. Ct. 1985); *Norwood Hosp. v. Munoz*, 564 N.E.2d at 1023.

39. In re *Requena*, 517 A.2d 886, 891 (N.J. Ch. Div.), aff'd, 517 A.2d 869 (App. Div. 1986). Note also Justice Stevens's remark in *Cruzan*, 110 S. Ct. at 2885, that a patient's choice to reject life-preserving medical intervention "presupposes no abandonment of the desire for life."

40. *Farrell*, 529 A.2d at 411.

41. See *Satz v. Perlmutter*, 362 So. 2d at 162; *Superintendent of Belchertown State School v. Saikewicz*, 370 N.E.2d 417, 425–26 (Mass. 1977); In re *Quinlan*, 355 A.2d 647, 663–64 (N.J. 1976); Pollock, supra note 14, at 516.

42. The issue is particularly important in light of statutory measures in some states which ostensibly confine the effect of "living wills" or powers of attorney to situations where an incompetent patient's death is "imminent." It is conceivable that such measures are unconstitutional. The nature and effect of such statutory measures will be addressed in chapter 3.

43. I specify "a naturally occurring dying process" in order to avoid connotations of suicide. The relevance of suicide to rejection of life-preserving medical intervention is discussed in the next subsection.

44. See *Fosmire v. Nicoleau*, 551 N.E.2d at 82–83; In re *Peter*, 529 A.2d 419, 423 (N.J. 1987); *Bartling v. Superior Court*, 209 Cal. Rptr. 200, 224 (Ct. App. 1984).

45. See *McKay v. Bergstedt*, 801 P.2d at 624–25.

46. Id. See also *Bartling*, 209 Cal. Rptr. at 224; *McAfee*, 385 S.E.2d at 652.

47. The whole concept of "terminal" conditions is somewhat problematic. The dividing line between terminal illness and chronic, degenerative illness may be difficult to define and may or may not be relevant, depending on the context. See Sandra H. Johnson, "From Medicalization to Legalization to Politicization: O'Connor, Cruzan, and Refusal of Treatment in the 1990's," 21 Conn. L. Rev. 685, 704 (1989). Further discussion is devoted in chapter 3 to the meaning of terminal illness in the context of living wills and other advance directives.

48. See *Guardianship of Browning*, 568 So. 2d at 9–10; *McConnell v. Beverly Enterprises*, 553 A.2d 596, 609 (Conn. 1989) (Healy, J., concurring); Developments, "Medical Technology and the Law," 103 Harv. L. Rev. 1519, 1667 (1990); see also *Guardianship of L.W.*, 482 N.W.2d at 60, 74 (suggesting that state interests in preserving life weaken as a patient's chance of recovery wanes).

49. See James F. Childress, *Who should Decide? Paternalism in Health Care* 164–65 (1982).

50. There are commentators who read *McKay v. Bergstedt*, 801 P.2d at 617, 630–31, as endorsing the possible judicial override of a nonterminal patient's determination to reject life-preserving medical care. See Thomas A. Eaton & Edward J. Larson, "Experimenting With the Right to Die in the Laboratory of the States," 25 Ga. L. Rev. 1253, 1274–75 (1991); M. Lisa Wilson-Clayton & Mark Clayton, "Two Steps Forward, One Step Back: *McKay v. Bergstedt*," 12 Whittier L. Rev. 439, 456 (1991). That seems to me to be an erroneous interpretation of

Bergstedt. McKay v. Bergstedt, 801 P.2d at 621, does talk about a separate state interest in encouraging humane care of incapacitated persons whose lives can be significantly extended. The opinion explains that the state interest requires a careful effort to inform a patient about all rehabilitative opportunities before acquiescing in the patient's decision to reject continued life support; see id. at 625, 627, 630. This emphasis on providing information to a patient does not undermine judicial recognition of the patient's ultimate entitlement to determine his or her own medical fate.

51. See, e.g., *Public Health Trust of Dade County v. Wons*, 541 So. 2d 96, 97–98 (Fla. 1989); In re *Milton*, 505 N.E.2d 255 (Ohio 1987); In re *E. G.*, 549 N.E.2d 322, 327 (Ill. 1989); In re *Estate of Brooks*, 205 N.E.2d 435 (Ill. 1965); Charlotte K. Goldberg, "Choosing Life After Death: Respecting Religious Beliefs and Moral Convictions in Near Death Decisions," 39 Syracuse L. Rev. 1197 (1988).

52. *Norwood Hosp. v. Munoz*, 564 N.E.2d at 1021.

53. See *Fosmire v. Nicoleau*, 551 N.E.2d at 77; cf. *Peter*, 529 A.2d at 423.

54. All this is not to say that nonreligious patients who are salvageable to a healthful existence will widely seek to invoke a prerogative to reject lifesaving medical intervention. Most salvageable patients desire lifesaving treatment. Resistance from nonreligious patients comes primarily when the preservable existence is highly debilitated and therefore distasteful to the patient.

55. See, e.g., *McAfee*, 385 S.E.2d at 652; *McKay v. Bergstedt*, 801 P.2d at 624; *Bouvia v. Superior Court*, 225 Cal. Rptr. at 300; *Lane v. Candura*, 376 N.E.2d 1232 (Mass. App. Ct. 1978).

56. See Laurence H. Tribe, *American Constitutional Law*, § 15-11, at 1367–68 (2d ed. 1988); Peters, supra note 22, at 932.

57. See *Georgetown College*, 331 F.2d at 1008–09; *John F. Kennedy Hospital v. Heston*, 279 A.2d 670 (N.J. 1971), overruled by *Conroy*, 486 A.2d at 1209.

58. *Cruzan*, 110 S. Ct. at 2859.

59. See, e.g., *Fosmire v. Nicoleau*, 551 N.E.2d at 82; *Brophy*, 497 N.E.2d at 635; *Rasmussen v. Fleming*, 741 P.2d 674, 685 (Ariz. 1987). For more detailed discussion of the relation between suicide and rejection of medical treatment, see Norman L. Cantor, *Legal Frontiers of Death and Dying* 46–51 (1987); Robert F. Weir, *Abating Treatment with Critically Ill Patients* 295–98 (1989); Matthews, supra note 22, at 729–43; Fisher, supra note 33, at 244–50; Sanford H. Kadish, "Letting Patients Die: Legal and Moral Reflections," 80 Cal. L. Rev. 857, 864–68 (1992).

60. "It is possible for a patient to refuse treatment precisely because she ignores or denies the intrinsic value of her own life." Blake, supra note 35, at 8. See also Mathews, supra note 22, at 732, 738–41. For an example of a refusal of care grounded on the conviction that the patient's existence has become too painful or frustrating, see *Bouvia*, 225 Cal. Rptr. at 297, 304.

61. See New Jersey Commission on Legal and Ethical Problems in the Delivery of Health Care, *Problems and Approaches in Health Care Decisionmaking* 56 (1990); *McKay v. Bergstedt*, 801 P.2d at 625.

62. This distinction may blur where the patient has had some role in causing the fatal condition precipitating a decision to resist life-preserving treatment. For example, a patient who launches a hunger strike, or who causes a fatal condition by intentionally neglecting himself or herself, is not simply "letting nature take its course." Such a patient is behaving like a suicide. For discussion of hunger strikers, see Cantor, supra note 59, at 51–53.

63. See *Cruzan*, 110 S. Ct. at 2851–52; *Fosmire v. Nicoleau*, 551 N.E.2d at 80–81; In re *Greenspan*, 558 N.E.2d 1194, 1201 (Ill. 1990).

64. "Asserting the right to refuse medical treatment is not tantamount to committing suicide." *Rasmussen v. Fleming*, 741 P.2d at 685. See also *Bouvia*, 225 Cal. Rptr. at 306.

65. *Norwood Hosp. v. Munoz*, 564 N.E.2d at 1022 n.5.

66. See Richard J. Bonnie, "The Dignity of the Condemned," 74 Va. L. Rev. 1363, 1375–77, 1389–90 (1988).

67. See *Bouvia*, 225 Cal. Rptr at 301–02; *McKay v. Bergstedt*, 801 P.2d at 631; *McAfee*, 385 S.E.2d at 652.

68. See also *Farrell*, 529 A.2d at 411; *Requena*, 517 A.2d at 870; *Rodas*, No. 86PR139, slip op. at 28.

69. *McKay v. Bergstedt*, 801 P.2d at 617.

70. Id. at 634.

71. See, e.g., *By No Extraordinary Means: The Choice to Forgo Life-Sustaining Food & Water* (Joanne Lynn ed., 1986); Johnson, supra note 47, at 700–01; Kamisar, supra note 12, at 1220–24.

72. See Developments, supra note 48, at 1662 n.142. For discussion of the idea that a "fundamental" societal value may be viewed at different levels of abstraction, see Wojciech Sadurski, "Conventional Morality and Judicial Standards," 73 Va. L. Rev. 339, 377–79 (1987).

73. For a discussion of the artificial nutrition issue in the context of permanently unconscious patients, see Norman L. Cantor, "The Permanently Unconscious Patient, Non-Feeding, and Euthanasia," 15 Am. J.L. & Med. 381, 384–98 (1989).

74. See, e.g., Bonnie Steinbock, "The Removal of Mr. Herbert's Feeding Tube," 13:5 Hastings Cent. Rep. (Oct. 1983), 13–14; William E. May et al., "Feeding and Hydrating the Permanently Unconscious and Other Vulnerable Persons," 3 Issues in L. & Med. 203 (1987).

75. See *Requena*, 517 A.2d at 888; *McConnell*, 553 A.2d at 608–09.

76. For an analysis of causation parallel to the one presented here, see *Rodas*, No. 86PR139, slip op. at 26–27. *Rodas* involved a 34 year old man who was permanently paralysed from the neck down and afflicted by a "locked-in" syndrome. The court upheld the competent patient's right to order withdrawal of artificial nutrition maintaining his existence, and it viewed the trauma to the brainstem which had ended the swallowing reflex as the determinative cause of death.

77. See, e.g., Daniel Callahan, "On Feeding the Dying," 13:5 Hastings Cent. Rep. 22 (Oct. 1983).

78. See Robertson, supra note 12, at 1156.

79. See Charles L. Sprung, "Changing Attitudes and Practices in Forgoing Life-Sustaining Treatments," 263 JAMA 2211, 2212 (1990).

80. See *Barber v. Superior Court*, 195 Cal. Rptr 484, 490, 147, Cal. App. 3d 1006 (1983); *Conroy*, 486 A.2d at 1226.

81. *Brophy*, 497 N.E.2d at 641 n.2.

82. Ronald E. Cranford, "Neurological Syndromes and Prolonged Survival: When Can Artificial Nutrition and Hydration Be Forgone?" 19 Law, Med. & Health Care 13, 18 (1991); Joanne Lynn & Glover, "Ethical Decision Making in Enteral Nutrition," in *Enteral and Tube Feeding* 577 (Rombeau & Caldwell eds., 2d ed. 1990); see also Evan R. Collins, Jr., and Doran Weber, *The Complete Guide to Living Wills*, 51, 56 (1991).

83. Cranford, supra note 82, at 18.

84. Current Opinions of the Council on Ethical and Judicial Affairs of the A.M.A. § 2.18 (1986). For citation to other medical bodies which have adopted a similar posture, see *Peter*, 529 A.2d at 428.

85. President's Commission for the Study of Ethical Problems in Medicine and Biomedical and Behavioral Research, *Deciding to Forego Life-Sustaining Treatment*, 88–90 (1983); The Hastings Center Task Force on Death and Dying, *Guidelines on the Termination of Life-Sustaining Treatment and the Care of the Dying* 57–62 (1987).

86. E.g., *Guardianship of L.W.*, 482 N.W.2d at 66–67. See Martyn & Bourguignon, supra note 17, at 826 n.50, for a list of relevant cases. Only the Washington State Supreme Court

has been equivocal with regard to equating artificial nutrition with customary medical treatment; see *Farnum v. Crista Ministries*, 807 P.2d 830, 842–44 (Wash. 1991) (Dore, C.J., dissenting).

87. Robert I. Simon, "Silent Suicide in the Elderly," 17:1 Bull. Am. Acad. Psychiatric Law 83, 86 (1989).

88. *Estate of Longeway*, 549 N.E.2d at 296.

89. There are commentators who do argue that a patient does have a right to reject manual feeding. See Robertson, supra note 12, at 1175. Professor Yale Kamisar sees a possible dividing line between artificial nutrition and "natural" feeding, but he doubts whether courts will adhere to that line; see Kamisar, supra note 12, at 1224–27.

90. *Cruzan* 110 S. Ct. at 2852.

91. See In re *Caulk*, 480 A.2d 93, 96–97 (N.H. 1984); Contra *Zant v. Prevatte*, 286 S.E.2d 715 (Ga. 1982). For discussion of hunger strikers, see Cantor, supra note 59, at 26–30.

92. See *Department of Public Welfare v. Kallinger*, 580 A.2d 887, 892 (Pa. Common. Ct. 1990); *Von Holden v. Chapman*, 450 N.Y.S.2d 623, 624–25 (App. Div. 1982).

93. See In re *Plaza Health and Rehabilitation Center*, order dated Feb. 2, 1984 (N.Y. Sup. Ct., Onondaga County); In re *Brooks, and Good Samaritan Nursing Home*, decision dated June 9, 1987 (N.Y. Sup. Ct., Albany County). See also *A.B. v. C.*, 477 N.Y.S.2d 282, 284 (Sup. Ct. 1984) (dictum in petition of a severely incapacitated person whose petition was dismissed as being prematurely filed).

94. But see *Bouvia v. Superior Court* (*Bouvia I*), No. 159780 (Calif. Super. Ct., Riverside County, 1983), referred to in *Bouvia v. Superior Court*, 225 Cal. Rptr. 297, 300 (Ct. App. 1986).

95. See Justice O'Connor's concurring opinion in *Cruzan*, 110 S. Ct. at 2856; In re *Hier*, 464 N.E.2d 959, 964 (Mass. App. Ct. 1984); George J. Annas, "Foreclosing the Use of Force: A.C. Reversed," 20:4 Hastings Cent. Rep. 27, 29 (July 1990); B. Lo, "The Clinical Use of Advance Directives," in *Medical Ethics: A Guide for Health Professionals* 210 (J. Monagle ed., 1988).

96. For example, in In re *Storar*, 420 N.E.2d 64 (N.Y.), cert. den. 454 U.S. 858 (1981), the court authorized blood transfusions for a mentally disabled leukemia patient even though the patient had to be physically restrained; likewise, the result in *Conroy*, 486 A.2d at 1209, was to suggest maintenance of artificial nutrition for the incompetent, debilitated patient despite the patient's resistance. See also *Bouvia I*, supra note 94.

97. See Robert J. Moss & John LaPuma, "The Ethics of Mechanical Restraints," 21:1 Hastings Cent. Rep. 22 (Jan. 1991).

98. See, e.g., George P. Smith, II, "All's Well that Ends Well: Toward a Policy of Assisted Rational Suicide or Merely Enlightened Self-Determination?" 22 U.C. Davis L. Rev. 275 (1989); Steven J. Wolhandles, Note, "Voluntary Active Euthanasia for the Terminally Ill and the Constitutional Right to Privacy," 69 Cornell L. Rev. 363 (1984); Linda Carl, Note, "The Right to Voluntary Euthanasia," 10 Whittier L. Rev. 489 (1988); Kadish, supra note 59, at 864–68.

99. *Donaldson v. Vandekamp*, 4 Cal. Rptr. 2d 59, 64 (Ct. App. 1992).

2. Advance Directives and Problems of Prospective Autonomy

1. For perceptive discussions of the difficulties of future-oriented decisions, see Allen E. Buchanan & Dan W. Brock, *Deciding for Others* 101–07 (1989); Donald L. Beschle, "Autonomous Decisionmaking and Social Choice: Examining the Right to Die," 77 Ky. L.J. 319, 335–45 (1988–89); Sanford H. Kadish, "Letting Patients Die: Legal and Moral Reflections," 80 Cal. L. Rev. 857, 873–76 (1982).

2. See President's Commission for the Study of Ethical Problems in Medicine and Biomedical and Behavioral Research, *Deciding to Forego Life-sustaining Treatment* 140 (1983); David S. Rosettenstein, "Living Wills in the United States: The Role of the Family," 4 Conn.

Prob. L.J. 27, 32 (1988); Stuart J. Eisendrath & Albert R. Jonsen, "The Living Will: Help or Hindrance?" 249 JAMA 2054, 2055 (1983).

3. See *John F. Kennedy Hosp. v. Heston*, 279 A.2d 670 (N.J. 1971), overruled by In re *Conroy*, 486 A.2d 1209 (N.J. 1985); In re *President and Directors of Georgetown College*, 331 F.2d 1000 (D.C. Cir.), cert den., 377 U.S. 978 (1964); *United States v. George*, 239 F. Supp. 752 (D. Conn. 1965); *Powell v. Columbian Presbyterian Medical Center*, 267 N.Y.S.2d 450 (Sup. Ct. 1965); cf. *Holmes v. Silver Cross Hosp.*, 340 F. Supp. 125 (N.D. Ill. 1972).

4. See generally George J. Annas & Leonard H. Glantz, "The Right of Elderly Patients to Refuse Life-Sustaining Treatment," 64 Milbank Q. Supp. 2, at 95 (1986); Martha A. Matthews, Note, "Suicidal Competence and the Patient's Right to Refuse Lifesaving Treatment," 75 Cal. L. Rev. 707, 724–28 (1987); Edmund D. Pellegrino & David C. Thomasma, *For the Patient's Good* 148–62 (1988).

5. See In re *Westchester County Medical Center*, 531 N.E.2d 607, 613, 534 N.Y.S.2d 886, 892 (N.Y. 1988); Nancy M.P. King, *Making Sense of Advance Directives* 65–67 (1991).

6. The limited scope of a person's predictive capacity might become a factor influencing the interpretation of advance directives. In that context, limited predictive capacity serves as a reason to afford flexibility to the agent ultimately charged with administration of an advance directive. But limitations of predictive capacity ought not preclude enforcement of advance directives, especially if the directive is clearly expressed and the product of deliberation.

7. For perceptive discussion of the difficulties of future-oriented decisions, see Beschle, supra note 1, at 335–45; Buchanan & Brock, supra note 1, at 106–07.

8. Buchanan & Brock, supra note 1, at 107, 153.

9. See Rebecca S. Dresser & John A. Robertson, "Quality of Life and Non-Treatment Decisions for Incompetent Patients: A Critique of the Orthodox Approach," 17 Law, Med. & Health Care 234, 236 (1989); John A. Robertson, "Cruzan and the Constitutional Status of Nontreatment Decisions for Incompetent Patients," 25 Ga. L. Rev. 1139, 1180–82, 1185 (1991).

10. See John A. Robertson, "Second Thoughts on Living Wills," 21:6 Hastings Cent. Rep. 7 (1991); Bernard Lo, "Caring for Incompetent Patients: Is There a Physician on the Case?" 17 Law, Med. & Health Care 214, 215–16 (1989).

11. Dan W. Brock, "Trumping Advance Directives," 21:5 Hastings Cent. Rep. S5 (1991).

12. See, e.g., John A. Robertson, "Prior Agreements for Disposition of Frozen Embryos," 51 Ohio St. L.J. 407, 421 (1990).

13. Many commentators note the practical obstacles to advance directives but favor them as the best way to honor self-determination in the death-and-dying context. See Laurence A. Tribe, *American Constitutional Law*, § 16-31, at 1599 n.29 (2d ed. 1988); Robert M. Veatch, *The Patient as Partner* 59 (1987); Philip G. Peters, Jr., "The State's Interest in the Preservation of Life: From Quinlan to Cruzan," 50 Ohio St. L.J. 891, 936 (1989); Susan M. Wolf, "Nancy Beth Cruzan: In No Voice at All," 20:1 Hastings Cent. Rep. 39 (Jan. 1990)

14. "Patients who feel secure that their wishes will be respected are relieved of anxiety and are more likely to seek medical advice in a timely and open manner." Hackler, Mosely, & Vawter, *Advance Directives in Medicine* 4 (1989). See also Peters, supra note 13, at 938.

Professor Robert A. Burt laments people's lack of confidence in terminal care and in the "nurturant potential in our common social life." He analogizes the nurturant aspects of terminal care to positive "images of childhood and infancy." See Burt, "Withholding Nutrition and Mistrusting Nurturance: The Vocabulary of In re *Conroy*," 2 Issues in L. & Med. 317, 320–21 (1987). Unfortunately, most people don't want to complete their life cycle by returning to an infant's status, even if the care process carries with it certain symbolic value.

15. See Special Committee on Aging, U.S. Senate, *A Matter of Choice: Planning Ahead for Health Care Decisions* 4 (1989).

16. Kent W. Davidson et al., "Physicians' Attitudes on Advance Directives," 262 JAMA 2415, 2417 (1989).

17. Thomas Wm. Mayo, "Constitutionalizing the Right to Die", 49 Md. L. Rev. 103, 146 (1990); Developments, "Medical Technology and the Law," 103 Harv. L. Rev. 1519, 1164–65 (1990).

18. See In re *Estate of Longeway*, 549 N.E.2d 292, 303 (Ill. 1990) (Ward, J., dissenting).

19. See, e.g., Beschle, supra note 1, at 360; Rebecca Dresser, "Life, Death, and Incompetent Patients: Conceptual Infirmities and Hidden Values in the Law," 28 Ariz. L. Rev. 373, 389 (1986); Rebecca Dresser, "Relitigating Life and Death," 51 Ohio St. L.J. 425 (1990).

20. Concerning the deep Anglo-American respect for personal choice, see Bruce J. Winick, "Competency to Consent to Treatment: The Distinction Between Assent and Objection," 28 Hous. L. Rev. 15, 36–37 (1992); Gerald Dworkin, *The Theory and Practice of Autonomy* (1988).

21. Justices Brennan and Stevens, in their dissenting opinions in *Cruzan v. Director, Missouri Dep't of Health*, 110 S. Ct., were sensitive to people's legitimate concern about the images and recollections to be left with loved ones. They saw this element as a critical reason to respect people's death and dying choices. Id. at 2868 (Brennan, J., dissenting); id. at 2883–84 (Stevens, J., dissenting).

22. In re *Conroy*, 486 A.2d 1209, 1229 (N.J. 1985); *Brophy v. New England Sinai Hosp.*, 497 N.E.2d 626, 633–34 (Mass. 1986); *John F. Kennedy Memorial Hosp., Inc. v. Bludworth*, 452 So. 2d 921, 923 (Fla. 1984); In re *Guardianship of L.W.*, 482 N.W.2d 60, 65 (Wis. 1992); see George J. Alexander, "Death by Directive," 28 Santa Clara L. Rev. 67, 79 (1988); Jeffrey J. Delaney, Note, "Specific Intent, Substituted Judgment and Best Interests: A Nationwide Analysis of an Individual's Right to Die," 11 Pace L. Rev. 565, 571–89 (1991).

23. See In re *Spring*, 405 N.E.2d 115, 119 (Mass. 1980); *Superintendent of Belchertown State School v. Saikewicz*, 370 N.E.2d 417, 431 (Mass. 1977); Delaney, supra note 22, at 592–616.

24. See *Kennedy Hosp. v. Bludworth*, 452 So. 2d at 926; James F. Childress, "Dying Patients: Who's in Control?" 17 Law, Med. & Health Care 227, 229 (1989); Sandra H. Johnson, "From Medicalization to Legalization to Politicization: O'Connor, Cruzan and Refusal of Treatment in the 1990's," 21 Conn. L. Rev. 685, 692–93 (1989).

25. See, e.g., *Gray v. Romeo*, 697 F. Supp. 580, 587 (D.R.I. 1988); In re *Guardianship of Browning*, 543 So. 2d 258, 267 (Fla. Dist. Ct. App. 1989), aff'd, 568 So. 2d 4 (Fla. 1990); In re *Peter*, 529 A.2d 419, 423 (N.J. 1987).

26. *Thompson v. Oklahoma*, 108 S. Ct. 2687, 2693 n.23 (1988).

27. See *Conroy*, 486 A.2d at 1231: "[I]n the absence of adequate proof of the patient's wishes, it is naive to pretend that the right of self-determination serves as the basis for substituted decision-making." See also *Guardianship of Browning*, 543 So. 2d at 267, 269, 272–73.

28. "[T]he state must recognize the dignity and worth of such a person [a PVS patient] and afford to that person the same panoply of rights and choices it recognizes in competent persons." *Brophy*, 497 N.E.2d at 634. See also Tracy L. Merrit, "Equality for the Elderly Incompetent: A Proposal for Dignified Death," 39 Stan. L. Rev. 689, 704 (1987).

29. See *Youngberg v. Romeo*, 457 U.S. 307, 317 (1982).

3. Choosing the Best Format in Light of the Statutory Framework for Advance Directives

1. A helpful state-by-state summary is provided in Evan R. Collins, Jr., & Doron Weber, *The Complete Guide to Living Wills* (1991), a paperback published by the Society for the Right

to Die (now known as Choice in Dying). That same organization also publishes a compendium of state advance directive legislation, under the title *Refusal of Treatment Legislation*.

2. For citations to living-will type laws in 43 states, see George J. Alexander, "Time for a New Law on Health Care Advance Directives," 42 Hastings L.J. 755, 758 nn.14–15 (1991). For a chronicle of the development of living-will laws, see Marguerite A. Chapman, "The Uniform Rights of the Terminally Ill Act: Too Little, Too Late?" 42 Ark. L. Rev. 319, 322–49 (1989).

3. Concerning the forms often contained in living-will laws, see Craig P. Goldman, "Revising Iowa's Life-Sustaining Procedures Act: Creating a Practical Guide to Living Wills in Iowa," 76 Iowa L. Rev. 1137, 1153–54 (1991).

4. See generally Pat M. McCarrick, Scope Note No. 2, "Living Wills and Durable Powers of Attorney: Advance Directive Legislation and Issues," Kennedy Institute of Ethics (1990); Nancy M. P. King, *Making Sense of Advance Directives* (1991); Evan R. Collins & Doron Weber, *The Complete Guide to Living Wills* (1991); Alan Meisel, *The Right to Die* §§ 12.1 to .10 (1989); Elizabeth D. McLean, Note, "Living Will Statutes In Light of *Cruzan v. Director, Missouri Department of Health*: Ensuring That a Patient's Wishes Will Prevail," 40 Emory L.J. 1305 (1991); Craig K. Van Ess, Note, "Living Wills and Alternatives to Living Wills: A Proposal—The Supreme Trust," 26 Val. U. L. Rev. 567 (1992).

5. See White, "Living Will Statutes: Good Public Policy?" in *Advance Directives in Medicine* 46–47 (Andrew Hackler et al., eds., 1989); Sandra H. Johnson, "Sequential Domination, Autonomy and Living Wills," 9 W. New Eng. L. Rev. 113, 120–22 (1987).

6. See David Orentlicher, "Advance Medical Directives," 263 JAMA 2365, 2367 (1990) (reporting about a 1988 survey conducted for the A.M.A.); Times Mirror Center for the People and the Press, *Reflections of the Times: The Right to Die* 19 (June 1990) (reporting on a poll indicating that 14% of all adults and 24% of people over 64 had a living will); Gene C. Anderson et al., "Living Wills: Do Nurses and Physicians Have Them?" 86 Am. J. Nursing 271 (1986). A December 1991 report indicated that somewhere between 4% and 24% of adults have signed living wills. Susan M. Wolf et al., "Sources of Concern About the Patient Self-Determination Act," 325 New Eng. J. Med. 1666, 1667 (1991).

7. Alexander M. Capron, "The Burden of Decision," 20:3 Hastings Cent. Rep. 36 (June 1990).

8. A 1990 poll of 1,213 adults nationwide showed that 28% think that little or no attention is ultimately paid to a patient's prior instructions. See Times Mirror Center, supra note 6, at 1.

9. Joel M. Zinberg, "Decisions for the Dying: An Empirical Study of Physicians' Responses to Advance Directives," 13 Vt. L. Rev. 445, 475, 477–79, 491 (1989); David A. Peters, "Advance Medical Directives: The Case for the Durable Power of Attorney for Health Care," 8:3 J. Leg. Med. 437, 460 (1987); Elizabeth G. Patterson, "Planning for Health Care Using Living Wills and Durable Powers of Attorney," 42 S.C. L. Rev. 525, 549 (1991).

10. Concerning physicians' fear of liability as an influence on extending life-preserving medical intervention, see Lawrence J. Nelson & Ronald E. Cranford, "Legal Advice, Moral Paralysis, and the Death of Samuel Linares," 17 Law, Med. & Health Care 316 (1989); B. D. Colen, *The Essential Guide to a Living Will* 14–16 (1991).

11. See James F. Childress, "Ethical Criteria for Procuring and Distributing Organs for Transplantation," in *Organ Transplantation Policy* 91–92 (James Blumstein & Frank Sloan eds., 1989).

12. Patient Self-Determination Act of 1990 (PSDA), Pub. L. No. 101-508 § 4206, codified at 42 U.S.C.A. § 1395cc (West 1992).

13. See generally Kelly C. Mulholland, Note, "Protecting the Right to Die: The Patient Self-Determination Act of 1990," 28 Harv. J. on Legis. 609 (1991); Susan Wolf et al., supra note 6.

14. Living-will statutes tend to be "riddled with restrictions presumably attributable to excessive caution and lack of experience." Alexander, supra note 2, at 766. See also Marni J. Lerner, Note, "State Natural Death Acts: Illusory Protection of Individuals' Life-Sustaining Treatment Decisions," 29 Harv. J. on Legis. 175 (1992).

15. See Meisel, supra note 4, § 11.12; Gregory Gelfand, "Living Will Statutes: The First Decade," 1987 Wis. L. Rev. 737, 740–44; Lerner, supra note 14, at 188–97.

16. Robert M. Veatch, *Death, Dying and the Biological Revolution* 159 (2d ed. 1990).

17. See Idaho Code § 39-4503 (3) (1991); Md. Health-Gen. Code Ann. 5-601 (g) (1990); Tenn. Code Ann. § 32-11-103 (g) (Michie Supp. 1991); Lerner, supra note 14, at 189; Susan R. Martyn & Lynn B. Jacobs, "Legislating Advance Directives for the Terminally Ill: The Living Will and Durable Powers of Attorney," 63 Neb. L. Rev. 779, 779–91 (1984). The wording is sometimes "incurable or irreversible," but the terms are read conjunctively. See N.D. Cent. Code § 23-06.4-02 (7) (1991); cf. Uniform Rights of the Terminally Ill Act § 1 (9), 9B U.L.A. 612 (1987 & Supp. 1992) [hereinafter URTIA].

18. See In re *Spring*, 405 N.E.2d 115, 118 (Mass. 1980); In re *Lydia E. Hall Hosp.*, 455 N.Y.S. 706, 708 (Sup. Ct. 1982).

19. In a number of jurisdictions, the living-will statutes have been amended to include permanent unconsciousness as a point at which life sustaining care may be withdrawn. But this does not help patients with chronic debilitated conditions and degenerative diseases.

20. Many commentators have recognized this truism. See, e.g., Meisel, supra note 4, at § 11.12. A few states have amended their living-will statutes to clarify that a condition is "terminal" if it would cause death in the absence of the disputed medical intervention. See Mont. Code Ann. § 50-9-102 (14) (1991); Ohio Rev. Code Ann. § 2133.01 (AA) (Anderson Supp. 1991); Iowa Code Ann. § 144A.2 (8) (West 1989); S.C. Code Ann. § 44-77-20 (4) (Law Co-op Supp. 1991).

21. In re *Greenspan*, 558 N.E.2d 1194, 1203–04 (Ill. 1990).

22. Id. See also In re *Guardianship of Browning*, 568 So. 2d 4, 17 (Fla. 1990) (interpreting Florida's living-will statute in a similar fashion).

23. See, e.g., Iowa Code Annn. § 144A.2 (8) (West 1989); Tex. Health & Safety Code Ann. § 672.002 (6) (West Pamph. 1992); Ohio Rev. Code. Ann. § 2133.01 (AA) (Anderson Supp. 1991); Mo. Ann. Stat. § 459.010 (3), (6) (Vernon Supp. 1992); URTIA, supra note 17, § 1 (9) (Supp. 1992); Daniel D. King et al., "Where Death Begins While Life Continues," 31 So. Tex. L. Rev. 145, 180–81 (1990); Lerner, supra note 14, at 191–94. See also *Guardianship of Browning*, 568 So. 2d at 17 (achieving a similar result by judicial interpretation).

24. Collins & Weber, supra note 1, at 7.

25. See In re *Peter*, 529 A.2d 419, 425 (N.J. 1987).

26. See *Satz v. Perlmutter*, 362 So. 2d 160 (Fla. Dist. Ct. App. 1978), aff'd, 379 So. 2d 359 (Fla. 1980).

27. See generally Philip G. Peters Jr., "The State's Interest in the Preservation of Life: From *Quinlan* to *Cruzan*," 50 Ohio St. L.J. 891 (1989).

28. See Yale Kamisar, "When Is There a Constitutional "Right to Die"? When Is There No Constitutional "Right to Live"?" 25 Ga. L. Rev., 1203, 1211–12 (1991); Lerner, supra note 14, at 186.

29. See White, supra note 5, at 46–47. Johnson, supra note 5, at 120–22.

30. Ariz. Rev. Stat. Ann. § 36-3201 (4) (Supp. 1991); Wyo. Stat. § 35-22-101 (a)(iii) (1991); Wis. Stat. Ann. § 154.03 (Interim Supp. 1992) (allowing for withdrawal of artificial nutrition and hydration); Me. Rev. Stat. Ann. tit 18A, § 5-701 (b)(4) (West Supp. 1991).

31. Tenn. Code Ann. § 32-11-103 (5) (Michie Supp. 1991); Okla. Stat. Ann. tit. 63, § 3103 (West Supp. 1992); N.H. Rev. Stat. Ann. § 137-H:3 (Supp. 1991); Colo. Rev. Stat. Ann. § 15-18-104 (2.5)(A) (West Supp. 1991); Idaho Code § 39-4504 (Supp. 1991); Fl.

Stat. Ann. § 765.075 (1)(a) (West Supp. 1991); Haw. Rev. Stat. Ann. § 327 D-4 (Michie 1991); Md. Health-Gen. Code § 5-605 (Michie 1990) as interpreted by 73 Op. Att'y Gen. (Oct. 17 1988); S.C. Code Ann. § 44-77-20 (2) (Law Co-op Supp. 1991); Ore. Rev. Stat. Ann. § 127.580 (1990) (elective provision is in DPOA-HC law).

32. Ga. Code Ann. § 31-32-2 (5)(A) (Michie 1991); Mo. Ann. Stat. § 459.010 (3) (Vernon Supp. 1992); Ind. Code Ann. § 16-8-11-4 (West 1992); Iowa Code Ann. § 144A.2 (5) (West 1989); Utah Code Ann. § 75-2-1103 (6) (b) (Michie Supp. 1991); Ky. Rev. Stat. Ann. § 311.624 (5)(b) (Michie Supp. 1990). Another statute is silent as to whether artificial nutrition and hydration can be foregone, but it places on the physician the responsibility to provide any nutrition and hydration needed to alleviate pain; see Mont. Code Ann. § 50-9-202 (2) (Michie 1991).

33. Ill. Rev. Stat., ch. 110 1/2, para. 702 (d) (Smith-Hurd Supp. 1992).

34. N.D. Cent. Code § 23-06.4-07 (3) (1991). For assessment of the living-will laws regarding nutrition, see Lerner, supra note 14, at 199–204.

35. E.g., Colo. Rev. Stat. Ann. § 15-18-103 (7) (West Supp. 1991); R.I. Gen. Laws § 23-4.11-2 (d) (Supp. 1991); Tex. Health & Safety Code Ann. § 672.002 (6) (West Pamph. 1992).

36. See, e.g., Va. Code Ann. § 54.1-2982, 2984 (Michie 1991); Fla. Stat. Ann. § 765.05 (1) (West Supp. 1992); R.I. Gen. Laws § 23-4.11-2 (d), (3) (Supp. 1991); S.C. Code. Ann. § 44-77-50 (Law. Co-op Supp. 1991); URTIA, supra note 17, §§ 1 (4), 2 (B) (Supp. 1992).

37. This language has been criticized as delegating uninformed discretion to those ultimately in charge of terminal care for an incompetent patient. See Thomas J. Marzen, "The Uniform Rights of the Terminally Ill Act: A Critical Analysis," 1 Issues in L. & Med. 441, 459, 470 (1986); C. Everett Koop and Edward R. Grant, "The "Small Beginnings" of Euthanasia: Examining The Erosion of Legal Prohibitions Against Mercy-Killing," 2 Notre Dame J.L. Ethics & Pub. Pol'y 585, 609, 615 (1986). See also Chapman, supra note 2, at 388; George J. Annas & Leonard H. Glantz, "The Right of Elderly Patients to Refuse Life-Sustaining Treatment," 64 Milbank Q. Supp. 2, at 95, 142–43 (1986) (contending that the formulation has no practical application because it would only forbid treatment which would be medically inappropriate anyway).

38. See Molly C. Dyke, Note, "A Matter of Life and Death: Pregnancy Clauses in Living Will Statutes," 70 B.U. L. Rev. 867 (1990); Goldman, supra note 3, at 1157–59.

39. See Alexander, supra note 2, at 764.

40. See Fla. Stat. Ann. § 765.06 (West 1986); R.I. Gen. Laws § 23-4.11-4 (a) (Supp. 1991); Iowa Code Ann. § 144A.4 (1) (West 1989).

41. Annas & Glantz, supra note 37, at 143; see also Goldman, supra note 3, at 1161–62.

42. New Jersey Commission on Legal and Ethical Problems in the Delivery of Health Care, *Problems and Approaches in Health Care Decision Making* 106 (1990) [hereinafter Report of the New Jersey Bioethics Commission]; David S. Rosettenstein, "Living Wills in the U.S.: The Role of the Family," 4 Conn. Prob. L.J. 27, 38–39 (1988).

43. See Chapman, supra note 2, at 357.

44. See, e.g., Utah Code Ann. § 75-2-1108 (Michie Supp. 1991); cf. N.Y. Pub. Health Law § 2985 (1) (Consol. Supp. 1992).

45. The issue of how to relate to the expressions of incompetent patients is considered further in chapter 5 on administration and interpretation of advance directives.

46. Capron, supra note 7, at 41.

47. See California Medical Association, Committee on Evolving Trends in Society Affecting Life, "What Health Care Providers Should Know About Foregoing Life-sustaining Treatment," Calif. Physician, Nov. 1989, at 67; Report of the New Jersey Bioethics Commission, supra note 42, at 89–90.

48. See Peters, supra note 9, at 451. The advocacy role of a health-care agent is considered in more depth in chapter 7, which deals with enforcement of advance directives.

49. See sources cited supra note 9; see also New York State Task Force on Life and the Law, *Life-Sustaining Treatment: Making Decisions and Appointing a Health Care Agent* 77 (1987).

50. See Orentlicher, supra note 6, at 2365, 2366; Patterson, supra note 9, at 571.

51. Ben A. Rich, "The Values History: A New Standard of Care," 40 Emory L.J. 1009, 119 n.38 (1991) (provides citations for 34 DPOA-HC laws); see also Cathaleen A. Roach, "Paradox and Pandora's Box: The Tragedy of Current Right-to-Die Jurisprudence," 25 U. Mich. J. Law Reform 133, 162 (1991).

52. See *Guardianship of Browning*, 568 So. 2d at 4; In re *Westchester County Medical Center*, 531 N.E.2d 607, 612 n.2 (N.Y. 1988); *Peter*, 529 A.2d at 426.

53. See, e.g., Cal. Civ. Code § 2430 (b) (West Supp. 1992); Idaho Code 39-4505 (Supp. 1991); Kan. Stat. Ann. § 58-629 (Supp. 1991); Nev. Rev. Stat. Ann. § 449.830 (Michie 1991); Tex. Civ. Prac. & Remedies § 135.002 (a) (West Supp. 1992).

54. N.Y. Pub. Health Law § 2982 (1) (Consol. Supp. 1992).

55. Ohio Rev. Code Ann. § 1337.13 (B)(1), (E) (Anderson Supp. 1991); Ore. Rev. Stat. §§ 127.540, .580 (1990); Tenn. Code Ann. § 34-6-204 (d) (1991); Fla. Stat. Ann. § 765.05 (2) (West 1986).

56. Ky. Rev. Stat. Ann. § 311.978 (1) (Michie Supp. 1990).

57. See, e.g., Md. Health-General Code Ann. § 20-107 (d)(1) (Supp. 1991); Utah Code Ann. § 75-2-1105 (2) (Supp. 1991); Va. Code Ann. § 37.1-134.4 (1991); Nev. Rev. Stat. Ann. § 449.626 (2) (1991); Veatch, supra note 16, at 163–64. See Judith Areen, "Advance Directives Under State Law and Judicial Decisions," 19 Law, Med. & Health Care 91, 97–98 (1991); David M. Schultz, Note, "Procedures and Limitations for Removal of Life-Sustaining Treatment from Incompetent Patients," 34 St. Louis U. L.J. 277, 279–80 (1990).

58. See Conn. Gen. Stat. § 19a-571 (West Supp. 1991); Fla. Stat. Ann. § 765.07 (West 1986 & Supp. 1992); Iowa Code § 144A.7 (West 1989); Me. Rev. Stat. Ann. tit. 18A, § 5-707 (West Supp. 1991); Nev. Rev. Stat. Ann. § 449.626 (Michie 1991).

59. Richard F. Uhlmann et al. "Physicians' and Spouses' Predictions of Elderly Patients' Resuscitation Preferences," 43 J. Gerontology: Medical Sciences M115, M117–20 (1988). The study analyzed the wishes of 258 elderly, chronically ill persons compared to the assumptions of surrounding physicians and family. The results suggested that "surrogate resuscitation decisions for elderly patients would often not approximate patients' wishes, even when surrogate decisionmakers appear to know the patients well and believe they are exercising substituted judgment." Id. at M120.

60. See King, supra note 4, at 91.

61. Susan J. Nanovic, Note, "The Living Will: Preservation of the Right-to-Die Demands Clarity and Consistency," 95 Dick. L. Rev. 209, 229 (1990).

62. The possibility of justifiable deviations from the substantive terms of an advance directive is addressed in chapter 5 dealing with administration of an advance directive.

63. Ill. Ann. Stat., ch. 110 1/2, para. 804-11 (Smith-Hurd Supp. 1992).

64. The only deviation from this pattern comes in a few states whose living-will laws do not give conclusive effect to the declarant's instructions. See Conn. Gen. Stat. Ann. § 199-571 (West Supp. 1992); Nev. Rev. Stat. Ann. § 449-640 (1) (Michie 1991): N.D. Cent. Code § 23-06.4-04 (Michie 1990); Ind. Code Ann. § 16-8-11-11 (6) (West 1992).

65. Even a health-care provider with conscientious objections to the declarant's wishes must either implement the living will or seek transfer of the patient to another provider. The impact of health-care providers' scruples will be discussed in chapter 5, which deals with administration of advance directives.

66. Not long ago, I published a suggested advance directive. See Norman L. Cantor, "My Annotated Living Will," 18 Law, Med. & Health Care 114 (1990). In that publication, I called the document a *living will*. I've changed my mind, at least with regard to jurisdictions with significant statutory limitations on the scope of living wills. In such instances, I would now recommend labeling the document a *nonstatutory advance directive* or *instruction directive*, unless the limitations contained in the relevant living-will law do not interfere with the particular declarant's wishes.

67. For endorsement of the idea of nonstatutory instruction directives, see King, supra note 4, at 9–10, 17, 97–98; Patterson, supra note 9, at 538–40.

68. Idaho Code § 39-4508 (1985); Iowa Code Ann. § 144A.11 (5)(1989); Fla. Stat. Ann. § 765.15 (West 1986); Cal. Health and Safety Code § 7195.5 (d) (West Supp. 1992); Gelfand, supra note 15, at 784 n.202; see also Lerner, supra note 14, at 191 n.72.

69. Chapters 1 and 2 already explained the great extent to which American jurisprudence has embraced self-determination in the context of shaping medical intervention in the dying process.

70. In re *Finsterbach* (N.Y. Sup. Ct., Oneida County 1990).

71. See In re *Gardner*, 534 A.2d 947, 952 n.3 (Me. 1987); *Camp v. White*, 510 So. 2d 166, 169–70; and cases cited in Tribe, *American Constitutional Law* § 15-12, at 1370 (2d Ed. 1988). Cf. *Bouvia v. Superior Court*, 179 Cal. App. 3d 1127, 1139–40, 225 Cal. Rptr. 297, 302–03 (1986) (regarding the import of a preservation of rights provision in a living-will law).

72. For comments supporting such a possible interpretation of legislative intent, see Report of the New Jersey Bioethics Commission, supra note 42, at 112–13; Prefatory Note and Comments to Section 2 of URTIA, supra note 17, § 2 (noting that the Act does not in any way affect authority under existing law). See also In re *Guardianship of Browning*, 543 So. 2d 258, 265 (Fla. App. 1989), aff'd 568 So. 2d 4 (Fla. 1990).

73. See Collins & Weber, supra note 1, at 45–46, 66, 87; King, supra note 4, at 102–03.

74. *Cruzan v. Harmon*, 760 S. W.2d 408, 419–20 (Mo. 1988), aff'd sub. nom., *Cruzan v. Director, Missouri Dept. of Health*, 110 S. Ct. 2841 (1990).

75. *Cruzan v. Harmon*, 760 S. W.2d at 420, 426. In December 1990, though, a Missouri trial court approved the removal of artificial nutrition from Ms. Cruzan. Missouri had adopted a DPOA-HC law permitting the removal of artificial nutrition in some circumstances.

76. *Couture v. Couture*, 549 N.E.2d 571 (Ohio Ct. App. 1989).

77. Ohio Rev. Code 1337.13 (B)(3) (1989).

78. *Couture*, 541 N.E.2d at 576. The same argument was accepted by the dissenting opinion in In re *Estate of Longeway*, 549 N.E.2d 292, 307–14 (Ill. 1989). In Illinois, however, the supposed public policy was more murky, since the DPOA-HC authorized cessation of nutrition while the living-will law did not. See *Greenspan*, 558 N.E.2d at 1200–04, and In re *Lawrance*, 579 N.E.2d 32, 40 (Ind. 1991). There have been post-Couture developments in Ohio. See *Anderson v. St. Francis Hosp.*, slip op. at 6 (Ohio Ct. Common Pleas 1989).

79. In my estimation, a careful analysis of the U.S. Supreme Court's 1990 Cruzan decision does not undercut that judicial trend. But see James Bopp, Jr., & Daniel Avila, "The Due Process 'Right to Life' in Cruzan and its Impact on 'Right-to-Die Law'," 53 Pitt. L. Rev. 193 (1991).

80. See Lerner, supra note 14, at 205–06.

81. See *Guardianship of Browning*, 568 So. 2d at 4; *Rasmussen v. Fleming*, 741 P.2d 674 (Ariz. 1987); In re *Crabtree*, No. 86-0031 (Haw. Fam. Ct., 1st Cir., April 26, 1990).

82. E.g., In re *Conroy*, 486 A.2d 1209, 1229 (N.J. 1985); *Brophy v. New England Sinai Hosp.*, 497 N.E.2d 626, 633 (Mass. 1986).

83. See *Guardianship of Browning*, 568 So. 2d at 9; *State v. McAfee*, 385 S.E.2d 651, 652 (Ga. 1989); In re *Drabick*, 245 Cal. Rptr. 840, 860 (Dist. Ct. App. 1988), cert. denied, 488 U.S. 958 (1989).

4. Drafting Advance Instructions

1. Charles P. Sabatino, *Health Care Powers of Attorney* 3 (A.B.A. pamphlet 1990) (distributed by the American Association of Retired Persons) [hereinafter *ABA Power of Attorney*]. The formula is offered in the A.B.A. document as an option, not as a recommended provision.

2. Concerning the multiplicity of factors which might influence the preparation of an advance directive, see, e.g., New Jersey Commission on Legal and Ethical Problems in the Delivery of Health Care, *Problems and Approaches in Health Care Decisionmaking* 87–88 (1990); Nancy R. Zweibel, "Measuring Quality of Life Near the End of Life," 260 JAMA 839, 840 (1988); Stuart J. Eisendrath & Albert R. Jonsen, "The Living Will; Help or Hindrance," 249 JAMA 2054 (1983); Linda L. Emanuel & Ezekiel J. Emanuel, "The Medical Directive: A New Comprehensive Advance Care Document," 261 JAMA 3288 (1989).

3. Joanne Lynn, "Why I Don't Have a Living Will," 19 Law, Med. & Health Care 101 (1991).

4. Id. at 101–04.

5. Letter from Ellen Friedland, Esq., December 1991.

6. See Robert S. Olick, "Approximating Informed Consent and Fostering Communication: The Anatomy of an Advance Directive," 2 J. Clinical Ethics 181, 185 (1991). Olick describes there how Professor George Annas recommends that the health-care agent receive a private letter from the principal, a letter to be disclosed and used only if necessary to convince health-care providers to cooperate with the agent.

7. Even Dr. Lynn advises that written instructions might be useful if the declarant's wishes deviate from what common medical approaches would normally dictate. Lynn, supra note 4, at 104.

8. See generally, Nancy M.P. King, *Making Sense of Advance Directives* 67, 112–13 (1991).

9. Concern for Dying recently merged with the Society for the Right to Die to form an organization known as Choice in Dying.

10. Quoted in Eisendrath & Jonsen, supra note 2, at 2055.

11. See Leflar, "A Framework for Legal Analysis of Advance Directives in Health Care," in *Advance Directives in Medicine* 60 (Andrew Hackler et al. eds., 1989)

12. See supra note 9.

13. An identical form appears in Pat M. McCarrick, "Living Wills & Durable Powers of Attorney: Advance Directive Legislation and Issues," Scope Note No. 2 (Kennedy Institute of Ethics 1990).

14. For criticism of the vagueness of many short-form living wills, see, e.g., King, supra note 8, at 10–11; Robert M. Veatch, *Death, Dying and the Biological Revolution* 149–52 (rev. ed. 1989); Olick, supra note 6, at 183.

15. See, e.g., Va. Code Ann. § 54.1-2984 (Michie 1991); Ariz. Rev. Stat. Ann. § 36-32-2 (Supp. 1991); Idaho Code § 39-4504 (Supp. 1991).

16. See, e.g., Me. Rev. Stat. Ann. tit. 18-A, § 5-702 (b) (West Supp. 1991); Uniform Rights of the Terminally Ill Act § 2(b), in 9B U.L.A. Supp. 1992, at 101.

17. Veatch, supra note 14, at 154–55.

18. *ABA Power of Attorney*, supra note 1, at 3.

19. *Evans v. Bellevue Hosp.* (N.Y. Sup. Ct. 1987), reported in N.Y.L.J., July 28, 1987, at 1, 11.

20. King, supra note 8, at 139–40; B. D. Colen, *The Essential Guide to a Living Will* 26, 117 (1991); Evan R. Collins, Jr., & Doron Weber, *The Complete Guide to Living Wills* 76

(1991); Ben A. Rich, "The Values History: A New Standard of Care," 40 Emory L.J. 1109, 1121–22 (1991).

21. Colen recommends a videotape as an additional index of the declarant's seriousness and determination. Colen, supra note 20, at 131–37.

22. See Collins & Weber, supra note 20, at 22; Elizabeth G. Patterson, "Planning for Health Care Using Living Wills and Durable Powers of Attorney: A Guide for the South Carolina Attorney," 42 S.C. L. Rev. 525, 579 (1991). Veatch, supra note 14, at 152.

23. For another commentary explaining why it is usually pointless to specify types of medical intervention in an advance directive, see Allan S. Brett, "Limitations of Listing Specific Medical Interventions in Advance Directives," 266 JAMA 825, 826–27 (1991).

24. See Colen, supra note 20, at 128–29. Ms. Colen explains that writing, playing guitar, and photography are the pursuits which make life worthwhile for her, so that permanent loss of mental acuity would be personally intolerable.

25. See Collins & Weber, supra note 20, at 64.

26. New Jersey Commission on Legal and Ethical Problems in Medicine, *Advance Directives for Health Care: Planning Ahead for Important Health Care Decisions* (1991); see also Appendix C.

27. Norman L. Cantor, "My Annotated Living Will," 18 Law, Med. & Health Care 114 (1990).

28. Upon reflection, I might add a sentence indicating that the directive is aimed at binding any ultimate decision maker on my behalf, in the event that neither designated agent were available. Such a provision ought to be unnecessary, for its content ought to be self-evident; but it might be added out of an excess of caution.

29. For a more detailed enumeration of a health-care agent's powers, see the sample power of attorney for health care drafted by Charles Sabatino, *ABA Power of Attorney*, supra note 1, at 1–2. A version of that useful sample document is provided as Appendix B.

30. See Ronald E. Cranford, "Neurological Syndromes and Prolonged Survival: When Can Artificial Nutrition and Hydration be Forgone?" 19 Law, Med. & Health Care 13, 19–20 (1991); Eric J. Cassell, "Recognizing Suffering," 21:3 Hastings Cent. Rep. 24, 26–27 (May 1991).

31. See Brett, supra note 23, at 826; Alan B. Handler, "Individual Worth," 17 Hofstra L. Rev. 493 (1989).

32. In an earlier version of my advance directive, I included a sentence providing a "standard of proof" for my designated agent. I stated: "In line with my normal preference and respect for life, any such terminal decision should be made only when that decision is *clearly* in my best interests." Upon further reflection, I've dispensed with that admonition. I am apprehensive that the word "clearly" would inhibit my agent in sound administration of the document. The substantive terms of my advance directive indicate that life-preserving treatment is to be withheld only when I have reached a status of extreme debilitation. Good-faith implementation of those instructions should foreclose any premature withdrawal of life support. Good-faith implementation is the minimum standard that the law would demand in any event, and I see no need to specify any further standard of proof.

33. See A.M.A. Council on Scientific Affairs and the Council on Ethical and Judicial Affairs, "Persistent Vegetative State and the Decision to Withdraw or Withhold Life Support," 263 JAMA 426 (1990); Ronald E. Cranford "The Persistent Vegetative State: The Medical Reality," 18:1 Hastings Cent. Rep. 27 (Feb. 1988).

34. Nonlife-extending palliative care should always be provided. Sometimes, though, a preventive medical measure may itself diminish a patient's self-defined dignity. For example, a tracheotomy designed to prevent choking in a patient who has lost a gag reflex can have negative consequences for the communication abilities of the patient. See Eisendrath & Jonsen, supra note 2, at 2056.

35. Alan Lieberson, letter to the editor, New York Times, Dec. 21, 1991, at A18.

36. King, supra note 8, at 90; Olick, supra note 6, at 183; Linda Emanuel, "PSDA in the Clinic," 21:5 Hastings Cent. Rep. S6 (Oct. 1991).

37. After an advance directive is prepared, further discussion must ensue. That is, the declarant ought to discuss the contents of his or her directive both with any agent designated in the document and with any physician likely to be attending during a subsequent dying process.

38. See Rich, supra note 20, at 1141–43, 1155–58; Olick, supra note 6, at 182–83.

39. Pam Lambert et al., "The Values History: An Innovation in Surrogate Medical Decision Making," 18 Law, Med. & Health Care 202 (1990); see also David J. Doukas & Laurence B. McCullough, "Assessing the Values History of the Elderly Patient Regarding Critical and Chronic Care," in *Handbook of Geriatric Assessment* 111–25 (J. Gallo et al. eds., 1988).

40. Not surprisingly, the compilers of the values history recommend preparation of a separate advance directive. They view their values history merely as an informational tool to assist future interpretation of a separate advance directive. Lambert, supra note 39, at 210; see also Collins & Weber, supra note 20, at 104–05.

41. Emanuel & Emanuel, supra note 2, at 3288, 3290.

42. Id. at 3290.

43. See Ezekiel J. Emanuel & Linda L. Emanuel, "Living wills: Past, Present, and Future," 1 J. Clinical Ethics 9 (1990).

44. Veatch, supra note 14, at 152.

45. See Collins & Weber, supra note 20, at 52; see also Appendix B.

46. See, e.g., Ala. Code § 22-8A-7 (1990); Ark. Code Ann. § 20-17-208 (Michie 1991); Iowa Code Ann. § 144A.9 (2) (West 1989).

47. Colen, supra note 20, at 130.

5. Interpretation and Administration of Advance Directives

1. These include living-will forms distributed by various right-to-die organizations as well as documents circulated as either required or suggested forms pursuant to living-will statutes.

2. Allan S. Brett, "Limitations of Listing Specific Medical Interventions in Advance Directives," 266 JAMA 825, 826 (1991).

3. An assessment of suffering is itself a herculean task. See Eric J. Cassell, "Recognizing Suffering," 21:3 Hastings Cent. Rep. 24 (May-June 1991).

4. See Nancy M.P. King, *Making Sense of Advance Directives* 58–60 (1991) (rejecting any heightened standard of capacity for the making of an advance directive).

5. This does not mean that compliance with the declarant's wishes is the exclusive guideline. There are a few jurisdictions which indicate that the administrator of a living will need only "consider" or "give great weight" to the declarant's wishes. See Nev. Rev. Stat. Ann. § 449.640 (1) (Michie 1991) (immunity to physicians who "give great weight to the declaration" but "consider other factors. . . . "); Conn. Gen. Stat. Ann. § 19a-571 (a) (West Supp. 1992) (immunity to physicians who used "best medical judgment [and] . . . considered the patient's wishes"); Ind. Code Ann. § 16-8-11 (f) (West 1992); N.D. Cent. Code § 23-06.4-04 (1991).

6. Haw. Rev. Stat. § 327D-19 (1991) (family court may be petitioned for appointment of a guardian for declarant whose living will is not being followed); Del. Code Ann. tit. 16, § 2506 (a) (1983); Me. Rev. Stat. Ann. tit. 18-A, § 5-707 (f) (West Supp. 1992).

7. See, e.g., *Brophy v. New England Sinai Hosp., Inc.*, 497 N.E.2d 626, 639 (Mass. 1986); In re *Gardner*, 534 A.2d 947 (Me. 1987).

8. See, e.g., Elizabeth D. McLean, Note, "Living Will Statutes in Light of *Cruzan v. Director, Missouri Department of Health*: Ensuring That a Patient's Wishes Will Prevail," 40 Emory L.J. 1305, 1316–17 (1991).

9. See, e.g., Cal. Civ. Code § 2433 (a) (West Supp. 1992); Idaho Code § 39-4505 (Supp. 1991); N.Y. Pub. Health Law § 2982 (2) (Supp. 1992); Miss. Code Ann. § 41-41-163 (Supp. 1992); Ore. Rev. Stat. Ann. § 127.550 (1)(b) (1990); R.I. Gen. Laws § 23-4.10-2 (1989); Nev. Rev. Stat. Ann. § 449.830 (Michie 1991). Not all DPOA-HC laws confer such expansive authority on an appointed agent. For example, West Virginia confines the agent's authority to withdraw life-sustaining care to situations where medical intervention offers "no medical hope of benefit." W. Va. Code § 16-30A-4 (c)(6) (1991).

10. See Michael P. Kane, "The Application of the Substitution of Judgment Doctrine in Planning an Incompetent's Estate," 16 Vill. L. Rev. 132, 133 (1970); In re *Turner*, 305 N.Y.S.2d 387, 389 (Sup. Ct. 1969).

11. In re *Peter*, 529 A.2d 419, 426 (N.J. 1987); In re *Guardianship of L.W.*, 482 N.W.2d 60, 70 (Wis. 1992); See Craig K. Van Ess, Note, "Living Wills and Alternatives to Living Wills: A Proposal—The Supreme Trust," 26 Val. U.L. Rev. 567, 584 (1992).

12. Robert S. Olick, "Approximating Informed Consent and Fostering Communication: The Anatomy of an Advance Directive," 2:3 J. Clinical Ethics 181, 186 (1991).

13. See Mich. Stat. Ann. § 27.5496 (7)(f), (9) (Callaghan 1992); Van Ess, supra note 11, at 588 n.125; N.J. Stat. Ann. §§ 26:2H-63(d), -64(b) (West Supp. 1992).

14. Several jurisdictions beside Missouri impose a clear and convincing evidence standard when an incompetent patient's life-sustaining care is withdrawn in reliance on the patient's prior instructions. See In re *Westchester County Medical Center*, 531 N.E.2d 607, 613 (N.Y. 1988); *Gardner*, 534 A.2d at 952; In re *Longeway*, 549 N.E.2d 292, 300 (Ill. 1989). It's not clear, though, that these jurisdictions demand clear-cut prior instructions as the exclusive predicate for withdrawal of life support. Neither *Longeway* nor *Gardner*, for example, determines whether a patient's best interests might be used as a rationale for withdrawing life support in the absence of prior instructions. See *Longeway*, 549 N.E.2d at 300; *Gardner*, 534 A.2d at 952. And none of the above three cases involves action by an appointed health-care agent. A DPOA-HC type statute might well have changed the result in New York and Illinois. See N.Y. Pub. Health Law § 2982 (2) (McKinney Supp. 1992) (1990 law allowing agent to make all decisions without clear-cut evidence, except withholding of artificial nutrition and hydration).

15. *Browning v. Herbert*, 568 So. 2d 4 (Fla. 1990).

16. See In re *Conroy*, 486 A.2d 1209, 1230–31 (N.J. 1985); Allen E. Buchanan & Dan W. Brock, *Deciding for Others* 119–22 (1989).

17. See N.J. Stat. Ann. § 26:2H-57(b)(1) (West Supp. 1992).

18. Expressions inconsistent with an advance directive's contents might also be uttered *after* the declarant has become incompetent. The appropriate status of such post-competence expressions is considered later in this chapter.

19. See, e.g., Louise Harmon, "Falling Off the Vine: Legal Fictions and the Doctrine of Substituted Judgment," 100 Yale L.J. 1, 38 (1990); Larry R. Churchill, "Trust, Autonomy, and Advance Directives," 28 J. Religion and Health 175 (1989).

20. However, evidence of a patient's altruism must be used with caution. Arguably, the interests of others (family, friends, or health care providers) should be weighed in terminal care decisions only if so provided by the declarant. See Norman L. Cantor, "*Conroy*, Best Interests, and the Handling of Dying Patients," 37 Rutgers L. Rev. 543, 576–77 (1985).

21. This language was used by a declarant in *Saunders v. State*, 492 N.Y.S.2d 510, 512 (Sup. Ct. 1985).

22. Cf. Ohio Rev. Code Ann. § 1337.13 (f) (Anderson Supp. 1991).

23. For consideration of this issue relating to family members' interests, see Lawrence J. Schneiderman & Roger C. Spragg, "Ethical Decisions in Discontinuing Mechanical Ventilation," 318 New Eng. J. Med. 984, 987 (1988); Bernard Lo, "Caring for Incompetent Patients: Is There a Physician on the Case?" 17:3 Law, Med. & Health Care 214 (1989).

24. President's Commission for the Study of Ethical Problems in Medicine and Biomedical and Behavioral Research, *Deciding to Forego Life-Sustaining Treatment* 137 (1983) [hereinafter President's Commission].

25. New Jersey Commission on Legal and Ethical Problems in the Delivery of Health Care, *Problems and Approaches in Health Care Decisionmaking* 103, 155 (1990) [hereinafter Report of the New Jersey Bioethics Commission].

26. Marion Danis et al., "Patients' and Families' Preferences for Medical Intensive Care," 260 JAMA 797, 802 (1988).

27. See John A. Robertson, "Second Thoughts on Living Wills," 21:6 Hastings Cent. Rep. 6 (Nov. 1991).

28. See In re *Estate of Greenspan*, 558 N.E.2d 1194, 1197 (Ill. 1990) (patient repeatedly said he would rather die than live in a nursing home); Newark Star Ledger, Feb. 8, 1992, at 17 (letter to Ann Landers describing a living will dictating that no medical intervention be provided if the declarant "must enter a nursing home").

29. Surveys disclose that many persons wish to avoid future medical maintenance in a state of total and permanent dependence on others. Times Mirror Center for the People and the Press, *Reflections of the Times: The Right to Die* 6 (1990).

30. For a more complete explanation of my views, see Norman L. Cantor, "Prospective Autonomy—On the Limits of Shaping One's Post-Competence Medical Fate," 8 J. Contemp. Health L. & Pol'y 13 (1992).

31. For another view condemning use of a standard demanding "appropriate" or adequate contemplation of a directive's consequences on the part of a declarant, see King, supra note 4, at 57–59, 67–68.

32. Discussion of this issue is continued in chapter 6.

33. Uniform Rights of Terminally Ill Act 1989 § 4 (a), 9B U.L.A. 106 (Supp. 1992) [hereinafter URTIA]; Del. Code Ann. tit. 16, § 2504 (a) (1983); Me. Rev. Stat. Ann. tit. 18-A, § 5-704 (a) (West Supp. 1991). See Thomas A. Eaton & Edward J. Larson, "Experimenting with the "Right to Die" in the Laboratory of the States," 25 Ga. L. Rev. 1253, 1305 (1991). Not every state so readily accepts a revocation. In South Carolina, for example, a revocation must be "clearly expressed" in order to be effective. See Elizabeth G. Patterson, "Planning for Health Care Using Living Wills and Durable Powers of Attorney: A Guide for the South Carolina Attorney," 42 S.C. L. Rev. 525, 579 (1991).

34. See Norman L. Cantor, *Legal Frontiers of Death & Dying* 68–82 (1987); Jeffrey J. Delaney, Note, "Specific Intent, Substituted Judgment and Best Interests: A Nationwide Analysis of an Individual's Right to Die," 11 Pace L. Rev. 565, 591, 617–23 (1991) (concerning the legal standards generally applicable to the handling of incompetent patients who have left no clear instructions).

35. See Marguerite A. Chapman, "The Uniform Rights of the Terminally Ill Act: Too Little, Too Late?" 42 Ark. L. Rev. 319, 356 (1989); George J. Annas & Leonard H. Glantz, "The Right of Elderly Patients to Refuse Life-Sustaining Treatment," 64 Milbank Q. Supp. 2, at 95, 107 (1986).

36. A gravely incapacitated patient may fluctuate in resolve or give contradictory signals. See In re *O'Brien*, 517 N.Y.S.2d 346, 348 (Sup. Ct. 1986).

37. *Kurzweil v. Harrison*, No. 14810/91, slip op. at 3 (N.Y. Sup. Ct., N.Y. County).

38. See President's Commission, supra note 24, at 152.

39. See George J. Annas, *Judging Medicine* 255–56 (1988); Annas & Glantz, supra note 35, at 107. Both these sources criticize In re *Hier*, 464 N.E.2d 959 (Mass. App. 1984). See also Rebecca S. Dresser & John A. Robertson, "Quality of Life and Non-Treatment Decisions for Incompetent Patients: A Critique of the Orthodox Approach," 17:3 Law, Med. & Health Care 234, 238–39 (1989).

40. In In re *O'Brien*, 517 N.Y.S.2d 346 (Sup. Ct. 1986), the 83-year-old victim of a severe stroke had attempted 15 times to remove a nasogastric feeding tube. The court nonetheless refused to authorize detachment of the life-preserving device. The opinion commented: "This court is not prepared to order discontinuance of this life support based upon gestures of irritation or annoyance." Id. at 348. See also *Conroy*, 486 A.2d at 1243, where the court essentially disregarded a patient's moaning and attempts to remove a feeding tube because it was not clear whether the conduct was intentional or reflexive.

41. For a provision requiring a health-care agent to discuss treatment options with a now incompetent principal and to "take the patient's expressed wishes into account in the decision-making process," see N.J. Stat. Ann. § 26:2H-63(b) (West Supp. 1992).

42. Consultation with the incompetent person and consideration of that person's wishes and feelings do not compel adherence to those incompetent wishes. If an incompetent but comprehending minor were involved, it would be evident that the patient ought to be consulted even though the patient's substantive wishes would not necessarily be followed. Cf. Charles R. Tremper, "Respect for Human Dignity and Minors: What the Constitution Requires," 39 Syracuse L. Rev. 1293, 1314 (1988); John H. Garvey, "Freedom and Choice in Constitutional Law," 94 Harv. L. Rev. 1756, 1784 n.30 (1981).

43. Concerning the significance of "assent" from an incompetent person, see Annas & Glantz, supra note 35, at 119; Nancy L. Dubler, "Refusals of Medical Care in the Home Setting," 18:3 Law, Med. & Health Care 227, 231–32 (1990); Bruce J. Winick, "Competency to Consent to Treatment: The Distinction Between Assent and Objection," 28 Hous. L. Rev. 15, 37–42 (1991). Cf. Robert M. Veatch, *The Patient as Partner* 58–60 (1987). See also Sanford H. Kadish, "Letting Patients Die: Legal and Moral Reflections," 80 Cal. L. Rev. 857, 874–76 (1992).

44. In addition, there is always some chance that the consultation with the patient might yield surprising responses which reflect a level of function beyond that previously attributed to the patient. This would be a basis to reassess the patient's mental status.

45. Report of the New Jersey Bioethics Commission, supra note 25, at 104, 161. In In re *Clark*, 510 A.2d 136, 138 (N.J. Super. Ct. Ch. Div. 1986), in deciding that the burdens of the patient's continued existence did not outweigh the benefits, the court noted that the incompetent patient had answered "yes" when asked if she was happy. In In re *Storar*, 420 N.E.2d 64 (N.Y., 1981), cert. den., 454 U.S. 858 (1981), the lower court interpreted the incompetent patient's resistance to blood transfusions as expressing pain and anxiety, which furnished a basis for withholding further intervention. The New York Court of Appeals, however, refused to permit termination of life support in the absence of clear-cut prior expressions by the now incompetent patient. See also In re *Hier*, 464 N.E.2d 959 (Mass. App. 1984).

46. See In re *Guardianship of Grant*, 747 P.2d 445, 457 (Wash. 1987), amended by 757 P.2d 534 (Wash. 1988); In re *Guardianship of Ingram*, 689 P.2d 1363, 1370 (Wash. 1984).

47. *Ingram*, 689 P.2d at 1370.

48. Courts frequently solicit the views of an incompetent patient when the issue is sterilization or abortion. See In re *C.D.M.*, 627 P.2d 607, 612–13 (Alaska 1981); In re *A.W.*, 637 P.2d 366, 375 (Colo. 1981); In re *Hayes*, 608 P.2d 635, 641 (Wash. 1980). In those instances, the courts acknowledge that the weight to be given to the incompetent patient's pronouncements depend on the patient's understanding of the procedure being contemplated.

49. Perhaps this is what the New Jersey Bioethics Commission had in mind when it prescribed, in draft legislation, that a "clearly expressed" wish by an incompetent patient to continue treatment should take precedence over a contrary advance directive. See Report of the New Jersey Bioethics Commission, supra note 25, at 43–44.

50. See sources cited in chapter 3, note 9.

51. See Current Opinions of the Council on Ethical and Judicial affairs of the A.M.A. §
2.19 (1986) [hereinafter Current Opinions of the AMA Council] (indicating that aggressive
intervention should ordinarily be maintained for an incompetent patient who is neither terminally
ill nor irreversibly comatose).

52. King, supra note 4, at 39.

53. Ben A. Rich, "The Values History: A New Standard of Care," 40 Emory L.J. 1109,
1145–56 (1991).

54. See *Rust v. Sullivan*, 111 S. Ct. 1759, 1171–72 (1991). The disputed federal rules
have been discontinued in the Clinton administration.

55. See, e.g., George J. Annas et al., *American Health Law* 657 (2d ed. 1990).

56. *Conroy*, 486 A.2d at 1225; see also Alexander Capron, "The Burden of Decision,"
20:3 Hastings Cent. Rep. 37 (June 1990).

57. See, e.g., *Brophy*, 497 N.E.2d at 639; *Gray v. Romeo*, 697 F. Supp. 580, 591 (D.R.I.
1988).

58. Chapter 2 addressed the way in which principles of autonomy have been respected in
the context of advance medical instructions.

59. See, e.g., S.D. Codified Laws Ann. § 59-7-2.5 (Supp. 1991); URTIA, supra note 33,
§ 9 (b); Chapman, supra note 35, at 387.

60. URTIA, supra note 33, § 9 (b); see also Alaska Stat. § 18.12.060 (1991); Ark. Code
Ann. § 20-17-208 (b) (Michie 1991); Cal. Health & Safety Code § 7190.5 (West Supp.
1992); Iowa Code Ann. § 144A.9 (2) (West 1989).

61. Conn. Gen. Stat. Ann. § 19A-571 (West Supp. 1992).

62. Del. Code Ann. tit. 16, § 2505 (1983).

63. As will be discussed a few pages hence, this is almost certainly true when the practitioner's reluctance to comply with a patient's wishes is based on a claim of personal conscience—a deeply felt moral position. The conflict between a patient's wishes and practitioner's
conscience will be resolved by transfer of the patient, if feasible. A similar framework probably
applies where the practitioner's reluctance is based on a claim of professional judgment or
sound medical practice. See American Hospital Association, *Patient's Choice of Treatment Options* (Feb. 1985).

64. See Mont. Code Ann. § 50-20-111 (1) (1991); Mass. Ann. Laws ch. 112, § 12 I
(Law Co-op 1991); *Swanson v. St. John's Lutheran Hosp.*, 597 P.2d 702, 709–10 (Mont. 1979);
Bruce G. Davis, "Defining the Employment Rights of Medical Personnel Within the Parameters
of Personal Conscience," 1986 Det. C. L. Rev. 847, 862–85.

65. See *Conservatorship of Morrison*, 253 Cal. Rptr. 530, 534 (Ct. App. 1988); In re
Farrell, 529 A.2d 404, 412 (N.J. 1987).

66. Approximately 10 jurisdictions say that, in the event of conscientious objection to
implementing a living will, the physician "shall promptly transfer" responsibility to another
physician. Ariz. Rev. Stat. Ann. § 36-3204 (c) (1991); Van Ess, supra note 11, at 577.
Approximately 20 jurisdictions require only that the physician take "reasonable steps" to effect
transfer. Iowa Code Ann. § 144 A.8 (1) (West 1989); Craig P. Goldman, "Revising Iowa's
Life-Sustaining Procedures Act: Creating a Practical Guide to Living Wills in Iowa," 76 Iowa
L. Rev. 1137, 1160 (1991); URTIA, supra note 33, § 8.

Not all states place responsibility upon a physician to arrange a transfer. For example,
Alabama "permits" transfer of the patient but doesn't require the physician to arrange it. Ala.
Code § 22-8A-8 (a) (1990). Kentucky simply provides that a physician shall not impede a
transfer. Ky. Rev. Stat. Ann. § 311.634 (Michie Supp. 1990).

67. See John B. Boyle, "Religious Employers and Gender Employment Discrimination," 4
Law & Ineq. J. 637, 646–51 (1986); Davis, supra note 64, at 853–54.

68. See *Warthen v. Toms River Community Memorial Hosp.*, 488 A.2d 229, 233–34 (N.J. Super. Ct. App. Div.), cert. den., 501 A.2d 926 (N.J. 1985); *Pierce v. Ortho Pharmaceutical Corp.*, 417 A.2d 505, 514 (N.J. 1980).

69. In re *Requena*, 517 A.2d 886 (N.J. Super. Ct. Ch. Div.), aff'd, 517 A.2d 869 (N.J. Super. Ct. App. Div. 1986).

70. See In re *Jobes*, 529 A.2d 434, 450 (N.J. 1987) (institution estopped by lack of having given prior notice of its conscientious policy; discomfort of individual providers acknowledged but apparently overridden).

71. See *Bartling v. Superior Court*, 209 Cal. Rptr. 220, 225 n.7 (Ct. App. 1984). But see In re *Bayer*, No. 4131, slip op. at 8–9 (Burleigh County Ct., N.D., Dec. 11 1987). After 200 physicians refused to accommodate the patient's wishes, the court refused to compel the attending physician to violate his conscience; the patient was permitted to die at home.

72. See Robert M. Veatch & Carol M. Spicer, "Medically Futile Care: The Role of the Physician in Setting Limits," 18 Am. J.L. & Med. 15, 27–28 (1992).

73. It might be argued that a patient's request for continued medical intervention (deemed futile by the physician) is distinguishable from a request for withdrawal of medical intervention. In the latter event, the patient is invoking an interest in bodily integrity and asking that the medical invasion of that integrity be withdrawn. By contrast, a patient seeking continued intervention is asking the physician to affirmatively introduce medical measures into the body (contrary to the professional judgment of the physician). The patient's interest in bodily integrity may not include the prerogative to introduce substances or medical instrumentalities into the body. Yet, even in the absence of full-blown bodily integrity, the patient's interest in continued medical attention ought to be recognized. The patient is still asserting a self-determination interest in attaining life-preserving medical intervention. That self-determination interest is legitimate and cognizable.

74. See, e.g., Allan S. Brett & Laurence B. McCullough, "When Patients Request Specific Interventions," 315 New Eng. J. Med. 1347, 1349 (1986); Linda L. Emanuel & Ezekiel J. Emanuel, "The Medical Directive: A New Comprehensive Advance Care Document," 261 JAMA 3288, 3292 (1989); Schneiderman and Spragg, supra note 23, at 984; Nancy Jecker, "Knowing When to Stop: The Limits of Medicine," 21:3 Hastings Cent. Rep. 5, 7 (May–June 1991).

75. The best discussion of this issue which I have seen is found in Veatch & Spicer, supra note 72, at 17–18.

76. This point is made by numerous sources. See, e.g., Felicia Ackerman, "The Significance of a Wish," 21:4 Hastings Cent. Rep. 27, 28 (July–Aug. 1991); Daniel Callahan, "Medical Futility, Medical Necessity: The Problem-Without-a-Name," 21:4 Hastings Cent. Rep. 30, 32 (July–Aug. 1991); Ronald E. Cranford, "Helga Wanglie's Ventilator," 21:4 Hastings Cent. Rep. 23, 23–24 (July–Aug. 1991).

77. Yale Kamisar, "Who Should Live—Or Die? Who Should Decide?" Trial, December 1991, at 24.

78. 18:12 Report of the Society for Critical Care Medicine 1435–39 (1990); see Michael A. Rie, "The Limits of a Wish," 21:4 Hastings Cent. Rep. 24, 25 (July–Aug. 1991).

79. In re *Conservatorship of Wanglie*, PX-91-283, slip op. (Minn. Prob. Ct. 1991).

80. Lisa Belkin, "As Family Protests, Hospital Seeks an End to Woman's Life Support," New York Times, Jan. 10, 1991, at A1, D22.

81. In point of fact, there was considerable dispute about what the patient had previously said or indicated. See Cranford, supra note 76, at 23.

82. "Those vested by society with a licensed monopoly of skill to preserve life have a duty to provide that life preservation as long as it is believed to be a benefit by the patient. . . . " Veatch & Spicer, supra note 72, at 31.

83. For another interesting clash between prior instructions of incompetent patients and professional preferences, see Alexander Gold et al., "Is There a Right to Futile Treatment? The Case of a Dying Patient With AIDS," 1 J. Clinical Ethics 19 (1990). There, the authors conclude that if health-care providers regard the patient's advance instructions as calling for futile medical treatment which they are unwilling to furnish, those providers ought to make their position known in advance so that the patient or the patient's representative can seek care from other sources; see id. at 22. I go further and suggest an affirmative obligation of the providers to assist in arranging alternative care.

84. "Life should be cherished despite disability and handicaps, except when the prolongation would be inhumane and unconscionable." Current Opinions of the AMA. Council, supra note 51, § 2.16. This quote is from a section dealing with incompetent patients who have not articulated their wishes, but it seems relevant to the context of advance directives as well.

85. Andrew H. Malcolm, "Missouri Family Renews Battle over Right to Die," New York Times, Nov. 2, 1990, at A14.

86. See Judith W. Ross, "The Puzzle of the Permanently Unconscious," 22:3 Hastings Cent. Rep. 2 (May–June 1992).

87. See, e.g., *Conroy*, 489 A.2d at 1231; *Rasmussen v. Fleming*, 741 P.2d 674, 688–89 (Ariz. 1987); Jeffrey J. Delaney, Note, "Specific Intent, Substituted Judgment and Best Interests: A Nationwide Analysis of an Individual's Right to Die," 11 Pace L. Rev. 565, 617–23 (1991).

88. See, e.g., In re *Lawrance*, 579 N.E.2d 32, 34 (Ind. 1991); In re *Moorhouse*, 593 A.2d 1256 (N.J. App. Div. 1991); In re *Crum*, 580 N.E.2d 876, 882 (Ohio Prob. Ct. 1991). Notice also that a number of states have amended their living-will laws to permit persons to prospectively reject life support in a permanently unconscious state.

89. For a more expansive statement of my views on treatment of PVS patients, see Norman L. Cantor, "The Permanently Unconscious Patient, Non-Feeding and Euthanasia," 15 Am. J.L. & Med. 384 (1989).

90. The judge in *Wanglie* refused to remove the husband as guardian; see *Conservatorship of Wanglie*, supra note 79.

91. See Rie, supra note 78, at 25; Alexander M. Capron, "In re Helga Wanglie," 21:5 Hastings Cent. Rep. 26, 27 (Sept.–Oct. 1991).

92. See Veatch & Spicer, supra note 72, at 29.

93. See, e.g., *Gray v. Romeo*, 697 F. Supp. at 583.

94. George J. Annas, "Transferring the Ethical Hot Potato," 17:1 Hastings Cent. Rep. 20, 21 (Feb. 1987); Robert Schwaneberg, Medical Ethics Panel Proposes Giving Legal Recognition to "Living Wills," The Star Ledger, Feb. 11, 1988, at 17.

95. Steven H. Miles et al., "Conflicts Between Patients' Wishes to Forego Treatment and the Policies of Health Care Facilities," 321 New Eng. J. Med. 48 (1989); James F. Childress, "Dying Patients: Who's in Control?" 17 Law, Med. & Health Care 227, 230 (1989).

96. On the meaning of "conscience," see James F. Childress, "Appeals to Conscience," 89 Ethics 315, 318–22 (1979).

97. Many state legislatures and the U.S. Congress adopted laws exempting private institutions from performing abortions in violation of institutional scruples. See, e.g., 42 U.S.C. § 300a-7 (d) (1989); Alaska Stat. § 18.16.010 (b) (1991); Colo. Rev. Stat. Ann. § 18-6-104 (West 1990). For an example of accommodation in the public sector, see *Poelker v. Doe*, 432 U.S. 519, 520–21 (1977).

98. See *Planned Parenthood Ass'n v. Ashcroft*, 655 F.2d 848 (8th Cir. 1981); *Greco v. Orange Memorial Hosp.*, 513 F.2d 873 (5th Cir. 1975); *Chrisman v. Sisters of St. Joseph*, 506 F.2d 308 (9th Cir. 1974).

99. *Brophy*, 497 N.E.2d at 639; *Grace Plaza of Great Neck v. Elbaum*, 1992 N.Y. App.

Div. LEXIS 10728 (App. Div., Sept. 21, 1992); *Gray v. Romeo*, 697 F. Supp. at 591; *Morrison*, 253 Cal. Rptr. at 534.

100. See, e.g., *Jobes*, 529 A.2d at 450.

6. The Moral Boundaries of Shaping Post-Competence Medical Care

1. While analgesics can relieve the vast majority of pain, there are still some kinds of terminal conditions which are accompanied by unrelievable pain. Alternatively, the directive itself might preclude palliatives or analgesics because either they might violate the patient's religious precept that suffering has important redemptive value or the patient might wish to remain as lucid as possible.

2. See Allen E. Buchanan & Dan W. Brock, *Deciding for Others: The Ethics of Surrogate Decision Making* 185 (1989).

3. By future "persona" I mean the changed, incompetent version of the previously competent person who propounded an advance directive.

4. On the various interests underlying autonomy in the context of advance medical directives, see New Jersey Commission on Legal and Ethical Problems in the Delivery of Health Care, *Problems and Approaches in Health Care Decisionmaking* 86 (1990); Buchanan & Brock, supra note 2, at 91–92; Philip G. Peters, "The State's Interest in the Preservation of Life: From *Quinlan* to *Cruzan*," 50 Ohio St. L.J. 891, 930–31 (1989).

5. See, e.g., *Brophy v. New England Sinai Hosp., Inc.*, 497 N.E.2d 626, 635 (Mass. 1986); In re *Gardner*, 534 A.2d 947, 953 (Me. 1987).

6. See In re *Guardianship of Browning*, 568 So. 2d 4, 13 (Fla. 1990); In re *Estate of Greenspan*, 558 N.E.2d 1194, 1202 (Ill. 1990); In re *Peter*, 529 A.2d 419, 425 (N.J. 1987).

7. Implicit in this statement is the judgment that prolongation of life is not always in the best interests of a moribund patient.

8. Such measures commonly instruct a health-care agent to implement the wishes of the principal as gleaned from the advance directive or elsewhere. "Best interests" of the incompetent patient must guide the agent when the patient's wishes cannot be determined. See, e.g., Cal. Civ. Code § 2500 (West Supp. 1992); Idaho Code § 39-4505 (Supp. 1991); Miss. Code Ann. § 41-41-163 (Supp. 1991); N.Y. Pub. Health Law § 2982 (2) (McKinney Supp. 1992); R.I. Gen. Laws § 23-4.10-2 (1989).

9. See Buchanan & Brock, supra note 2, at 154–59; Rebecca Dresser, "Relitigating Life and Death," 51 Ohio St. L.J. 425, 432 (1990).

10. Professor Dresser's initial analysis was presented in Rebecca Dresser, "Life, Death, and Incompetent Patients: Conceptual Infirmities and Hidden Values in the Law," 28 Ariz. L. Rev. 373 (1986). A more developed explication of her position is presented in Rebecca Dresser, "Relitigating Life and Death," supra note 9. A joint presentation with Professor Robertson is found in Rebecca S. Dresser & John A. Robertson, "Quality of Life and Non-Treatment Decisions for Incompetent Patients: A Critique of the Orthodox Approach," 17 Law, Med. & Health Care 234 (1989). For Professor Robertson's separately stated position, see John A. Robertson, "*Cruzan* and the Constitutional Status of Nontreatment Decisions for Incompetent Patients," 25 Ga. L. Rev. 1139 (1991) [hereinafter Robertson, "Constitutional Status"]; John A. Robertson, "Second Thoughts on Living Wills," 21:6 Hastings Cent. Rep. 7 (Nov. 1992).

11. Dresser & Robertson, supra note 10, at 238; Dresser, supra note 9, at 430–31; see Robertson, "Constitutional Status," supra note 10, at 1158–59.

12. Such miraculous choice would reflect the patient's "current and future interests as incompetent individuals, not their past preferences." Dresser & Robertson, supra note 10, at 236.

13. Robertson, "Constitutional Status," supra note 10, at 1143, 1162, 1167.

14. This is not to say that an advance instruction must prevail against all countervailing

interests. For example, allocation of a scarce medical resource to another critically ill patient might necessitate overriding a patient's choice. The point is that the patient's interest in having a prior choice respected is affected in a meaningful fashion even if the plaintiff cannot sense the violation.

15. Professor Robertson suggests that the distaste experienced by observers, rather than the dignity interests of unsensing patients, accounts for any proscription of the practices involved. Robertson, "Constitutional Status," supra note 10, at 1162 n.94. For an unusual case in which a court suggested that an anencephalic neonate's nonvital organs could be harvested for the benefit of others, see "Organ Donations Barred by Judge," New York Times, March 28, 1992, at A7.

16. See Nancy K. Rhoden, "The Limits of Legal Objectivity," 68 N. C. L. Rev. 845, 864 (1990) [hereinafter Rhoden, "Legal Objectivity"]; Rhoden, "Litigating Life and Death," 102 Harv. L. Rev. 375, 417–18 (1988); Rhoden, "How Should We View the Incompetent?" 17 Law. Med. & Health Care 264, 266 (1989).

17. Rhoden, "Legal Objectivity," supra note 16, at 858.

18. Id. at 864. See also Peters, supra note 4, at 935–36.

19. James F. Childress, "Dying Patients: Who's in Control?" 17 Law, Med. & Health Care 227, 228 (1989).

20. The Dresser-Robertson position—that once incompetent, a person cannot experience the previously feared indignity associated with a grossly deteriorated status—is a shaky premise. I suggest that some patients, in some phases of mental incapacity, can be aware of, and suffer from, grossly reduced functioning. That is, the frustration, embarrassment, or humiliation originally feared by the patient may in fact materialize and inflict emotional suffering on some incompetent patients. Admittedly, it is difficult to identify and measure these phenomena in severely compromised patients. But there will be some such patients whose overall distress will be apparent. And there will be some less mentally deteriorated patients whose particular distress relating to indignity can be discerned (e.g., a senile incontinent patient, once proud, independent, and punctilious about personal hygiene, who now weeps each time that a diaper must be changed). In such instances as these, the patient's prior expressions, directives, or values may help observers understand the nature of the apparent distress. At stages in which the incompetent patient is still aware of the environment, loss of prior faculties can prompt real emotional consequences.

21. Ronald Dworkin, "Autonomy and the Demented Self," 64 Milbank Q. Supp. 2, at 4, 11 (1986). See also Buchanan & Brock, supra note 2, at 100 (acknowledging the legitimacy of future-oriented interests to individuals as well as their families).

22. In our culture, we attach great importance to the "embodiment" of our beings, whether that embodiment is competent, incompetent, or even dead. "We only know of our selves and each other in and through our bodies. . . . " Thomas H. Murray, "Are We Morally Obligated to Make Gifts of Our Bodies?" 1 Health Matrix 19, 24 (1991).

23. Cruzan v. Director, Missouri Dept. of Health, 110 S. Ct. at 2841, 2885–86; see also id. at 2892.

24. See, e.g., Gardner, 534 A.2d at 953; Delio v. Westchester County Medical Center, 516 N.Y.S.2d 677, 691 (App. Div. 1987).

25. See Buchanan & Brock, supra note 2, at 99–100; Ronald E. Cranford, "Going Out in Style, The American Way, 1987," 17 Law, Med. & Health Care 208, 208 (1989).

26. Cruzan, 110 S. Ct. at 2869.

27. Times Mirror Center For the People and the Press, Reflections of the Times: The Right to Die 10 (June 1990).

28. See Buchanan & Brock, supra note 2, at 164.

29. See H. Frankfort, The Importance of What We Care About 83, 91 (1988).

30. My late stepbrother's will prescribed that a Dixieland band play at his wake and that the mourning family wear white. It was obvious to me that fulfillment of his wishes gave expression to his character and that to dishonor his instruction would have been an offense to his memory.

31. Recent court decisions indicate that a parent is entitled to reject life-preserving treatment so long as the minor is not totally abandoned (i.e., so long as a spouse or relative can care for the minor). Presence of emotional harm to the minor is not a basis to override the parent's medical decision. See *Norwood Hosp. v. Munoz*, 564 N.E.2d 1017, 1024 (Mass. 1991). At least one court has indicated that the parent's autonomy interest would be upheld even if the dependent minor would be totally abandoned; see *Fosmire v. Nicoleau*, 551 N.E.2d 77, 83 (N.Y. 1990).

32. This is not to say that a competent person who neglects his or her body and precipitates subsequent hardship during the post-competence stage of existence forfeits the moral prerogative of prospective control.

33. See generally James F. Childress, "Ethical Criteria for Procuring and Distributing Organs for Transplantation," in *Organ Transplantation Policy* 87 (James F. Blumstein & Frank A. Sloan, eds., 1989) (describing the effect of the Uniform Anatomical Gift Act); Erik S. Jaffe, Note, " 'She's Got Bette Davis['s] Eyes:' Assessing the Nonconsensual Removal of Cadaver Organs Under the Takings and Due Process Clauses," 90 Colum. L. Rev. 528 (1990) (discussing the substantive rights existing relative to the body and the family's disposition of the cadaver).

34. Dresser & Robertson, supra note 10, at 237.

35. See Rhoden, "Legal Objectivity," supra note 16, at 859.

36. See Dan W. Brock, "Trumping Advance Directives," 21:5 Hastings Cent. Rep. S5 (Sept. 1991); Dresser, supra note 9, at 432; Buchanan & Brock, supra note 2, at 154–59. For discussion of the personal identity issue, see Ben A. Rich, "The Values History: A New Standard of Care," 40 Emory L.J. 1109, 1122–32 (1991); Nancy M. P. King, *Making Sense of Advance Directives* 73–74 (1991).

37. See Robertson, "Constitutional Status," supra note 10, at 1157.

38. Buchanan & Brock, supra note 2, at 160–61.

39. Id. at 160, 185. Even in situations in which Buchanan and Brock consider personal identity to be unchanged, they wrestle with the conflict between a person's autonomy interests and the contemporaneous interests of the incompetent patient. To them, it would be immoral to accomplish the demise of an incompetent persona possessing clear capacity for net pleasure or satisfaction in life; see *id.* at 160. See also Sanford H. Kadish, "Letting Patients Die: Legal and Moral Reflections," 80 Cal. L. Rev. 857, 876–78 (1992).

40. Rich, supra note 36, at 1123.

41. Dworkin, supra note 21, at 5.

42. Rhoden, "Legal Objectivity," supra note 16, at 860.

43. For examples of judicial willingness to follow the perceptible best interests of a patient when the patient's prior contrary instructions were not clear-cut, see In re *Estate of Dorone*, 534 A.2d 452, 455 (Pa. 1987); *University of Cincinnati Hosp. v. Edmond*, 506 N.E.2d 299, 302 (Ohio Comm. Pleas 1986). See also Mo. Ann. Stat. §§ 459.025, .045 (Vernon Supp. 1992) (authorizing health-care providers to treat a patient in contravention of prior expressions if the treatment would be consistent with the best interests of the patient).

44. See Sean M. Dunphy & John H. Cross, "Medical Decision Making for Incompetent Persons: The Massachusetts Substituted Judgment Model," 9 W. New Eng. L. Rev. 153, 156 (1987); David A. Peters, "Advance Medical Directives: The Case for the Durable Power of Attorney for Health Care," 8 J. Leg. Med. 437, 454 (1987).

45. Dresser, supra note 9, at 433.

46. Buchanan & Brock, supra note 2, at 111, 188–89. See also Rhoden, "Legal Objectivity," supra note 16, at 859–60; King, supra note 36, at 75; Kadish, supra note 39, at 876–78.

47. See Bruce J. Winick, "Competency to Consent to Treatment: The Distinction Between Assent and Objection," 28 Hous. L. Rev. 15 (1991).

48. If the vitalist patient's advance directive is overridden, it must be based on some other rationale such as the moral impropriety of extending the suffering of a helpless, incompetent person on the basis of prior instructions. Such a sweeping rationale that an unambiguous advance directive must always yield to a patient's contemporaneous interests is difficult to accept.

49. See Irene P. Loftus, Note, "I have a Conscience Too: The Plight of Medical Personnel Confronting the Right to Die," 65 Notre Dame L. Rev. 699, 712 (1990); Anne L. Rubin & Mary E. Scrupski, Note, "When Ethics Collide: Enforcement of Institutional Policies of Non-Participation in the Termination of LIfe-Sustaining Treatment," 41 Rutgers L. Rev. 399, 425 (1988).

50. Buchanan & Brock sympathize with this position; see Buchanan & Brock, supra note 2, at 98. It's not clear, however, how this can be reconciled with their position that advance directives might not be permitted to dictate withdrawal of life-preserving care for an ostensibly happy incompetent; see id. at 186–89. Perhaps they are suggesting that a person should be able to dictate post-competence medical care by instructions in accord with the interests of an incompetent patient who is clearly enjoying his or her incompetency.

51. Gerald Dworkin, *The Theory and Practice of Autonomy* 98 (1988).

52. Restraints are often used to prevent institutionalized patients from harming themselves or others. Such restraints are not per se inhumane, although they may become inhumane, depending on their nature and duration.

7. Enforcing Advance Directives

1. See note 9 in chapter 3. See also Felicia Ackerman, "The Significance of a Wish," 21:4 Hastings Cent. Rep. 23, 29 n.1 (July 1991).

2. The PSDA requires all health-care institutions receiving federal funds (which includes the vast majority of health-care enterprises) to educate their staff and patients about advance directives and about the relevant state law applicable to advance directives; see Patient Self-Determination Act of 1990 (PSDA), Pub. L. No. 101-508, § 4206 (a), codified at 42 U.S.C.A. § 1395cc (f)(1)(E) (West 1992). See generally Kelly C. Mulholland, "Protecting the Right to Die: The Patient Self-Determination Act of 1990," 28 Harv. J. on Legis. 609 (1991); "Practicing the PSDA: A Hastings Center Report Special Supplement," 21:5 Hastings Cent. Rep. S1–S16 (Sept. 1991).

3. See Nancy M. P. King, *Making Sense of Advance Directives* 141 (1991).

4. Usually, medical staff will be the key factor. If a responsible relative had been available, the declarant would probably have designated that relative as health-care agent. So in many instances there will be no close family or friends surrounding a declarant's dying process. Of course, the picture may be complicated by the presence of relatives who are not sympathetic to implementation of the patient's advance directive.

5. See Willard H. Pedrick, "Dignified Death and the Law of Torts," 28 San Diego L. Rev. 387, 399 (1991); Richard P. Dooling, "Damage Actions for Nonconsensual Life-Sustaining Medical Treatment," 30 St. Louis L.J. 895, 917 (1986); M. Rose Gasner, "Financial Penalties for Failing to Honor Patient Wishes to Refuse Treatment," 11 St. Louis U. L. Rev. 499, 512–15 (1992).

6. See *Elbaum v. Grace Plaza*, 544 N.Y.S. 840, 847 (App. Div. 1989). In *Elbaum*, the trial court upheld a refusal to pay for medical care rendered by a hospital after the comatose patient's husband had requested cessation of treatment. The husband had sought withdrawal of

treatment on the ground that his wife would have wanted that course. The trial court's decision as to liability for medical care was recently overturned. *Grace Plaza of Great Neck v. Elbaum*, 1992 N.Y. App. Div. LEXIS 10728 (App. Div., Sept. 21, 1992). However, this latest decision does not vitiate the notion that payment can be withheld for unwanted medical services. The appellate court relied on its reading of New York law as requiring (in the absence of a proxy directive) a judicial determination that the now incompetent patient had previously given clear-cut instructions about withdrawal of life support. The hospital would be denied compensation for "unwanted" care only after such a judicial determination. New York's law on decision making for incompetent patients is particularly narrow. See also Alaska Stat. § 18.12.070 (a) (1991).

7. Norman Paradis, "Making a Living Off the Dying", New York Times, April 25, 1992, at 23.

8. For example, the New Jersey Division of Health Facilities requires that hospitals and other health facilities comply with the state's advance directive act. N.J. Admin. Code tit. 8, § 39-4.1 (a) (1992).

9. PSDA, Pub. L. No. 101-508, § 4206 (a), codified at 42 U.S.C.A. § 1395cc (f) (1)(D) (West 1992).

10. See Colo. Rev. Stat. Ann. § 15-18-113 (5) (West 1989); Kan. Stat. Ann. § 65-28, 107(a) (1985); Utah Code Ann. § 75-2-1112 (3) (Supp. 1991); Craig P. Goldman, "Revising Iowa's Life-Sustaining Procedures Act: Creating a Practical Guide to Living Wills in Iowa," 76 Iowa L. Rev. 1137, 1160 (1991). Technically, these statutory measures apply only to failure to abide by living wills conforming to statutory requirements (such as terminal condition limitations). However, because of constitutional and common-law mandates to respect an incompetent patient's prior instructions, the same kind of professional obligations exist with regard to nonstatutory advance directives (as discussed in chapter 3).

11. So long as the attending physician did not have a conscientious objection to the desired medical course, an order to comply with the advance directive would be plausible. In the event of personal or professional scruples, the order might be directed at compelling transfer of care to a more amenable professional.

12. See B. D. Colen, *The Essential Guide to a Living Will* 14–16 (1991).

13. See Alan Meisel, "Refusing Treatment, Refusing to Talk, and Refusing to Let Go: On Whose Terms Will Death Occur?" 17:3 Law, Med. & Health Care 221, 223 (1989) (indicating that litigation is more likely to flow from nonadherence to a living will than from implementation).

14. For an examination of the role of institutional ethics committees in the terminal decision making process see Maureen Cushing et al., "The Role of Hospital Ethics Committees in Decisions to Terminate Treatment," 29:2 Boston Bar J. 22 (March–April 1985).

15. See David C. Blake, "The Hospital Ethics Committee: Health Care's Moral Conscience or White Elephant?" 22:1 Hastings Cent. Rep. 6, 9 (Jan. 1992).

16. Paradis, supra note 7, at 23.

17. Concerning the possibility of health-care providers' liability for nonadherence to an advance directive, see, e.g., President's Commission for the Study of Ethical Problems in Medicine and Biomedical and Behavioral Research, *Deciding to Forego Life-Sustaining Treatment* 141 (1983); William C. Knapp and Fred Hamilton, " 'Wrongful Living': Resuscitation as Tortious Interference With a Patient's Right to Give Informed Consent," 19 N. Ky. L. Rev. 253, 261 (1992); Pedrick, supra note 5, at 396; Dooling, supra note 5, at 895; Gasner, supra note 5, at 504–12; *Estate of Leach v. Shapiro*, 469 N.E.2d 1047, 1054–55 (Ohio App. 1984).

18. While pain-and-suffering damages are not ordinarily awarded as a contract remedy, the situation is different with regard to an intimate matter such as physicians' services.

19. See Tenn. Code Ann. § 32-11-108 (a) (Supp. 1991); Md. Health-Gen. Code § 5-607 (a) (1990); R.I. Gen. Laws §23-4.11-9 (e) (Supp. 1991); Alaska Stat. § 18-12-.070 (1986).

20. A clear exception is Alaska, which specifies the civil liability involved. There, the offending physician may be liable for a civil penalty not to exceed $1,000—plus any costs associated with the unwanted medical treatment; see Alaska Stat. § 18.12.070 (a) (1991). New Jersey provides that a noncooperating institution is subject to a civil fine of up to $1,000 for each offense; see N.J. Stat. Ann. § 26:2H-78(b) (West Supp. 1992).

21. See James Moskop, "Advance Directives in Medicine: Choosing Among the Alternatives," in *Advance Directives in Medicine* 15 (Andrew Hackler et al. eds., 1989).

22. Id. Concerning the absence of enforcement machinery in living-will type statutes, see Ben A. Rich, "The Values History: A New Standard of Care," 40 Emory L.J. 1009, 1117 (1991); Susan R. Martyn & Lynn B. Jacobs, "Legislating Advance Directives for the Terminally Ill: The Living Will and Durable Power of Attorney," 63 Neb. L. Rev. 779, 794 (1984).

23. But see *Foster v. Tourtellotte*, 704 F.2d 1109, 1113 (9th Cir. 1983) (denying liability because of a lack of precedent indicating the scope of a patient's constitutional rights in this area). More recent cases seem to provide the authority *Foster* found lacking. See *Gray v. Romeo*, 697 F. Supp. 580, 587–88 (D.R.I. 1988) (patient's constitutional right to refuse life-sustaining treatment could be exercised based on evidence of conversations patient had with husband and sister); *Tune v. Walter Reed Army Hosp.*, 602 F. Supp. 1452 (D.D.C. 1985) (ruling that a patient does have a constitutional right to reject treatment and that it can be exercised via an advance directive). See also Gasner, supra note 5, at 506–08.

24. Many living-will type statutes accord immunity to physicians who conform to reasonable medical standards. See Marguerite A. Chapman, "The Uniform Rights of the Terminally Ill Act: Too Little, Too Late?" 42 Ark. L. Rev. 319, 387 (1989). I previously argued that professional preferences as to terminal treatment must yield to patient autonomy. But the issue is sufficiently open so that counsel for the health-care providers will be making the argument that physicians can rely on sound medical practice. A few states' advance directive laws give special support to the physicians' defenses. For example, Connecticut permits the attending physician to use "best medical judgment" and mandates only that the physician "consider" the patient's wishes; see Conn. Gen. Stat. Ann. § 19a-571 (West Supp. 1992). Also, a couple of states explicitly excuse a physician from liability for ignoring an advance directive. See Cal. Civ. Code § 2438 (c) (West Supp. 1992); Ohio Rev. Code Ann. § 1337.15 (b) (Anderson Supp. 1991)

25. In chapter 3, I noted the restrictions posed by some living-will type statutes. I advised there that declarants use a nonstatutory directive in order to try and avoid these statutory constraints.

26. Of course, I would argue that if reasonable efforts to transfer the patient are unavailing, the health-care providers should be required to fulfill the patient's advance instructions.

27. In *Bartling v. Glendale Adventist Medical Center*, 228 Cal. Rptr. 847 (Ct. App. 1986), where a hospital and physicians had resisted a competent patient's rejection of life-sustaining care, the defendants paid $160,000 in attorneys' fees. See Evan R. Collins, Jr. and Doron Weber, *The Complete Guide to Living Wills* 94 (1991). See also Gasner, supra note 5, at 515–16 (concerning the availability of attorneys' fees).

28. See *Estate of Leach v. Shapiro*, 469 N.E.2d at 1052; Pedrick, supra note 5, at 396; Rich, supra note 22, at 1160–67.

29. One lower court judge recently commented: "Ohio's public policy . . . disfavors imposing liability upon a health care provider who allegedly saved or sustained a human life," in *Anderson v. St. Francis Hosp.*, No. 8910187, slip op. at 6 (Ohio Ct. Common Pleas 1991). See also Knapp & Hamilton, supra note 17, at 266 n.72; Gasner, supra note 5, at 517–19.

30. For criticism of the judicial hesitance to award damages for "wrongful life," see Rich, supra note 20, at 1167. In some jurisdictions, an additional obstacle exists. A number of states say that a person's cause of action for mental suffering does not survive the person's death. See W. Page Keeton et al., *Prosser and Keeton on The Law of Torts* 949 (5th ed. 1984); Gasner, supra note 5, at 517.

8. New Jersey's Model Legislation

1. New Jersey Advance Directives for Health Care Act, N.J. Stat. Ann. §§ 26:2H-53 to -78 (West Supp. 1992).

2. Cf. George J. Alexander, "Time for a New Law on Health Care Advance Directives," 42 Hastings L.J. 755 (1991) (urging that provisions dealing with advance directives be combined in a single statute).

3. New Jersey Commission on Legal and Ethical Problems in the Delivery of Health Care, *Advance Directives for Health Care: Planning Ahead for Important Health Care Decisions* (1991) [hereinafter Booklet of the New Jersey Bioethics Commission].

4. In Massachusetts, Michigan, and New York, a DPOA-HC type statute is the sole legislative enactment concerning advance medical directives. See Mass. Ann. Laws ch. 201D, §§ 1–17 (Law Co-op Supp. 1991); Mich. Stat. Ann. § 27.5496 (Callaghan Supp. 1991); N.Y. Pub. Health Law §§ 2980–2994 (McKinney Supp. 1992).

5. N.Y. Pub. Health Law § 2982 (1) (McKinney 1992).

6. See Tracy E. Miller, "Public Policy in the Wake of *Cruzan*: A Case Study of New York's Health Care Proxy Law," 18 Law, Med. & Health Care 360, 362 (1990).

7. See New York State Task Force on Life and the Law, *Life Sustaining Treatment: Making Decisions and Appointing a Health Care Agent* 75–83 (1987) [hereinafter New York State Task Force].

8. Id. at 82–83; Miller, supra note 6, at 362.

9. New York State Task Force, supra note 7, at 78; Miller, supra note 6, at 362. This claim seems spurious. An advance substantive directive can be geared to the general conditions of an incompetent patient rather than to specific maladies. See chapter 4, which deals with the drafting of an advance directive.

10. N.J. Stat. Ann. § 26:2H-64 (West Supp. 1992). This provision governs so long as an instruction directive offers some discernible guidance as to the particular medical decision being faced. If the directive does not provide any guidance as to the wishes of the incompetent patient under the circumstances at hand, then the A.D. Act is not applicable and New Jersey's common law of death and dying governs. See New Jersey Commission on Legal and Ethical Problems in the Delivery of Health Care, *Problems and Approaches in Health Care Decisionmaking: The New Jersey Experience* 163–64 (1990) [hereinafter Report of the New Jersey Bioethics Commission].

11. N.J. Stat. Ann. § 26:2H-67(a)(2)–(4) (West Supp. 1992).

12. N.J. Stat. Ann. § 26:2H-55 (West Supp. 1992).

13. See Report of the N.J. Bioethics Commission, supra note 10, at 140 (rejecting a fixed life expectancy limitation as "artificial and unrealistic"); see also id. at 170 (criticizing a terminal condition limitation as "overly restrictive" of patients' rights and "contrary to widely held societal values").

14. In defining the best-interests test applicable to an incompetent patient who has not left clear-cut prior instructions, the New Jersey Supreme Court has thus far confined "burdens" to physical pain or suffering. In re *Conroy*, 486 A.2d 1209, 1232 (N.J. 1985). See also In re *Peter*, 529 A.2d 419 n.5 (N.J. 1987) (reserving decision on whether the burdens associated with the best-interests test should include interests other than physical pain and suffering).

15. The comment to this section in the report confirms that a health-care agent is intended to have "broad authority to make the same kinds of health-care decisions the patient would have the right to make on his or her own behalf." Report of the New Jersey Bioethics Commission, supra note 10, at 155.

16. See id. at 80, 85–87, 98, 104, 106.

17. Id. at 80.

18. N.J. Stat. Ann. § 26:2H-63(d), (e) (West Supp. 1992); See Report of the New Jersey Bioethics Commission, supra note 10, at 106.

19. Report of the New Jersey Bioethics Commission, supra note 10, at 104. Many sources recognize that an incompetent patient's best interests should be defined in terms of the patient's own values and preferences. See Gerald Dworkin, The *Theory and Practice of Autonomy* 98 (1988).

20. Report of the New Jersey Bioethics Commission, supra note 10, at 87.

21. In re *Peter*, 529 A.2d 419, 425 (N.J. 1987).

22. In re *Farrell*, 529 A.2d 404 (N.J. 1987), indicates that a New Jersey patient's right to decline life-sustaining medical treatment is grounded in the judicially developed common law, in the state constitution, and in the federal constitution; see id. at 410. I also contend that the United States Supreme Court's *Cruzan* decision in July 1990 reinforces the conclusion that constitutionally based autonomy rights include the prospective decision to decline life-preserving medical intervention, even if the incompetent patient is preservable for an indefinite period; see chapter 2.

23. In re *Conroy*, 486 A.2d 1209, 1229 (N.J. 1985). State courts in several other jurisdictions have taken a similar posture. See *Brophy v. New England Sinai Hosp.*, 497 N.E.2d 626 (Mass. 1986); *John F. Kennedy Hosp. v. Bludworth*, 452 So. 2d 921 (Fla. 1984).

24. See *Farrell*, 529 A.2d at 410; *Fosmire v. Nicoleau*, 551 N.E.2d 77 (N.Y. 1990); *Bartling v. Superior Court*, 209 Cal. Rptr. 220 (Ct. App. 1984); *State v. McAfee*, 385 S.E.2d 651 (Ga. 1989).

25. See *Peter*, 529 A.2d at 419, 425 (N.J. 1987); John D. Arras, "The Severely Demented, Minimally Functional Patient: An Ethical Analysis," 36 J. Am. Geriatric Soc'y 938, 939–41 (1988); Yale Kamisar, "When Is There a Constitutional "Right to Die"? When Is There No Constitutional "Right to Live"?" 25 Ga. L. Rev. 1203 (1991); Nancy K. Rhoden, "The Limits of Legal Objectivity," 68 N. C. L. Rev. 845, 849–52 (1990).

26. See "Combined Advance Directive for Health Care" (sample form), in Booklet of the New Jersey Bioethics Commission, supra note 3, at 3.

27. Id.

28. See also the option in the DPOA form prepared by Charles P. Sabatino and printed by the A.B.A. Commission on Legal Problems of the Elderly, *Health Care Powers of Attorney* 3 (1990). One option there instructs the agent to consider "relief of suffering, the expense involved, and the quality as well as the possible extension" of life.

29. S.1211, 204th Leg., 1st Sess. (1990).

30. Id. at § 16. The patient would also have to be in a situation where the burdens of continued therapy would likely outweigh the benefits of continued existence. The meaning of burdens in that context was not perfectly clear, as prior discussion has indicated. Section 16 explicitly permitted removal of artificial nutrition from a patient in a permanently unconscious state. *Id.*

31. Report of the New Jersey Bioethics Commission, supra note 10, at 173.

32. Id. at 236. Twelve of the Commission's 25 members filed a separate statement disagreeing with the bill's differentiation of artificial nutrition from conventional medical technology.

33. President's Commission for the Study of Ethical Problems in Medicine and Biomedical

and Behavioral Research, *Deciding to Forego Life-Sustaining Treatment* 87–90 (1983); New York Task Force, supra note 7, at 38–40; Hastings Center Task Force on Death and Dying, *Hastings Center Guidelines on the Termination of Life-Sustaining Treatment and the Care of the Dying* 57–62 (1987).

34. N.J. Stat. Ann. §§ 26:2H-64(a), -61(f) (West Supp. 1992).

35. N.J. Stat. Ann. §§ 26:2H-61(f), -63(e) (West Supp. 1992).

36. Report of the New Jersey Bioethics Commission, supra note 10, at 104 n.1; see also id. at 87, 98, 162.

37. N.J. Stat. Ann. § 26:2H-67(a)(4) (West Supp. 1992).

38. Report of the New Jersey Bioethics Commission, supra note 10, at 107.

39. Id. at 89.

40. Report of the New Jersey Bioethics Commission, supra note 10, at 103.

41. N.J. Stat. Ann. § 26:2H-63(c) (West Supp. 1992).

42. Id. See also Report of the New Jersey Bioethics Commission, supra note 10, at 162.

43. N.J. Stat. Ann. § 26:2H-64(b) (West Supp. 1992).

44. N.J. Stat. Ann. § 26:2H-61(f) (West Supp. 1992).

45. Report of the New Jersey Bioethics Commission, supra note 10, at 103, 155.

46. See also N.J. Stat. Ann. § 26:2H-64(b) (West Supp. 1992), which anticipates some possible deviations from the terms of an advance directive.

47. See Report of the New Jersey Bioethics Commission, supra note 10, at 161 (ascribing the statutory language to "a commitment to the preservation of life"); see also id. at 106.

48. Section 62(b) of the Act clearly states that a physician may not "abandon" a patient by declining to participate in the withholding or withdrawal of measures to sustain life. N.J. Stat. Ann. § 26:2H-62(b) (West Supp. 1992).

49. Report of the New Jersey Bioethics Commission, supra note 10, at 158.

50. N.J. Stat. Ann. § 26:2H-65(b) (West Supp. 1992). An objecting religiously affiliated institution is required to take "all reasonable steps" to effect the transfer of the patient to another facility; see N.J. Stat. Ann. § 26:2H-65(a)(4), (b) (West Supp. 1992).

51. Report of the New Jersey Bioethics Commission, supra note 10 at 117, 167.

52. See id.

53. *Doe v. Bridgeton Hospital*, 366 A.2d 641 (N.J. 1976), cert. denied, 433 U.S. 914 (1976).

54. "Moral concepts cannot be the basis of a [charitable] hospital's regulations where that hospital is holding out the use of its facilities to the general public." Id. at 647. The court specifically refrained from deciding whether religiously affiliated institutions could refuse to perform elective abortions. *Id.* The opinion, however, interpreted the New Jersey legislation protecting institutional conscience as applicable only to sectarian institutions. *Id.*

55. N.Y. Pub. Health Law § 2984 (3) (Consol. Supp. 1990).

56. Id. at § 2984 (3)(b). See also Miller, supra note 6, at 364.

Index

NORMAN L. CANTOR is Professor of Law, as well as Justice Nathan L. Jacobs Scholar, at Rutgers University School of Law, Newark. He was also a member of the faculty of law at Tel Aviv University. He has served as an advisor to counsel in the Karen Ann Quinlan case and as advisor to the New Jersey Bioethics Commission. He is author of *Legal Frontiers of Death and Dying*.

.

Milton Keynes UK
Ingram Content Group UK Ltd.
UKHW021821020923
427856UK00005B/113